HERALDRY

HERALDRY

Henry Bedingfeld, Rouge Croix Pursuivant
Peter Gwynn-Jones, Lancaster Herald
Foreword by the Duke of Norfolk, Earl Marshal

GREENWICH EDITIONS

First published in 1993 by
PRC Publishing Ltd
Kiln House
210 New Kings Road
London SW6 4NZ

Produced for Greenwich Editions
10, Blenheim Court
Brewery Road, London N7 9NT

ISBN 0-86288-279-6

Printed in China

PAGE 1:
The Royal Arms, 1603-88.

PAGE 2:
TOP: *The Royal Arms, 1340-c.1400.*

MIDDLE: *The Royal Arms, 1707-14.*

BOTTOM: *The Royal Arms, 1714-1801.*

CONTENTS

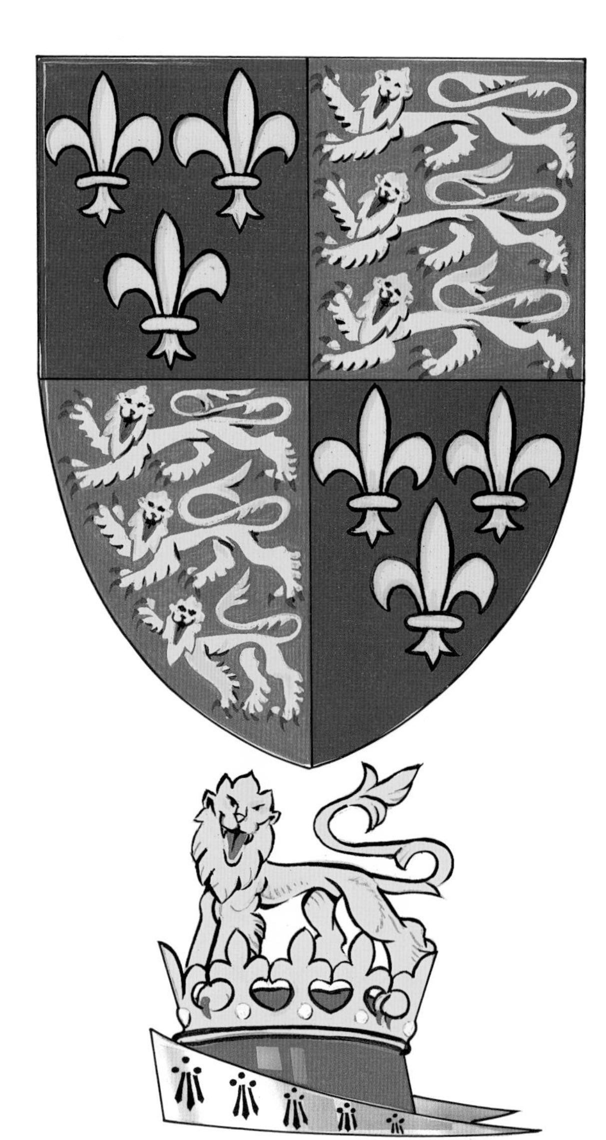

TOP: *The Royal Arms, 1801-16.*

BOTTOM: *The Royal Arms, c.1400-1603, and one of the crests used by Edward IV.*

OPPOSITE PAGE: *The arms of the Duke of Norfolk, surrounded by the Garter and ensigned by a duke's coronet.*

FOREWORD

by the Duke of Norfolk KG, GCVO, CB, CBE, MC
Earl Marshal of England

You will discover when you read this book that heraldry is a very old subject but, I am delighted to say, evergreen. From the period of the tournaments to the present day it has gradually evolved to fulfil the needs of the changing times, and today it is arguably more popular than ever before. Apart from the national Heraldry Society based in London, there are a number of provincial heraldry societies across Britain which cater for a proper study of the subject.

The two authors, Rouge Croix Pursuivant and Lancaster Herald, are full-time practising heralds at the College of Arms and are well versed in their chosen profession and the intricacies of heraldry. They have, I believe, given a fresh approach to this intriguing and colourful subject, and have taken many illustrations from the official records of the College of Arms which have not hitherto been published.

Norfolk.

1
ORIGINS

Henry Bedingfeld

LEFT: *Heralds' Roll*, c.*1280*.

Throughout Europe shields of arms are used to identify countries, counties, towns, cities and families and, partly as a result of past European colonial expansion, almost the whole world uses armorial symbolism, especially if national flags are included. The flag of the United States of America, said to have been based on the arms of George Washington, is even to be found on the moon, set in place by the first astronauts to land there.

The origins of armorial symbolism are diverse: there was no single 'great inventor' of heraldry. The original meaning of the word includes all the activities of heralds whether it be design of armorial insignia, genealogical research, ceremonial duties or, in the past, ambassadorial duties. Today the word has become synonymous with the study of armorial bearings and, because of this, it is used here in this context. If we have to pinpoint a time and place for the beginnings of heraldry it is almost certainly in Plantagenet Anjou and Maine in France in the mid-twelfth century, but the evidence for this is incomplete. The idea of painting a shield with simple, coloured designs fulfilled both the practical need of identifying one's opponent either in battle or during a tournament, and appealed to the individual's love of display. The twelfth-century Renaissance may have exercised a certain amount of cultural influence on the highest echelons of society, who may also have been drawn by Arthurian tales of courtly romance in which knights battled not merely to kill or capture an opponent, but in order to fulfil some sort of chivalric ideal. Above all, a brave and skilful knight would not wish to remain anonymous, and prominent insignia, either carried as a banner, or on his surcoat or shield, ensured that the world could recognise him.

The feudal system and the growth of large noble households may have encouraged magnates to display banners and flags bearing their own devices simply for the purpose of identification. On the battlefield, members of a lord's retinue needed to be able to identify their leader; in an illiterate age a magnate required a seal to authenticate his orders, and his mark had to be clearly recognisable. It became convenient for a nobleman's son to adopt his father's mark, and by the end of the twelfth century it is clear that armorial bearings had become hereditary. Heraldry started with the great magnates, whose vast landed

BELOW: *Bodiam Castle, Sussex.*

OPPOSITE, ABOVE: *The battle of Crécy, from Froissart's* Chronicle, *fifteenth century.*

possessions set them apart from ordinary knighthood; it gradually spread down the social ladder, so that by the fifteenth century, esquires and gentlemen adopted arms too. It undoubtedly spread throughout Western Europe from the mid-twelfth century as knights travelled to tournaments or to war.

Heralds, whose job was to proclaim the venues of tournaments, emerged as the first recorders of heraldry. They had to announce the lists of combatants by name and so needed to be able to recognise the insignia of the individuals. Heralds became expert in advising knights on the appropriate insignia to adopt and, from being mere recorders, grew to be controllers and, eventually, creators of armorial bearings.

Heraldry has been defined by Sir Anthony Wagner, Clarenceux King of Arms as, 'the systematic use of hereditary devices centred on the shield'. 'Systematic', because the science and art of heraldry developed a descriptive language and system of rules; 'hereditary devices', because certain designs passed from one generation of a family to another, usually from father to son; and 'centred on a shield', because the shield, with its simple, flat shape, was the best part of a knight's accoutrement upon which to paint devices. It provided a practical protection of the person as well as an ideological defence of family, territory, honour and virtue.

Today there are virtually no surviving medieval pennants, flags, or surcoats, and shields were destroyed in tournaments or on the battlefield. The only evidence of early heraldry is recorded in manuscripts such as rolls of arms, illuminated manuscripts,

BELOW: *The arms and crest of von Hassendorf, 1483, a modern painting.*

RIGHT: *A modern library painting of the armorial bearings of the Bowyers Company.*

chronicles and, to a certain extent, romances and poems, or on the seals used by kings and magnates to authenticate their charters and orders.

Heraldic seals seem to have appeared first in France, England and Germany in the second quarter of the twelfth century, and it is clear that they were used by several generations of the first owner's descendants. They provide the earliest practical evidence of heraldic designs and devices, most of which were simple geometric shapes.

The first seal of Waleran, Count of Meulan and Earl of Worcester, has been dated between 1136 and 1138 and shows the shield and horse trapper (a horse blanket reaching almost to the ground to protect the horse from blows) as checky; the counterseal (reverse side) shows the same checky pattern on shield, horse trapper and lance pennon. Waleran's maternal uncle, Ralph, Count of Vermandois, had a seal showing a checky lance flag, and in a second seal, on a charter of 1146, he bears the chequers on both flag and shield. The checky shield has claims to be the oldest in heraldry, but this example is particularly interesting as Waleran has clearly inherited it from his mother's family. The Counts of Vermandois continued to bear the checky shield, and later the descendants of his mother's second marriage, the Warenne Earls of Surrey, bore the same shield, as did another branch of the Warennes, the Earls of Warwick, who added an ermine chevron as a further distinguishing feature.

The de Clare family bore the simple shield of chevrons. The seal of Gilbert de Clare, Earl of Pembroke, has been dated at about 1141, but is only known from a later drawing, and that of his nephew Gilbert de Clare, Earl of Hertford, has been dated at about 1146.

BELOW LEFT: *Seal of Roger de Quincy, Earl of Winchester, c.1235.*

BELOW RIGHT: *Joanna Stuteville, c.1266. A rare seal showing a lady riding sidesaddle.*

ABOVE: *Seal of a Warenne Earl of Surrey.*

ABOVE: *The tomb plate of Geoffrey Plantagenet, Count of Anjou and Maine, d.1151.*

The shield shows six chevrons, but is better known in its later form with just three chevrons. It is the first surviving example of a fairly common design and instigated a whole series of arms, notably by changing the central chevron to a fess. A fess between two chevrons, in a variety of colour combinations and with certain additions, became common arms among feudal tenants in East Anglia in particular, notably the Fitzwalter, Pecche, Baynard, and Walpole families.

Another shield of this period is that almost certainly borne by Geoffrey de Mandeville, Earl of Essex (died 1144), which is quarterly gold and red. Variations of this shield were borne by a group of families, all connected to Geoffrey de Mandeville and his wife, including Say, Beauchamp of Bedford, Clavering, Vere, Lacy and others.

Elsewhere in Europe the existence of heraldry at this time is shown in the seals of Count Amadeus III of Savoy (died 1148); Henry the Lion, Duke of Saxony (died 1195); Raymond Berengar of Provence in 1150; Welf VI, Marquis of Tuscany and Prince of Sardinia in 1152; and of Raymond Berengar IV of Aragon in 1157.

Mention must be made here of the arms of Geoffrey Plantagenet, Count of Anjou and Maine (father of King Henry II of England). A Cluniac monk, Jean of Marmoutier Abbey in the Loire valley in France wrote a history of Anjou in about 1170-80, in which he describes Geoffrey's ceremony of knighthood in 1128 at Rouen. It took place a week before his marriage to Matilda, daughter of Henry I, King of England. In the ceremony, the king hung a shield bearing six golden lions about Geoffrey's neck. This passage has frequently been taken as the first written record of a shield of arms and thus the first mention of heraldry. Unfortunately Jean of Marmoutier is thought to be unreliable (Dr Elizabeth Hallam, editor of *The Plantaganet Chronicles*, describes Jean's tales as 'lively and often apocryphal'). Certainly Jean must have seen Geoffrey's enamel tomb plate at Le Mans Cathedral (he died in 1151), and it is quite possible that the chronicler, writing 20-30 years later, could have embellished his tale by adding the heraldic detail to the ceremony. However, if the written description of the first armorial shield cannot be believed, at least the tomb plate still exists in Le Mans Museum and is the first *coloured* example of heraldry that survives today. That it is heraldry is demonstrated by the fact that Geoffrey's bastard grandson, William de Longespée, Earl of Salisbury, bore the same shield, which today can be seen on his tomb in Salisbury Cathedral.

Rolls of arms are another important source of evidence for the origins, and particularly the development, of heraldry. The *Chronicles* of Matthew Paris, a Benedictine monk in the Abbey of St Albans, are illustrated with

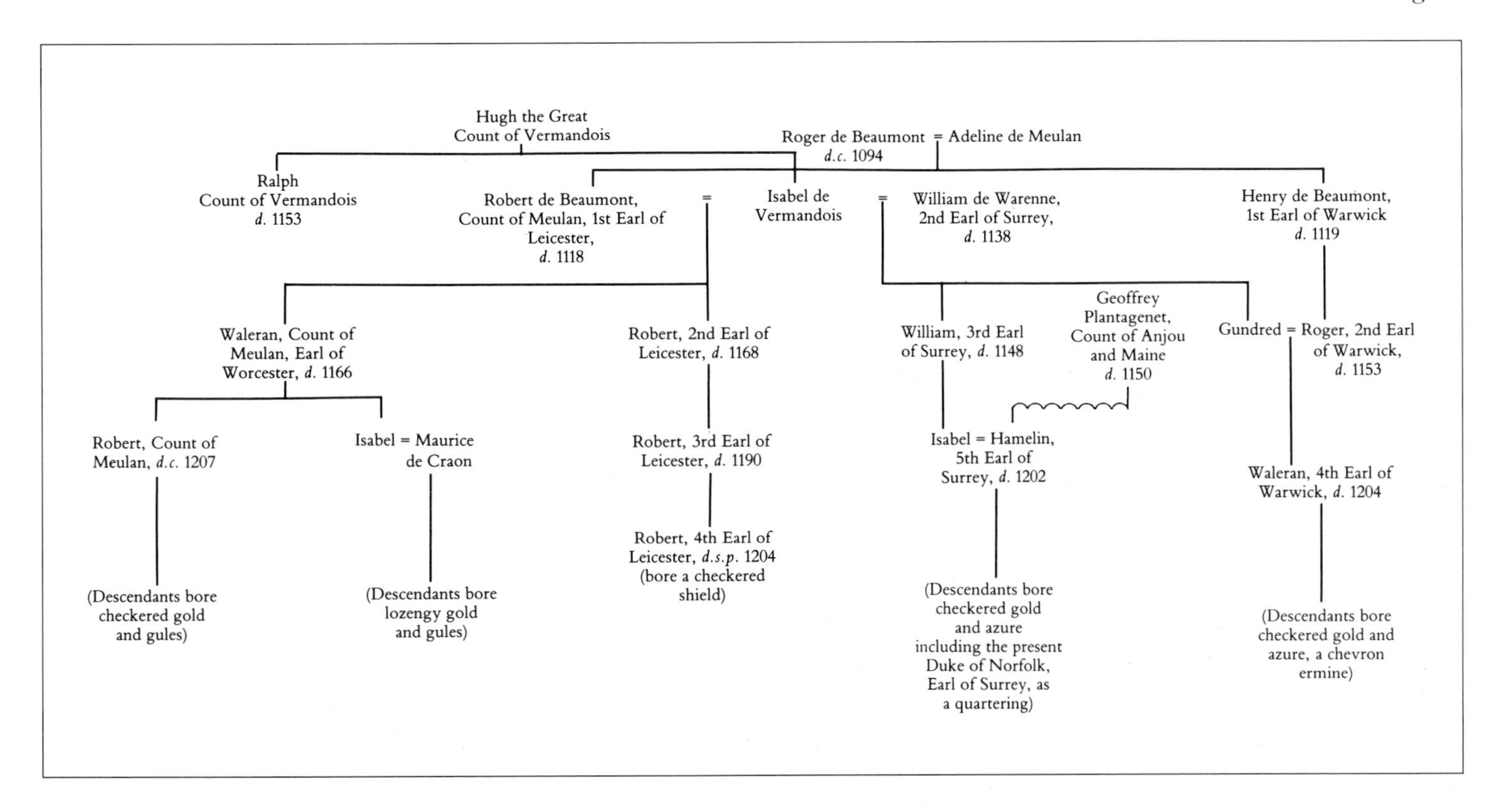

the shields of arms of figures mentioned in his text. Paris worked at St Albans between 1217 and his death in 1259, writing a variety of texts, one of which was a summary of events in England between 1200 and 1250. The heraldic record is secondary to the historic content of his work, but is nevertheless crucial to a study of early English heraldry. A day's journey from London, St Albans was visited by many of the eminent, including the

ABOVE: *Pedigree showing descent of checky arms.*

BELOW: Flower's Ordinary *c.1520, showing Warenne and other checky banners and shields.*

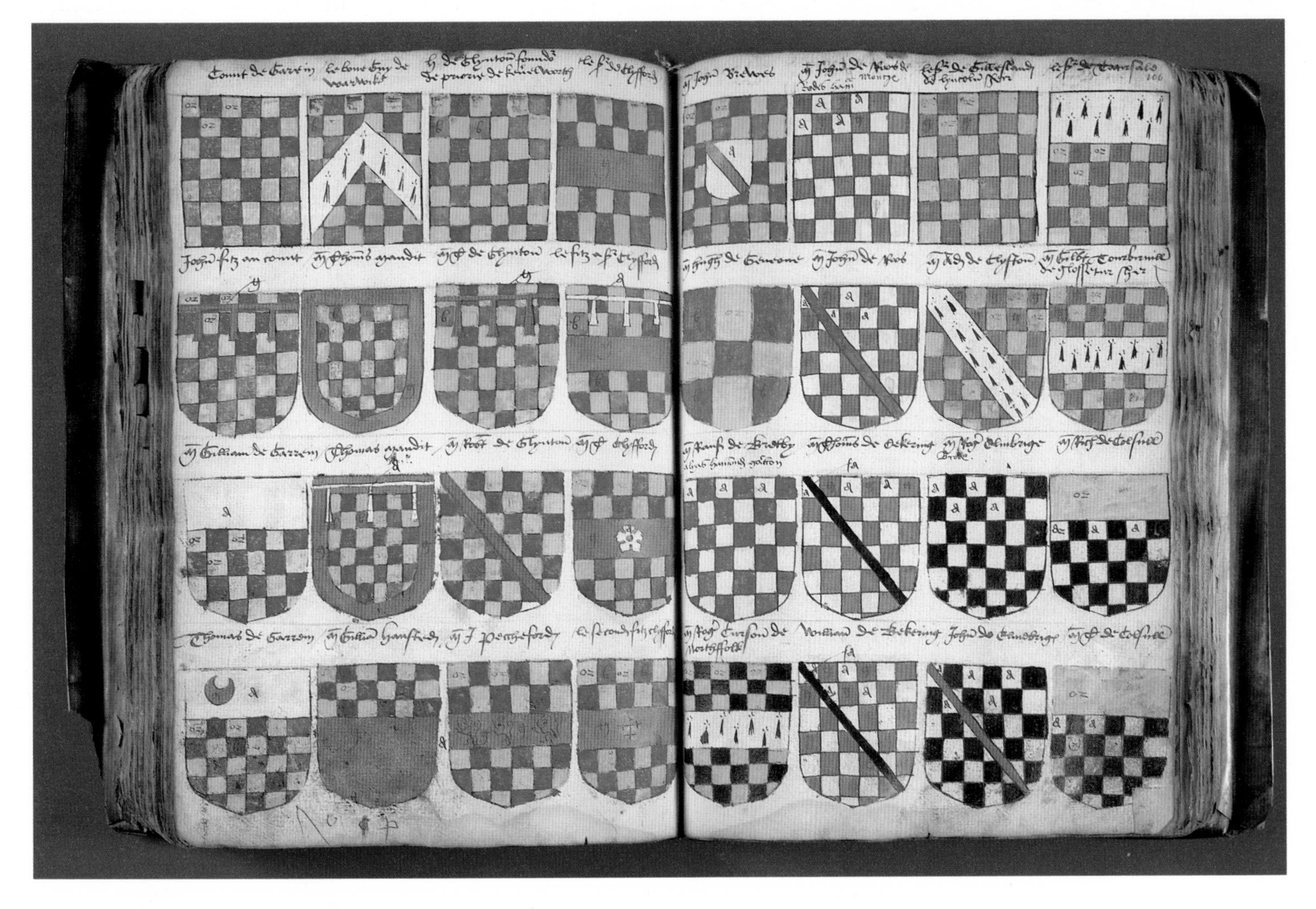

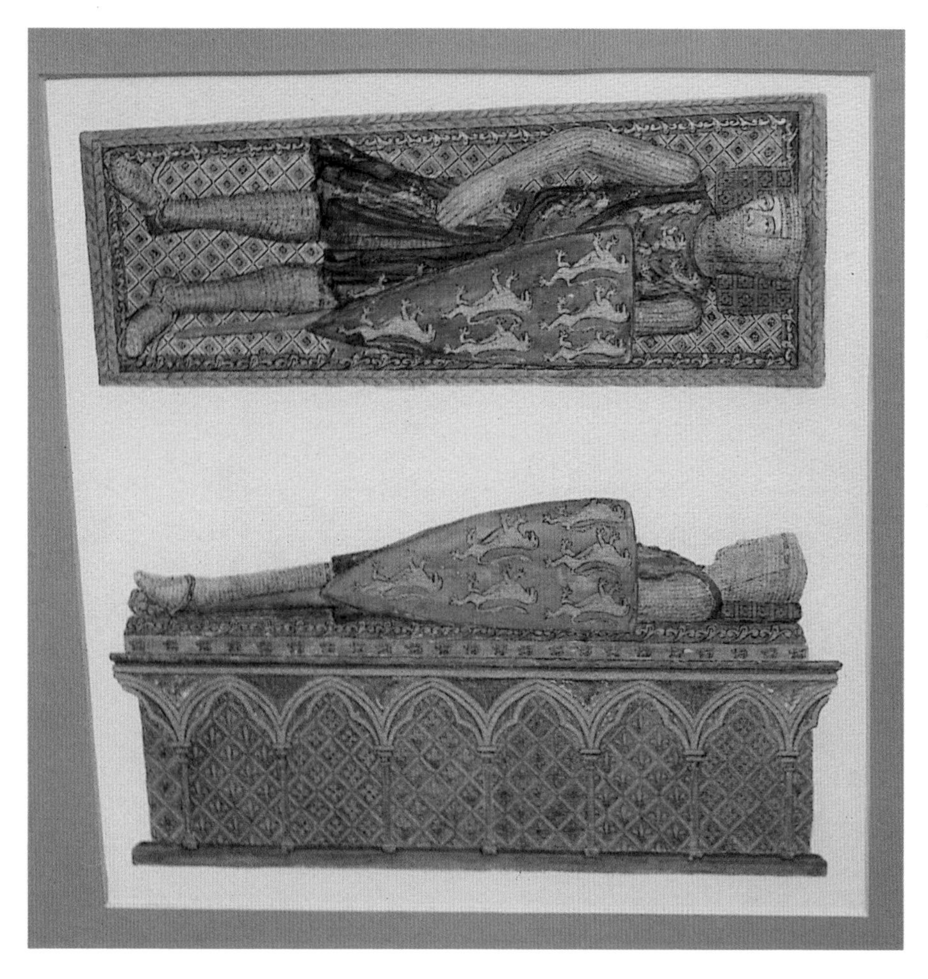

ABOVE: *A painting of the tomb of William de Longespée, Earl of Salisbury, an illegitimate grandson of Geoffrey of Anjou, at Salisbury Cathedral.*

king, Henry III. Matthew Paris was therefore able to gain a wide-ranging knowledge of events and people, including, of course, a record of their arms. Sir Anthony Wagner commented that 'the Matthew Paris shields are the work of a clerk, a keen and accurate observer, but one who looks at heraldry from the outside'. Other contemporary rolls of arms, such as Glover's and Walford's Rolls, are probably the work of heralds or even knights professionally involved with the subject.

The Bigot Roll, known from a seventeenth-century copy of the original, was composed after the campaign of Charles, Count of Anjou, in Hainault in 1254 against John, Count of Avesnes. It lists nearly 300 participants and gives their arms in blazon, the technical language used to describe arms. Glover's Roll (named after Robert Glover, Somerset Herald, 1570-88, who possessed a copy of the now lost medieval original) has been dated at 1255 or slightly earlier. It lists 55 names and the blazons of their arms, but unlike the Bigot Roll it is not a record of a discernible event, and it is not clear how the compiler decided on his choice of entrants. Starting with the king and his eldest son, it records the arms of earls, barons and knights from almost every English county. Walford's Roll, *c.*1275, exists as a nineteenth-century copy edited by W S Walford, and lists some 180 names and blazons. Like Glover's Roll, it seems to be a personal collection of the

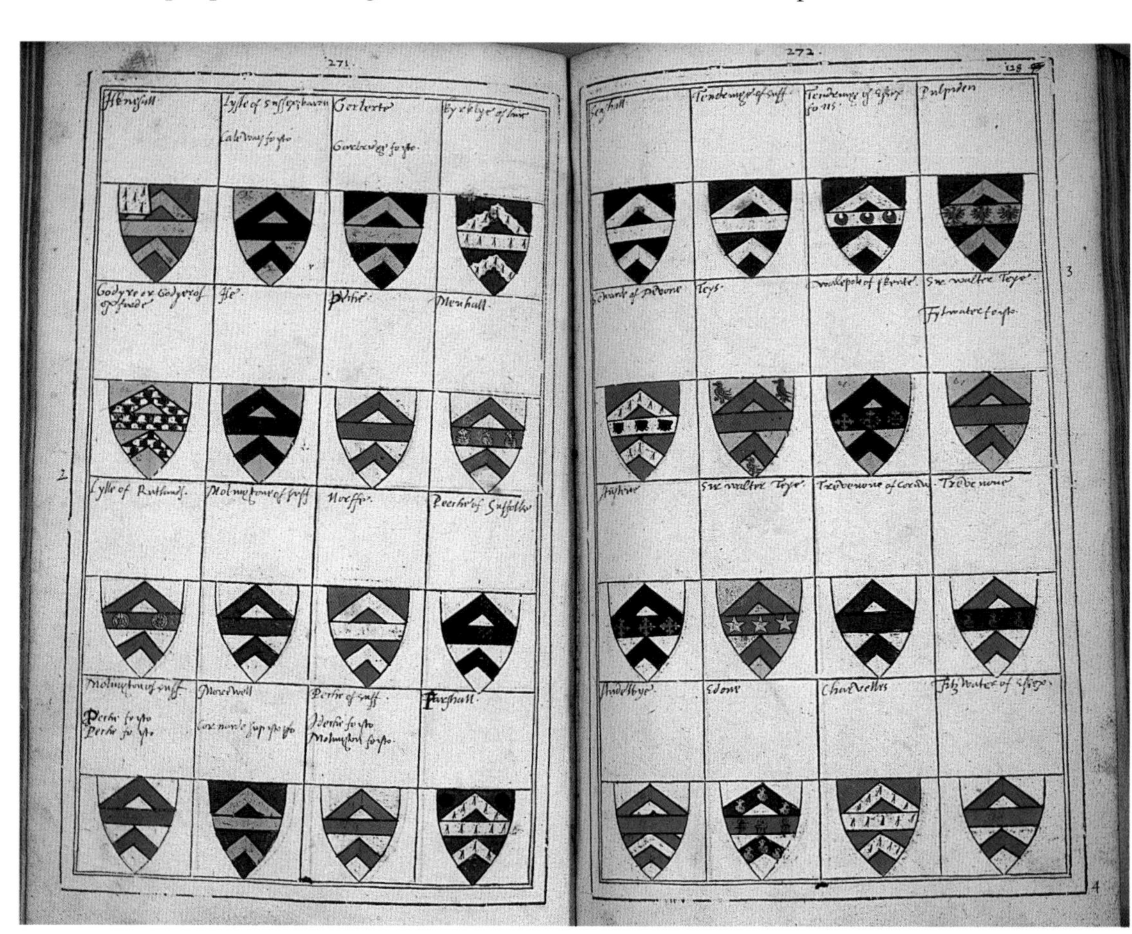

RIGHT: Holles Ordinary, *mid-seventeenth century. Arms derived from the Clare arms.*

FACING PAGE: *Matthew Paris shields, c.1244.*

RIGHT: Holles Ordinary; *various lozengy coats.*

FACING PAGE: *A miniature from the Westminster Psalter c.1250. It shows the typical equipment of a knight at the time.*

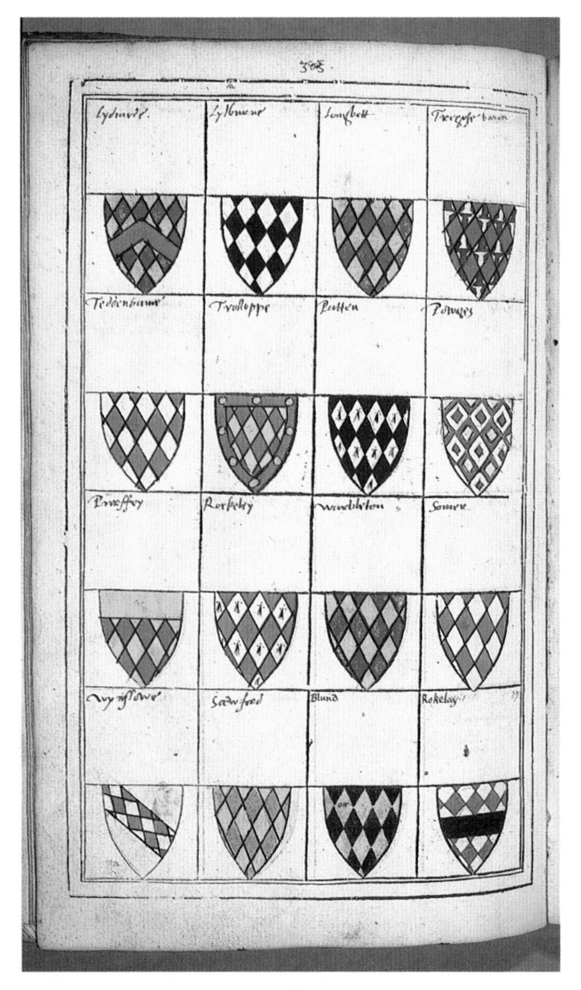

compiler, though as it also includes a number of foreign arms, it is likely that he was fairly well travelled. All the arms of these early rolls are described in Anglo-Norman blazon, the forerunner of a later-perfected system. The earliest roll commemorates a particular event, the Hainault campaign, and until 1500 it seems to have been fairly common for a herald to compile a roll after a military campaign, siege or tournament, recording the arms of the combatants.

Romances and poems are also important as heraldic records, but have a different relevance to that provided by seals and rolls of arms. The romances are primarily literary models of chivalry, drawn from a world of fiction and fantasy where men and events are larger than life. They were written from the end of the twelfth century – a century before the first rolls of arms were compiled – and provide the first literary references to heralds, banners, and shields of arms. Shield devices were mentioned as being used as a means of recognition on the field of combat, although descriptions of them are inevitably poetical, rather than by blazon. As Maurice Keen noted in *Chivalry*, the romances project an ideal world, 'the romantic authors habitually

BELOW: Holles Ordinary; *various quartered coats.*

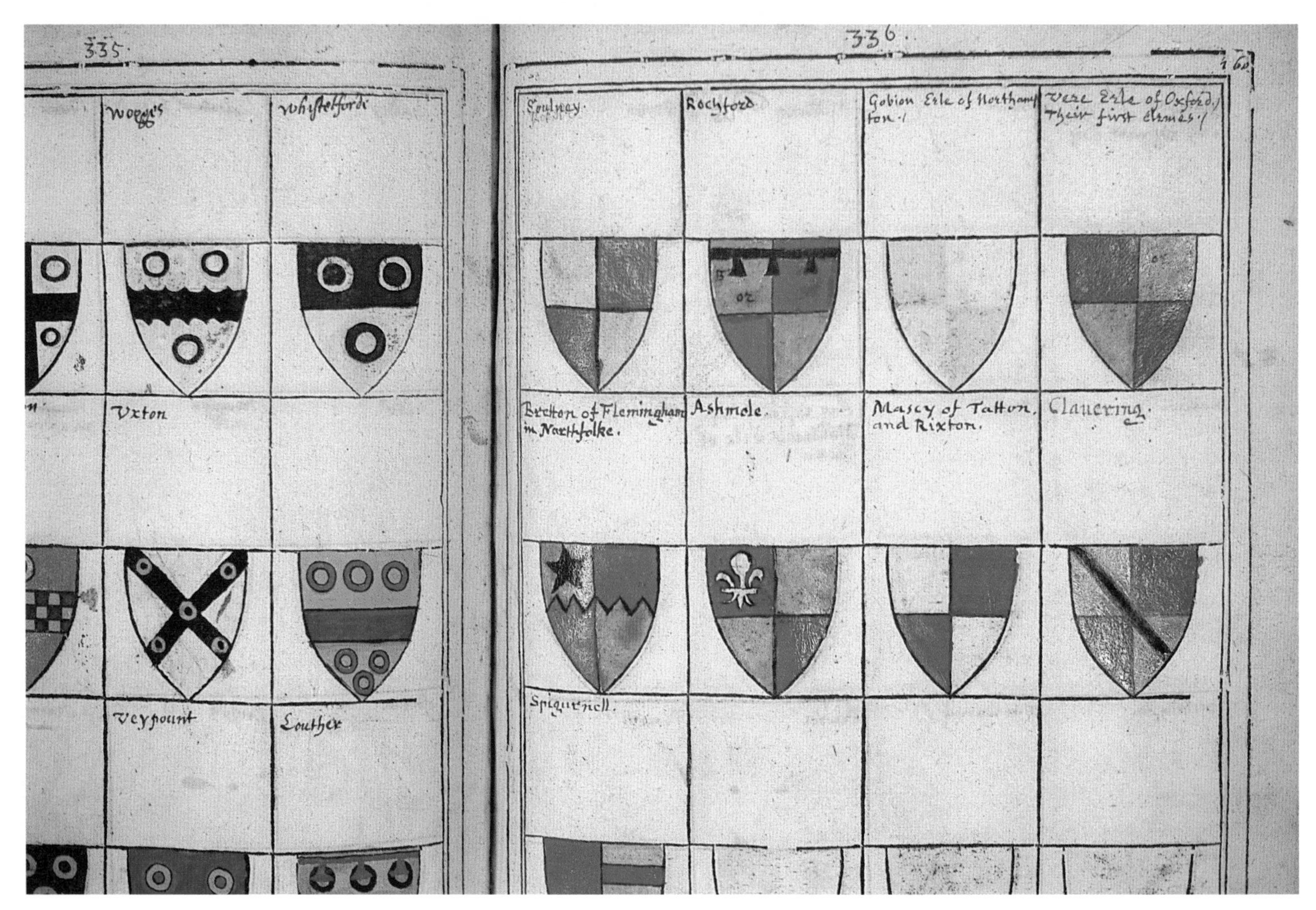

BRITISH
MUSEUM

associating together the classic virtues of good knighthood: *prouesse, loyauté, largesse, courtoisie,* and *franchise* (the free and frank bearing that is visible testimony to the combination of good birth with virtue)'. The romances were undoubtedly popular with contemporaries, but how much effect courtly ideals had on the behaviour of the average knight in the thick of battle or in the tournament mêlée is questionable. The harsh realities of life may have negated the civilising influence of chivalric principles.

Heraldry was an essential part of the chivalric ideal, the symbolic element of it in fact. Chivalry is a difficult concept to understand because it means different things to different people at different times. In essence it is an ideal by which a man achieved knighthood and by which he was supposed to live in honour and virtue. There are a number of surviving treatises on chivalry which provide an insight into the precise meaning of the concept. Their popularity lasted for centuries, and they were still being read in the fifteenth and sixteenth centuries. The *Ordene de Chevalerie*, written by an anonymous northern French poet before 1250, describes the ritual by which a man was created a knight, and explains the meaning of each part of the ceremony. The candidate underwent a ceremonial bathing to remove the stain of sin, supposedly emerging as clean as an infant from the baptismal font. This particular formality is still recalled in the modern order of chivalry, the Order of the Bath.

In the late thirteenth century the Majorcan writer, Ramon Lull, described the origins of chivalry, the duties of a knight and the qualities required of an esquire before he could attain knighthood, in the *Libre del ordre de Cavayleria*.

Geoffrey de Charny, himself a renowned warrior who was killed defending the French royal standard at the Battle of Poitiers in 1356, wrote three works, the *Livre*, the *Livre de Chevalerie*, and *Questions*, in which he discusses the joust, the tournament and war, and describes the different degrees of honour attached to each activity. Success in the joust is praiseworthy, but success in the tournament is better, and in war still more so. Gaining honour in war at home is accorded less prestige than battle honours acquired on a foreign battlefield.

BELOW: *Knights jousting c.1480, from the Military Roll of Arms.*

ABOVE: *The girding of a knight with a sword.*

Each of these authors shows a practical and humane understanding of what chivalry meant, and while the *Ordene* is entirely secular, Lull's and Charny's works have additional underlying Christian themes. There is a common thread running through all three works: that all candidates for knighthood must be of good birth, good lineage, and must have sufficient wealth to sustain their rank. Geoffrey de Charny extends these criteria to include men-at-arms as well as knights. From the time of early heraldry it was necessary to be well born to be a knight. This social distinction had a practical foundation, as any potential knight had to be wealthy enough to provide himself with at least one horse, as well as the other accoutrements of knighthood. The expense of knighthood thus helped to restrict the use of armorial bearings to those of the knightly class or above.

Heraldry, then, was an invention of the noble and knightly classes and evolved partly from the practical needs of combat, and partly from a desire to display. A combination of circumstances and ideas – feudalism, the chivalric ideal, the love of abstract decoration, and the desire for recognition in combat – fused together to produce conditions ideal for the development and flowering of heraldry. As Maurice Keen has commented, 'heraldry offered a means whereby both the class pride and the ideals of knighthood could be symbolically expressed, and the heralds, as experts in its history, literature and rituals became a kind of secular priesthood of chivalry'.

LEFT: *Seal of Margaret de Quincy, Countess of Winchester, c.1207-18.*

2
THE HERALDS

Henry Bedingfeld

LEFT: *The Garter stall plate of Ralph, Lord Basset of Drayton (d.1390), St George's Chapel, Windsor. It is the oldest surviving Garter stall plate.*

The first mention of a herald in literature seems to be in the romantic poem known as *Le Chevalier de la Charette*, written by Chrétien de Troyes between 1164 and 1174. At a joust the herald sees a shield which he does not recognise hanging outside a poor lodging. He enters barefoot, wearing only a shirt (he had pawned his other clothes for a drink at a tavern), in order to discover whose arms he has seen, and he finds Lancelot within. As Sir Anthony Wagner has written: 'It is unlucky that the first recorded act of the first recorded herald should be his failure to recognise a shield of arms!' But to be fair to our wayward herald, Lancelot was taking part in the joust in disguise, having been released from captivity on parole, and it is therefore not surprising that he was not recognised. Two things become apparent from this story. Heralds were known and written about as being involved in jousting in the third quarter of the twelfth century, and were evidently expected to be able to recognise arms only a short time after heraldry first came into being and before it became fully established as hereditary.

The tournament and joust, in fact, created the herald. It was he who had to proclaim the event, he who had to announce and acclaim the knight as he took to the field in combat, and he who had to be able to explain to the onlookers who was who. Chrétien de Troyes, in the *Chevalier au Lion*, calls them 'Li hera qui des vaillanz crie le ban?' In *Le Chevalier de la Charette* Chrétien de Troyes also points out the combatants to the Queen and her ladies: 'Do you see that knight yonder with a golden band across his red shield? That is Governau de Roberdic. And do you see that other one, who has an eagle and a dragon painted side by side on his shield? That is the son of the King of Aragon, who has come to this land in search of glory and renown. And do you see that other one beside him, who thrusts and jousts so well, bearing a shield with a leopard painted on a green ground on one part, and on the other azure blue? That is Ignaures the well-beloved, a lover himself and jovial. And he who bears the shield with the pheasants portrayed beak to beak is Coguillanz de Mautirec.' This is a vivid picture, at an early date, of the herald's skill of personal identification at a tournament.

Not only did the herald acclaim the knight entering the lists, but knowing a man's history gave him enough power to mar his reputation. He has been called the journalist of that age and perhaps because of this certain provincial newspapers include the word 'herald' in their names. Certainly present-day heralds are aware that they may be mistaken as a London representative of these journals.

For the first hundred years or so of heraldic history the French romantic poems seem to be the only sources that provide any mention of heralds and their activities, almost all of which were connected to the tournament. While they may not relate factual history, they do at least portray the conditions of the time. It is not until the latter part of the thirteenth century that we have the beginnings of documentary evidence mentioning heralds, rarely by name, but by title, and often in the company of minstrels or confused with them. The *Statutum Armorum* of 1292, containing new laws for the conduct of tournaments, forbade any king of heralds or min-

BELOW: *Two pursuivants followed by two heralds, all wearing tabards, in procession. Westminster Tournament Roll, 1511.*

strels from carrying hidden weapons or swords unless pointless, and ordered that kings of heralds should wear their surcoats of arms only. For making minstrelsy before Edward III at Christmas, a 1338 wardrobe document records a payment of wages to 'Master Conrod, King of the Heralds of Germany' and *ten other minstrels* of divers great lords of Germany. In 1348 payment was made to 'Magistro Andreae Roy Norreys' (Master Andrew Norroy King of Arms), Lybekin the piper, Hanekin, his son and *six other minstrels* of the king.

It is thought that heralds were originally minstrels who somehow managed to specialise in the tournament. Minstrels would undoubtedly have been present at tournaments as well as at the courts of magnates, and would have been familiar with who bore which shield of arms. There seems to have been a certain amount of rivalry between the two groups. There are a number of romantic poems which contain detailed heraldic references and which may have been written by heralds. However, judging by the number of disparaging comments about heralds, they are more likely to have been penned by a jealous minstrel: 'Heralds are boorish and deceitful and no one is greedier than a herald in pursuit of his perquisite of broken armour'. Heralds were entitled to collect broken armour when it had fallen from a

ABOVE: *The Earl of Warwick jousting at Calais, 1414. The Earl's herald stands holding two saddles, while on the left the joust is watched by an English royal herald sitting between two French royal heralds.*

90.

To all and Singuler noble and gentlemen of what estate dignytie, or degrees bearinge armes to whome theis p'nts shall come William Dethicke als Garter principall Kinge of Armes of Englande and of all other the Quenes mats kingdomes Domynions principallities Isles and provinces Knowe ye that by the aucthority and Custome of my office from her most royall and excellent matie and from her highnes most noble and victorious pro-

LEFT: *William Dethick, Garter King of Arms, depicted in the initial letter 'T' in a grant of arms to Charles Hewet of Dublin in 1597.*

Badges of Officers of Arms

knight, and probably resold it later in the tournament. There is a complaint that 'every knight has to maintain three or four heralds and cannot get rid of them' and another that 'there is no profession more convenient for an idle, greedy man, nor any in which one may talk so much and do so little'. It is not difficult to draw the conclusion that heralds, by specialising in tournament work, were in greater demand than minstrels and therefore financially more successful.

The heraldic fraternity was divided early on into three grades: Kings of Arms, heralds, and pursuivants. Kings of Arms controlled a given province and heralds acted under them, with pursuivants as followers learning their profession. In France and Germany in the Middle Ages there were hundreds of heralds but in England, it seems, not nearly so many. The king and the great magnates in England each had their own heralds and pursuivants, and so, too, did the rich knight, each herald

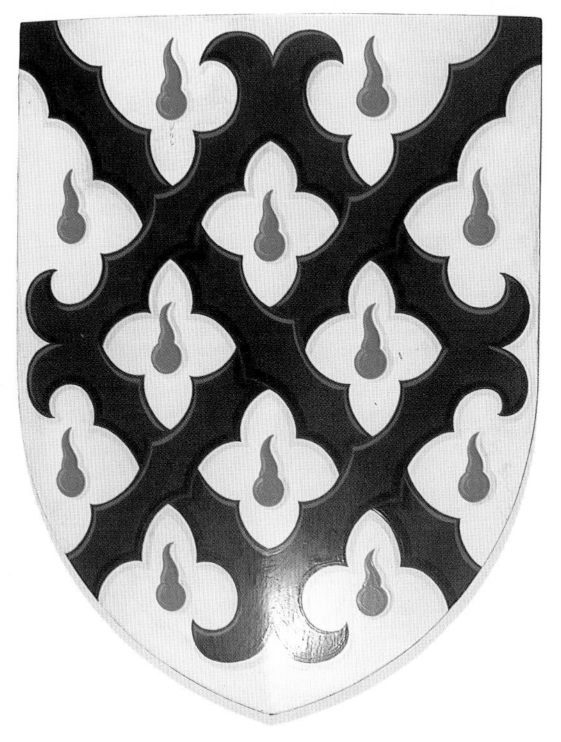

OPPOSITE PAGE: *The badges of office of the present English Heralds and Pursuivants in Ordinary.*

FAR LEFT: *The arms of Peter Gwynn-Jones, Lancaster Herald.*

LEFT: *The arms of Henry Bedingfeld, Rouge Croix Pursuivant.*

and pursuivant having a title of office. A study of the *College of Arms Monograph of the London Survey Committee, 1963* yields all the known names and titles of the English heralds. Apart from the obvious titles of territories conquered or acquired, such as Anjou,

LEFT: *Henry Bedingfeld wearing a tabard of the Royal Arms.*

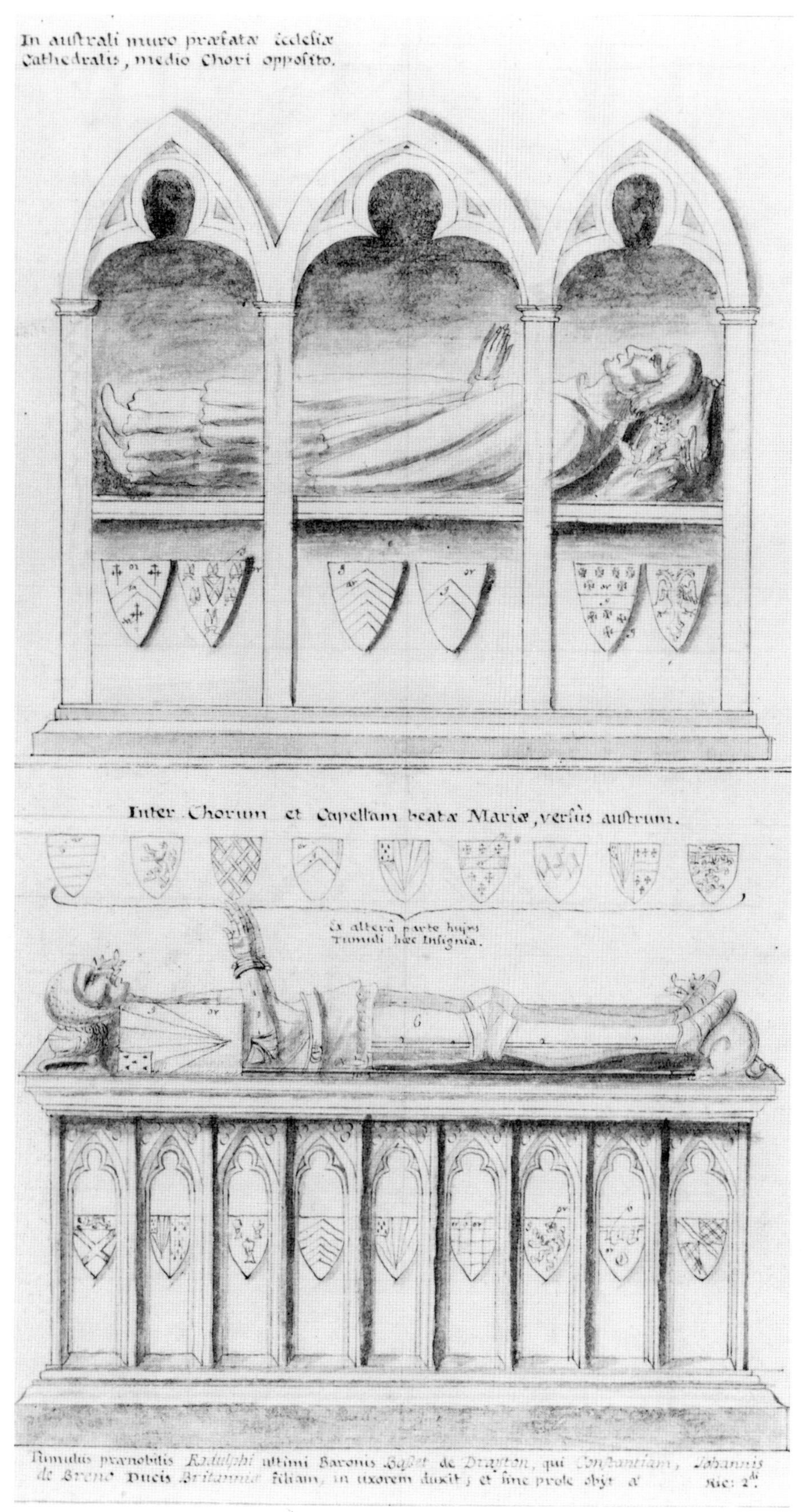

In australi muro præfatæ ecclesiæ
Cathedralis, medio Chori opposito.
Inter Chorum et Capellam beatæ Mariæ, versus austrum.
Ex alterâ parte hujus
Tumuli hæc Insignia.

ABOVE: *Drawings of two monuments in Lichfield Cathedral made at the Visitation of Staffordshire by William Dugdale, Norroy King of Arms in 1663/64. The lower one shows the effigy of Ralph, Lord Basset of Drayton, d.1390.*

Aquitaine or Guyenne, Ireland and Agincourt, Kings of Arms' and heralds' titles derived from lordships and castles like Lancaster (dating from 1347, both king and herald), Derby (1384), Nottingham (1399), Northumberland (1472), and Montorgueil (1494).

The titles of pursuivants are much more fanciful. These are taken from mottoes, badges and supporters, and include Bon Espoir (1419), Rouge Croix (1418/19), Il faut Faire (1443/44), Secret or Segret (1425), Bontemps (1434), Bonaventure (1445), Bon Rapport (1448), Tyger (1477) and Blanc Sanglier (*c.*1483, from the badge of Richard III). Lancaster Herald derives his name from the Earls and Dukes of Lancaster and his badge of office is the red rose of Lancaster royally crowned. The present incumbent is the forty-fifth to hold this office.

Rouge Croix Pursuivant was first created by Henry V and is named from the red cross of St George, badge of the Order of the Garter and sometime national flag of England. His badge of office is a red cross, and the present Rouge Croix is the eighty-second to hold this office.

Tyger Pursuivant, a title taken from the man-tyger supporters of Lord Hastings, from 1471 the Lieutenant-General of Calais, is known only from a letter from Edmund Bedingfeld, dated at Calais 17 August 1477, to Sir John Paston in Norfolk. Having conveyed local 'tydyngs' to Paston, and reported that King Louis XI of France is besieging St Omer, he goes on to say that 'the said French King within these three days railed greatly of my lord to Tyger Pursuivant, openly before 200 of his folks; wherefore it is thought here that he would feign a quarrel to set upon this town if he might get advantage'. Louis XI was using Tyger Pursuivant as a messenger, knowing that he would tell his master, Lord Hastings what he had heard.

Il faut Faire derives his name from Sir John Fastolf's motto. Secret or Segret, by name Laurence de Fugiers, was another of Fastolf's pursuivants and he and Roger Legh, Gloucester Herald (later to be Clarenceux King of Arms), suffered a most unfortunate incident in 1432 when they were robbed on the road between Rouen and Dieppe and barely escaped with their lives.

Before 1415 the chief of the English royal heralds held varying heraldic titles, but in that year Henry V created William Bruges Garter King of Arms, named after the Order of the Garter. Shortly after his creation he was present at the Battle of Agincourt with other English heralds, as was Montjoie, the French King of Arms. In 1406/07 the French royal heralds acquired the use of the Chapel of Saint Antoine le Petit in Paris and, endowed with a set of ordinances, had thus acquired corporate status. It was not until Richard III's charter of 1484 that the English royal heralds gained similar status, being

LEFT: *The College of Arms in Queen Victoria Street, London.*

BELOW: *The Garter feast in St George's Hall, Windsor Castle, 1672. The Hall was built by Edward III in 1363 and was completely altered in 1682. This engraving by Wenceslas Hollar shows the heralds standing in line before Charles II.*

PRECEDING PAGES: *St George's Hall, Windsor Castle, before fire destroyed the roof in November 1992. The arms of all Knights of the Garter were depicted here and the annual procession of the Knights of the Garter, preceded by the heralds, started from here.*

given a residence known as Coldharbour on the northern bank of the Thames in the City of London. This corporation is now known as the College of Arms. After the Battle of Bosworth in the following year, Henry VII removed Coldharbour from the heralds, who were obliged to conduct their business from the Court or their residences in London. This unhappy state of affairs was resolved in 1555 when Queen Mary gave them by charter a house in the City of London called Derby House. This was burnt down in the Great Fire of 1666, though the records were saved. A new College of Arms was built on this site and, with a lucky escape in World War II, it remains the home of the heralds today.

Tournaments must have been the chief occupation of the heralds until Tudor times, but from it they developed a further skill in ceremonial matters, whether for ceremonies of knighthood or coronation. They also acted as messengers between their masters and others. Certainly Tyger Pursuivant's diplomatic language must have been tested to the limit when he was railed at by the French king. Senior heralds were employed on special missions by the king (or queen), for example when taking the Order of the Garter to a foreign sovereign, and in their diplomatic capacity they had the equivalent of diplomatic immunity.

From the twelfth century the heralds' function evolved: from being observers and heraldic advisers at tournaments they became recorders, then controllers, then creators of arms. As the king's Court officials they came under the control of the High Constable and Earl Marshal and were in attendance upon their court, the Court of Chivalry, which regulated the use of arms. The growing number of armigerous individuals and complicated family descent involving arms meant that many cases were brought before it, one of the most celebrated being that of Scrope *v* Grosvenor, which lasted from 1385 to 1390. An argument over who had the right to bear *Azure a Bend Or* was finally decided in Scrope's favour by Richard II after a long case in which John of Gaunt and Geoffrey Chaucer were among the witnesses. The court still exists today as the Earl Marshal's Court, and the last case brought before it was in 1954.

Until the late thirteenth century, it seems that individuals could assume arms as they wished. Gradually, arms came to be regarded as property which could be inherited, and by

RIGHT: *The choir of St George's Chapel, Windsor, showing the banners and crests of the Knights of the Garter.*

the mid-fourteenth century it is clear that they were regarded as marks of privilege, dignity or nobility, grantable by royal authority through Letters Patent. The first known grant by Letters Patent was in 1338 by the Holy Roman Emperor Louis IV; the first known English grant, by Edward III, has not actually survived, but is referred to in a grant by Richard II. In 1393 he granted arms to Otes de Maundell, mentioning that this was a fresh grant to replace the one made to his father, Peter, at least 20 years earlier. The earliest surviving Letters Patent again dates from Richard II's reign and shows how arms had come to be regarded as a mark of distinction. In 1389, Richard granted arms to Johan de Kingeston so that he could 'faire certeins faitz et pointz d'armes' against a French knight in the tournament lists. He was raised to the rank of gentleman, the lowest rank of nobility, and then to esquire, but it is clear that without the right to bear arms, he was unable to respond to the challenge laid down by the French knight in tournament.

Richard II had a keen interest in heraldry, and made several grants during his reign, but generally grants of arms by English kings are rare. Unlike their European counterparts, they delegated the power to grant arms by Letters Patent to the Kings of Arms. Henry V appointed William Bruges Garter King of Arms in 1415, and the first of his grants that survives is to the Company of Drapers in London on 10 March 1438/39. The assumption of arms was obviously an area in which Henry wished to exercise control, because in 1417 he issued a writ to the sheriffs of Hampshire, Wiltshire, Sussex and Dorset, which referred to the assumption of 'Cotearmures' by men on recent military expeditions. He empowered them to stop this practice unless men had ancestral rights to arms, or had received an authoritative grant. Those that had borne arms with the king at Agincourt were, however, exempt, and could continue to use any arms they had assumed. This seems to lend credence to the words Shakespeare gave the king in his play *Henry V*:

BELOW: *The heralds in the Garter procession at Windsor Castle.*

For he today that sheds his blood with me
Shall be my brother; be he ne'er so vile
This day shall gentle his condition.

Another form of heraldic control, which started later but ran parallel to the Court of Chivalry, only to cease at the end of the seventeenth century, was the system of Heralds' Visitations. These developed from the production of rolls of arms and were heraldic surveys made from the mid-fifteenth century by the provincial Kings of Arms, ie Clarenceux, whose province is England south of the river Trent; Norroy, north of the Trent; and March, whose province was Wales and the west of England. March disappeared in Henry VII's reign and his province was divided between Clarenceux and Norroy. On appointment each King of Arms took an oath at his creation which required him to know and record the arms of noble gentlemen within his province. The earliest of these visitations was made by Roger Legh, Clarenceux (1435-60), the same man who was robbed in 1432 with Segret Pursuivant. In 1498-99 Henry VII issued a 'placard' or licence to John Writhe, Garter, and Roger Machado, Clarenceux, to visit the arms of gentlemen and to reform them if necessary, according to their oath at their creations.

In 1530 Henry VIII issued a Commission by Letter Patent under the Great Seal to Thomas Benolt, Clarenceux, to visit his province and 'to reform all false armory and arms devised without authority' and to 'deface and take away' all unlawful arms. Thus began a series of county visitations made by the provincial Kings of Arms or their deputies which lasted until the revolution of 1688, recording the lawful arms of the gentry visited, together with their pedigrees; those arms not acceptable had to be disclaimed. The series of visitations are a most important source of armorial and genealogical knowledge, unique in Europe, and they show that the royal heralds with direct royal authority had complete control over armorial matters during this period.

An unexpected controversy arose as a result of the 1530 Visitation Commission. Clarenceux and Norroy Kings of Arms both had clearly-defined provinces over which to exercise their jurisdiction, but Garter King of Arms, the senior heraldic officer, did not. With jurisdiction over Knights of the Garter and peers of the realm, Garter could, theoretically, grant arms to suitably qualified individuals in any area of the country. When he did this, he encroached on the territorial powers of the junior Kings of Arms and acrimonious disputes often resulted. It was not until 1680 that the Earl Marshal, who is responsible to the Crown for the College of Arms, was able to resolve the problem. He ordered in 1673 that all grants of arms were to be recorded at the College of Arms and, in 1680, that they were to be made jointly by Garter and Clarenceux in the south, and by Garter and Norroy in the north. A clause was also added to the Kings of Arms' patents of creation whereby they could only make grants with the Earl Marshal's consent by Warrant, and these orders apply to this day.

Since 1673 the College of Arms has kept a continuous series of grant volumes, which has now reached volume 158. Well over half these grants have been made in this century

ABOVE: *Rouge Croix Pursuivant reading the Letters Patent granting armorial bearings to Hampshire County Council. They were presented to the Lord Lieutenant of the county, Lt Col Sir James Scott, Bt, seated left. In the background is 'King Arthur's' Round Table, made in the late thirteenth century in the reign of Edward I.*

alone, and this is a clear indication that there is a strong and increasing demand for arms.

Heralds are visible to the public twice a year in full Court uniforms and tabards at the State Opening of Parliament and at the Garter Service in Windsor. They spend most of their time, however, engaged in heraldic and genealogical research. Regarded as learned officers of the Crown, they conduct themselves accordingly, but over the years there have been a few rogues entrusted with the job. Several have died of drink or insolvent in a debtors' gaol. William Radclyffe, Rouge Croix, however, did something far worse. In order to establish a claim to the estate of the Earls of Derwentwater, he entered a false pedigree in the College records, having forged a marriage entry in a parish register to act as proof. He was tried at York Assizes in 1820 and was sentenced to three months' imprisonment which he served still as Rouge Croix, not resigning his office until 1823. He died five years later. Others, such as Sir John Vanbrugh, seemed to have used their position as a sinecure. A celebrated architect and dramatist, Vanbrugh was not at all notable as Clarenceux King of Arms (1704-25). It was said of him that he knew nothing about heraldry and genealogy, and cared even less; in fact he ridiculed both and neglected his official duties.

Fortunately, many others have brought learning and considerable application to the

LEFT: *Her Majesty The Queen with her heralds at the time of the quincentenary of the foundation of the College of Arms, 1984.*

BELOW: *John Charles Brooke, Somerset Herald, 1778-94. Portrait painted on glass.*

NON PAREIL

TO ALL AND SINGULAR to whom these Presents shall come Sir Alexander Colin Cole Knight Commander of the Royal Victorian Order upon whom has been conferred the Territorial Decoration Garter Principal King of Arms Sends Greeting! **Whereas** The Right Honourable Charles Baron Forte Chairman of Lillywhites Limited hath represented unto The Most Noble Miles Francis Stapleton Duke of Norfolk Knight of the Most Noble Order of the Garter Knight Grand Cross of the Royal Victorian Order Companion of the Most Honourable Order of the Bath Commander of the Most Excellent Order of the British Empire upon whom has been conferred the Decoration of the Military Cross Earl Marshal and Hereditary Marshal of England that Lillywhites was first established by James Lillywhite as a sports goods shop in central London in 1863 and that on the Twenty-seventh day of January 1922 was incorporated as Lillywhites Limited under and by virtue of the terms of the Companies Acts 1908 to 1917 as athletic and general sports outfitters and in 1925 established premises at Piccadilly Circus in the City of Westminster That the management of the said Company is vested in a Board of Directors and whereas the said Directors being desirous that Lillywhites Limited as a corporate body should have Armorial Ensigns established under lawful authority and recorded in Her Majesty's College of Arms it having been submitted that the said Company by reason of its business record and general reputation was eligible so to petition have required him as Chairman of Lillywhites Limited and on behalf of the Board of Directors thereof to request the favour of His Grace's Warrant for My granting and assigning such Arms and Crest and in the same Patent such Supporters and such Device or Badge as are deemed suitable to be borne and used for ever hereafter by Lillywhites Limited on its Common Seal or otherwise according to the Laws of Arms and forasmuch as the said Earl Marshal did by Warrant under his hand and Seal bearing date the Twenty-seventh day of November 1991 authorize and direct Me to grant and assign the said Arms and Crest and Supporters and such Device or Badge accordingly Know Ye therefore that I the said Garter in pursuance of His Grace's Warrant and by virtue of the Letters Patent of My office granted by The Queen's Most Excellent Majesty to Me do by these Presents grant and assign unto the said LILLYWHITES LIMITED the Arms following that is to say Vert two Fleur-de-lis in chief and in base a Lily of the Field slipped Argent And for the Crest Upon a helm with a wreath Argent and Vert A Mount Vert thereon a Lily of the Field Argent seeded slipped and leaved proper between two Fleurs-de-lis also Argent Mantled Gules doubled Or and by the Authority aforesaid I do further grant and assign the Supporters following that is to say Upon a grassy compartment growing therefrom Lilies of the Valley on the dexter side a male figure being a representation of William Lillywhite as a bowler and on the sinister side a male figure being a representation of James Lillywhite as a batsman both habited as cricketers of the mid-19th century each in his own fashion and both proper And I do further grant and assign the following Device or Badge that is to say Within an Annulet fleury a figure representing Eros all Argent as the same are all in the margin hereof more plainly depicted to be borne and used forever hereafter by the said LILLYWHITES LIMITED on its Common Seal or otherwise according to the Laws of Arms In witness whereof I the said Garter have to these Presents subscribed My name and affixed the Seal of My office this Eighteenth day of August in the Forty-first year of the Reign of Our Sovereign Lady Elizabeth the Second by the Grace of God of the United Kingdom of Great Britain and Northern Ireland and of Her other Realms and Territories Queen Head of the Commonwealth Defender of the Faith in the year of Our Lord One thousand nine hundred and ninety two.

A. Colin Cole Garter

RIGHT: *The Letters Patent granting armorial bearings to Lillywhites Limited, showing a decorated border of lilies.*

job. William Camden, Clarenceux King of Arms (1597-1623) was a writer and antiquarian of note, as well as an extremely active herald who visited by deputy 20 counties in his southern province between 1612 and 1623. Probably the most famous member of the College was Sir William Dugdale, Garter King of Arms (1677-86). He accompanied Charles I to Oxford during the Civil War and at Charles II's restoration he was appointed Norroy King of Arms. He carried out Visitations to all ten of the counties in his province, usually with his clerk. A great benefactor to the College, he presented copies of his own works, some important transcripts, and arranged the gifts of many books and manuscripts by others. His clerk, Gregory King, was enormously talented; described as Dugdale's 'little clerk', he was not able to mount a horse from the ground for several years. He started working for Dugdale when he was 14 and, apart from his clerical duties, was also something of an artist. He was, by turn, a distinguished herald and genealogist, an engraver and cartographer, a draughtsman, one of the fathers of population studies, and a town planner. He laid out parts of Soho in London; Soho Square was originally named after him as King Square and the present-day Greek Street was originally Grig Street after his Christian name Gregory. He was Lancaster Herald from 1690 until 1712.

John Anstis, Garter (1719-44), was one of the most learned men of the College. It was mainly at his instigation that the Order of the Bath was instituted in 1725 by King George I.

He left a large manuscript collection to the College, and his most important published work is *The Register of the Order of the Garter.*

Elias Ashmole, Windsor Herald from 1660-75, gave Oxford University in 1672 a large collection of material he had acquired on the death of the naturalist John Tradescant, and he is best known as the founder of the Ashmolean Museum at Oxford. He had great ability as a herald and boundless energy, and wrote *The Institution of the Order of the Garter.* Sir Isaac Heard (Garter King of Arms from 1784 to 1822), fostered the Anglo-American connection. His first wife was a Bostonian and he visited America several times, corresponding with George Washington during his presidency. He is credited with being one of the first heralds to take an active interest in American genealogy, an interest continued by later heralds.

ABOVE: *Rouge Croix with the Lord Lieutenant of Hampshire, Lt Col Sir James Scott, Bt, with Mr F Emery-Wallis (left) and Councillor D A Keep, chairman of Hampshire County Council (right) in July 1992.*

LEFT: *The Letters Patent granting armorial bearings to Pickering Kenyon, solicitors. The decorated borders are composed of red and green filing tapes, and a symbol for each partner is included as a play on his name.*

DE MIEVLX EN MIEVLX
Rob. Cooke alias Clarencieulx
Roy Darmes

3
THE SCIENCE OF HERALDRY

Henry Bedingfeld

LEFT: *The armorial bearings of William Paston of Paston, Norfolk, signed by Robert Cooke, Clarenceux King of Arms, 1573. The quarterings show the arms of Paston, Peche, Leech, Somerton, Walcot, Barry, Hengrave, Watsam, Hetherset, Garbridge, Pevor and Mautby.*

BELOW: *A king showing the vair lining of his cloak, from the Westminster Psalter, c.1250.*

From the earliest heraldic times, or at least from the thirteenth century when the earliest rolls of arms were written, a language has been employed to describe shields of arms, crests, badges and supporters. Originally this language, which we 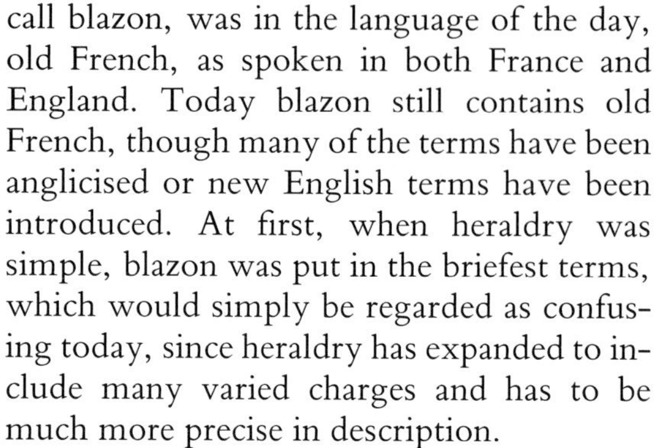 call blazon, was in the language of the day, old French, as spoken in both France and England. Today blazon still contains old French, though many of the terms have been anglicised or new English terms have been introduced. At first, when heraldry was simple, blazon was put in the briefest terms, which would simply be regarded as confusing today, since heraldry has expanded to include many varied charges and has to be much more precise in description.

The best-known shield of arms in England is the Royal Arms, which can be described in everyday speech as a red shield with three golden lions one above the other with their heads facing the viewer. This is both rather longwinded and somewhat inelegant. The earliest roll of arms, Glover's Roll of *c.*1255, has the first known blazon of the Royal Arms as follows: *Le Roy d'Angleterre port l'escu de gules oue trois Lupards d'Or* ('The King of England carries a red shield with three gold lions'). This was clearly sufficient at the time, and everybody would have known these arms well, but this blazon does not quite describe the arms precisely. Compare the earlier description with the latter blazon and the following modern blazon: *Gules three lions passant guardant in pale Or.* In early heraldry a lion passant guardant was called a leopard, or 'Lupard'; the term 'in pale' denotes that one lion should be placed above the other. The colours, '*Gules*' for red and '*Or*' for gold, are the same today as they were in the thirteenth century. (Heraldic convention has it that the claws and tongues of these lions are blue, though this is not blazoned.)

Fundamental to an understanding of heraldry is the fact that the left side of the shield is known as the *dexter* (the Latin word for right) and the right side of the shield is known as the *sinister* (the Latin for left). This is not a deliberate plot by heralds to confuse, but it describes the shield from the point of view of the *bearer* – the man carrying the shield.

The first step in blazoning a shield is to describe the background colour. This can be red (*Gules*), blue (*Azure*), black (*Sable*), green (*Vert*) or purple (*Purpure*) – these are called the tinctures. The other colours, gold (*Or*) and white (*Argent*) are called the metals. The background can also be patterned to show a fur, the principal ones being *Ermine* (black tails on white), *Vair* (a pattern of blue and white), and *Potent* (a crutch-like interlocking pattern). The background colour, called the field, can be a single metal, tincture, or fur; it can also be divided or parted. If the field

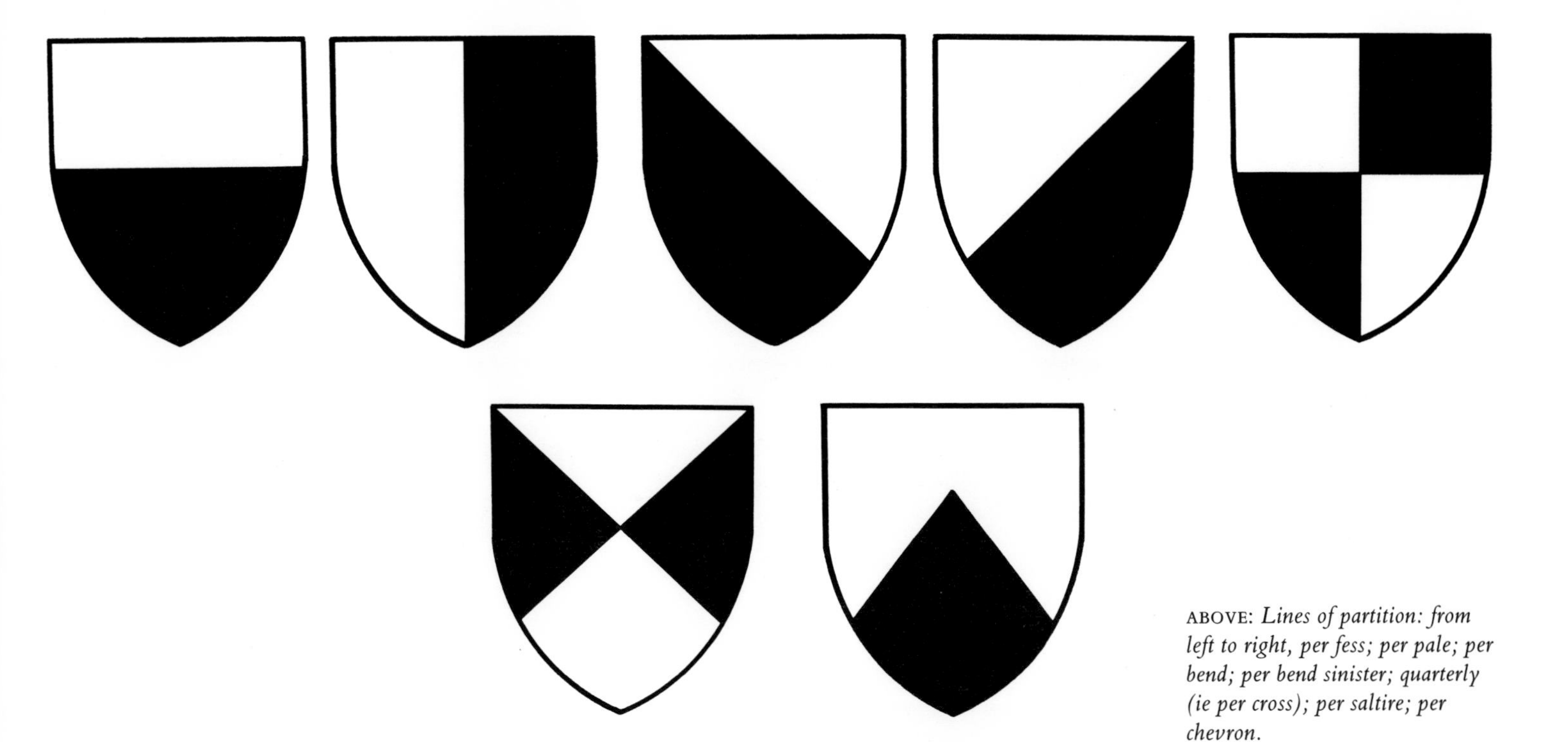

ABOVE: *Lines of partition: from left to right, per fess; per pale; per bend; per bend sinister; quarterly (ie per cross); per saltire; per chevron.*

is parted vertically it is *party per pale*; if horizontally it is *per fess*, if diagonally it is *per bend* or *per bend sinister*. It can also be *per chevron*, *per saltire* or *quarterly*. These partition lines can be multiplied so that many *per chevrons* on the shield becomes *chevronny*, *per saltire* multiplied becomes *lozengy*, and *quarterly* becomes *checky*. A multiplied *per pale* becomes *paly* and a multiplied *per bend* becomes *bendy*; they can be mixed so that *paly* combined with *bendy* becomes *pale bendy*. The straight lines of partition can also be decorated.

The second step in blazoning is to describe the principal shape or *charge* upon the shield. These geometrical shapes are usually referred to as the *Ordinaries* and are: *pale, fess, chevron, chief, bend, bend sinister, pile, pall, saltire* and *cross*. The width of these charges can vary, depending on whether they are plain or whether they have a device upon them. As a general rule, the *pale, fess* and *chief* are about one-third of the height or width of the shield, and the others are in the same proportion. They should be wider if they have charges upon them, and more narrow if they are between other charges. The edges of each can be straight, *engrailed* (indented in a series of curves which point outwards in a concave pattern) or *invected* (indented with a series of curves pointing inward). The most simple Ordinaries have diminutives: *pale* becomes *pallets*; *fess* becomes *bars* or *barry*; *bend*

BELOW: *The Ordinaries: from left to right, a bend; a bend sinister; a chief; a fess; a pale; a cross; a saltire; a pall; a chevron; a pile.*

ABOVE: *Differing forms of cross: from left to right, recercely; moline; patonce; fleuretty; fourché; crosslet; potent; crosslet fitchy; passion cross; pointed.*

becomes *bendlets*; and *chevron, chevronels*. There is no diminutive for *chief, pile* or *saltire*, and the cross has many variations.

If there is no Ordinary on the shield, the principal *charge* or charges are described next. A shield can have a single charge or figure, or a combination, and they are usually animals, mythical beasts, or inanimate shapes. The postures of animate charges must be described with terms such as *rampant* (a beast or monster standing on one hind leg), *passant* (walking past), *displayed* (a bird such as an eagle, with outstretched wings), *sejant* (seated erect).

In colouring charges, heralds observe a strict rule: tincture is not to be placed upon tincture, nor metal upon metal. Thus a red field with a black fess is not possible, nor a white field with a gold pale, for the simple reason that from a distance they would not be noticed.

The third step is to describe any secondary charges resting on the surface of the field. Thus the arms of de Montmorency are *Or a Cross Gules between four Eagles displayed Azure*, and those of the College of Arms are *Argent a Cross Gules between four Doves the dexter wing of each expanded and inverted Azure*.

The fourth step is to describe secondary charges placed upon the Ordinary, or main charge. Thus the arms of the City of York are, *Argent on a Cross Gules five Lions passant guardant Or* (recorded without tinctures at the Visitation of 1584). For a combination of the third and fourth steps, the arms of the University of Cambridge are *Gules on a Cross*

BELOW: *Various charges: from left to right, an eagle displayed; a lion rampant; a lion passant; a gryphon segreant; a boar sejant; a pheon; a pomegranate; a mullet; a maunch; a lymphad; a portcullis.*

Ermine between four Lions passant guardant Or a Bible lying fessways of the field clasped and garnished of the third the clasps in base (granted in 1573 and recorded at the Heralds' Visitation of 1575).

The fifth step is to describe important charges on the field which do not occupy a central position, such as a *chief, canton* or *bordure*. Therefore the arms of the Paston family are blazoned *Argent six Fleurs-de-lis 3, 2 and 1 Azure and a Chief indented Or*, those of Noel, (Earls of Gainsborough), *Or fretty Gules and a Canton Ermine*, and those of Montague (Earls of Sandwich), *Argent three Fusils conjoined in fess Gules within a Bordure Sable.*

The sixth step is to describe charges placed upon the chief, canton or bordure. Examples are *Azure a Fret Argent and on a Chief Or three Crescents Sable* (Hood) and *Quarterly 1st and 4th Azure three Fleurs-de-lis Or 2nd and 3rd Gules three Lions passant guardant in pale Or upon a Bordure Azure Fleurs-de-lis alternating with Martlets Or* (Henry Tudor as Earl of Richmond (Henry VII)).

It should be added that the field or Ordinaries can be *semy*, that is, strewn with charges as in the medieval French Royal Arms: *Azure semy-de-lis Or*, which shows many fleurs-de-lis strewn equally over the field. Another form of scattering is when droplets of liquid are displayed on the field, Ordinary or charge. Each of these droplets, or *gouttes*, has its own name. Droplets of water become *goutty d'eau* (white) and others are *goutty de sang* (red), *goutty des larmes* (blue), *goutty de poix* (black), *goutty d'huile* (green), and *goutty d'or* (gold).

Roundels (circles) also have their own picturesque descriptions. Gold roundels are *bezants* (when strewn they become *bezanty*), white roundels are *plates* (*platy* when strewn); a red roundel is a *torteau*, (*torteaux* when strewn); blue roundels are *hurts*; green roundels, *pomeis*; black roundels are *pellets* (*pellety* when strewn); and purple roundels are *golpes*. If the roundel is *barry wavy Argent and Azure* (representing water) then it is called a *fountain*.

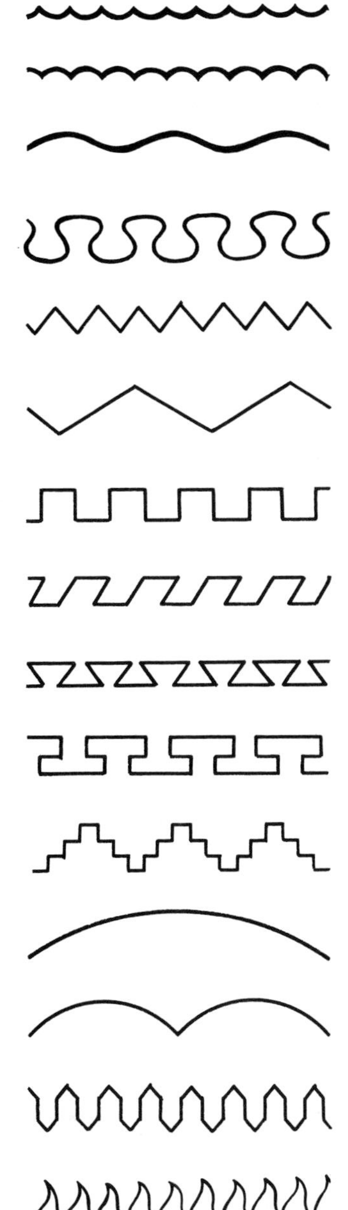

ABOVE: *Decorated lines of partition: from top to bottom, engrailed; invected; wavy; nebuly; indented; dancetty; embattled; raguly; dovetailed; potenty; embattled grady; arched; double arched; urdy; rayonny.*

LEFT: *The armorial bearings of Viscount and Viscountess Nelson.*

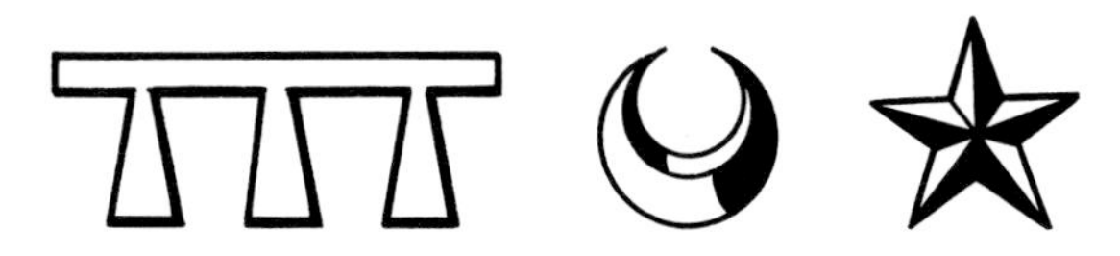

RIGHT: *Marks of cadency: eldest, second and third sons.*

Finally, marks of cadency are blazoned to denote the bearer as eldest, second, or third son etc; eldest sons bear labels, second sons, crescents, third sons, mullets, and so on.

When arms are shown with helmet, mantling, crest, supporters and motto, the whole combination is called the 'achievement of arms'. Next in importance to the shield of arms is the crest, which is three-dimensional and sits on top of the helmet. The full achievement is sometimes incorrectly referred to as the crest. From the helmet flows mantling on each side; this is depicted as a cut and shaped cape, thought originally to have shaded the knight from the heat of the sun or protected the neck from blows; it is coloured with a tincture on the outside and is lined with a metal. The mantling is held in place on top of the helmet with a crest wreath, depicted as twisted material coloured with an alternating metal and tincture (usually the first metal and the first tincture of the blazon), or a crest coronet. From either of these arises the crest.

BELOW: *The armorial bearings of Anthony Maria, 2nd Viscount Montagu, of Cowdray, Sussex.*

The helmet denotes the rank of the bearer: a steel tilting helm for esquires and gentlemen; steel with raised visor for baronets and knights; and steel with gold bars to the visor for all peers. The sovereign's helmet is wholly gold. Esquires' and gentlemen's helmets face the dexter; Baronets' and knights' and peers' face the dexter or can be *affronty* (facing the viewer). Supporters are an extra mark of honour and can only be borne by peers, Knights of the Garter and Thistle, and Knights Grand Cross of the orders of chivalry; only those of hereditary peers are inheritable. If the bearer is a Companion or Commander of one of the orders of chivalry, or more senior, or a Knight of the Garter or Thistle, then he can place the appropriate circlet of the order around his shield of arms and in addition show, suspended on ribbons below the shield, his orders and decorations. The motto can be in virtually any language though English, Latin and French are the most common. Mottoes are not part of a grant of arms but are adopted by the bearer and can be changed at any time.

So far we have discussed armorial bearings as borne by men, but women are subject to slightly different rules. Maiden ladies bear their paternal arms on a lozenge, a diamond shape that can have a decorated edge with a knotted bow at the top, known as a true lovers' knot. Married ladies bear their arms on a shield alongside those of their husbands; husband on the dexter, wife on the sinister. Widows continue to bear their marital coat, but on a lozenge rather than a shield, and divorcées revert to their paternal arms on a lozenge. Ladies do not bear crests because they do not wear helmets and are not combatant. However, it has recently been decided that women may take an 'active defence' role in the British armed services and, if commissioned, may in the future aspire to a grant of arms with crest, helm and mantling. History will have to relate as to whether the Kings of Arms will accede to this aspiration.

The marshalling of arms is a term used to describe the joining together of two or more coats of arms. Marshalling began with the compounding of arms, that is to say, taking part of one coat and adding to it part of another. John de Dreux, Duke of Brittany and Earl of Richmond, for example, was a grandson of Henry III and he placed the lions of England on a bordure around his own checky

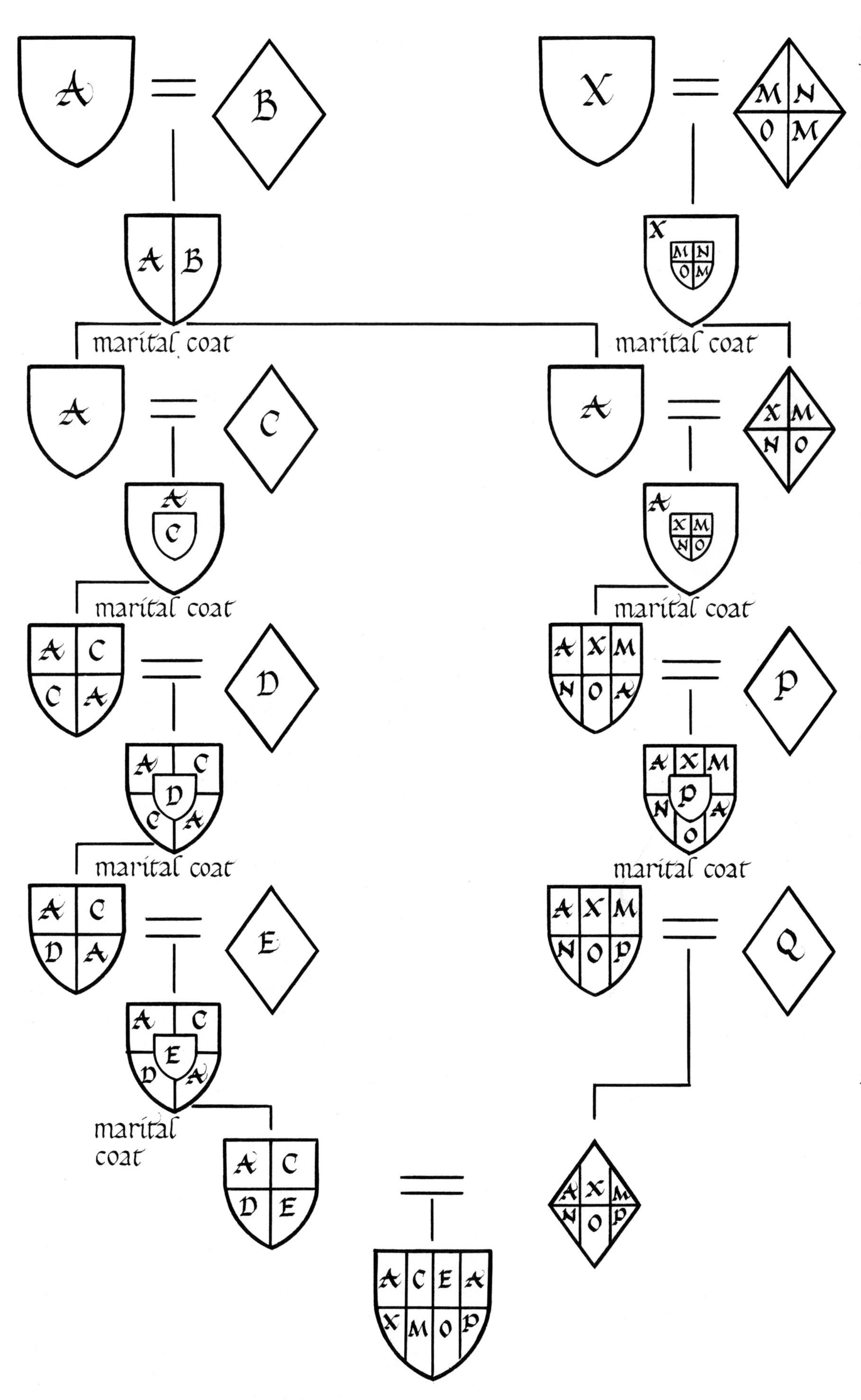

LEFT: *The system by which families may bear quarterings is based upon marriages to heraldic heiresses. A marries B who has brothers and is consequently not an heiress. A and B's marital coat shows the arms as impaled, but this arrangement ceases upon B's death. A and B have two sons; the first marries heiress C, and the marital coat shows the arms of A with an inescutcheon of pretence showing the arms of C, as A is said to be pretending to represent the family of C after C's father has died. After C's death their son can quarter the arms of C; the paternal arms A are placed in the first and fourth quarters, with C in second and third. This son then marries heiress D and the marital coat shows the quartered coat of AC with D on an inescutcheon of pretence. When D dies their son can then add the arms of D to his other quarterings so that his shield is quartered (1)A, (2)C, (3)D, (4)A. This system continues, and quarterings can be added whenever the family A marries other heiresses. The second generation of family A shows a second son (top right). He has married a Miss X, an heiress, who is already entitled to quarter the arms M, N and O. Their son, after X has died, can therefore quarter with his arms of A all those quarterings which his mother brought to the family. This process continues until one branch of A marries the heiress of the other branch of A, the son of this union being able to quarter A, C, D, E, A, X, M, N, O, P. Although the word 'quartering' would indicate only four divisions, in heraldry all the arms placed on one shield are termed as such, regardless of number.*

coat with a canton of Brittany overall. The arms of the de Bohun, Earls of Hereford, are said to have been compounded by adding the lions rampant of William de Longespée, Earl of Salisbury, to the attributed arms of two bends of Milo, Earl of Hereford. The arms of Prince John of Eltham: *England with a bordure of France*, is another example.

RIGHT: *The standard of Sir William Paston of Paston, Norfolk, 1532.*

Later, in the reign of Edward I, one sees the introduction of the practice of dimidiation, that is impaling (putting side by side) two coats on one shield, with each shield having first been cut in half vertically. This produced rather odd results. Edmund, Earl of Cornwall, dimidiated his shield of a lion rampant within a bordure of bezants (gold roundels) with the three chevrons of de Clare; being dimidiated the results show the lion cut vertically in half and the chevrons also, the latter appearing as three bendlets. Better known are the arms of the Cinque Ports, which consist of the arms of England dimidiating *Azure three ships hulls fesswise in pale Argent*, the result of which shows the front half of the lions joined to the back half of the ships' hulls. Another famous coat is that of Great Yarmouth in Norfolk, which shows the front halves of three lions joined to the rear halves of three herrings.

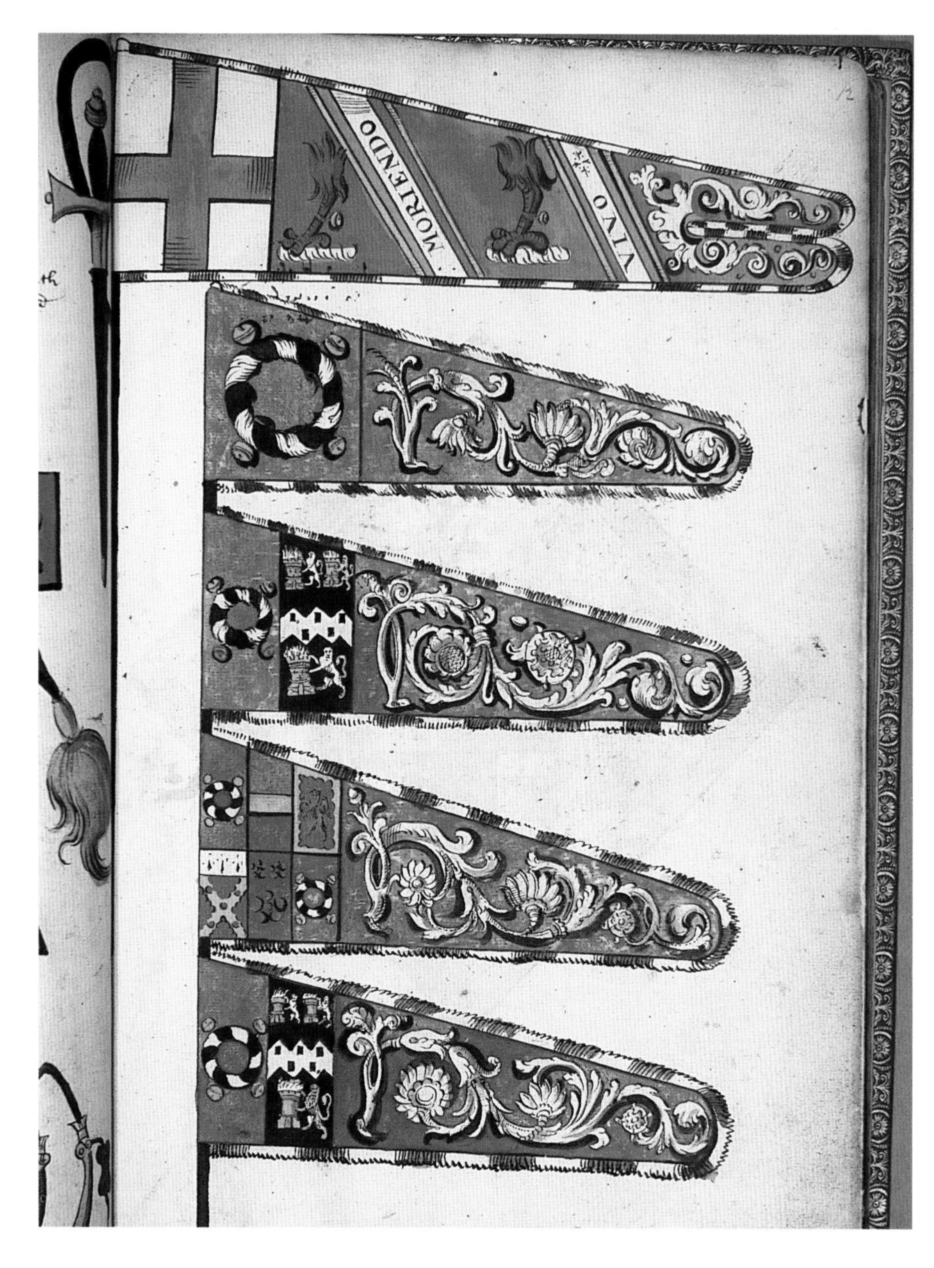

BELOW: *Standards of the Joscelyne family, part of a herald's funeral certificate, 1652-81.*

Dimidiation was clearly unsatisfactory, and in time it gave way to simple impalement. In personal heraldry, the husband's arms are placed in entirety on the left-hand side of the shield and the wife's arms in entirety on the right. Similarly, in arms of office, the arms of the corporation or institution are placed on the dexter and the arms of the head of that body are placed on the sinister, but only during his term of office. This applies to bishops, Kings of Arms, masters of livery companies, and chairmen of both civic and corporate bodies.

The marshalling of arms by quartering first occurred in England when Eleanor of Castile and Leon married Edward I. Her arms can be seen at Westminster, as the castle for Castile quartering the lion of Leon. Edward III's Great Seal of 1340 shows the ancient arms of France (*Azure semy de lis Or*) in the first and fourth quartering, with England in the second and third. King Edward's mother was Isabelle of France, the sister of kings Louis X, Philip V and Charles IV of France, who all died without male issue; and through his mother, Edward claimed the throne of France, reinforcing his claim heraldically by quartering the French arms. In about 1400 the French kings reduced the number of fleurs-de-lis on their arms to three, and the kings of England followed suit. British monarchs quartered the French Royal Arms until 1801, after the French mon-

LEFT: *Funeral accoutrements of a member of the Joscelyne family, from funeral certificates, 1652-81.*

archy had ceased to exist. Quartering indicates four divisions on a shield, but in fact the number of possible divisions is almost infinite. Families are entitled to quarterings if they have a descent in the male line from any forebear married to an heraldic heiress, that is, a woman entitled to arms who has no brothers (or deceased brothers without male issue). Marshalling by quartering is also possible when a 'name and arms' clause appears in a will. These were relatively frequent in the eighteenth and nineteenth centuries, and require beneficiaries to ask for a variation of the Laws of Arms, which state that arms descend down the legitimate male line. The beneficiary under the will (if unrelated) would need special permission from the sovereign (a Royal Licence) to put this clause into effect. This means that he could inherit property if he changes his name and arms to those of his benefactor, or adds the new name and arms to his.

Rychard
Anthony butler
wiffe to Edward West
Robert Morley de com norff
John paterson de London
Thomas Wood
William Tusser

4
THE ART OF HERALDRY

Peter Gwynn-Jones

LEFT: *Grants of William Hervey, Clarenceux King of Arms, made in 1559. These include arms for a woman, Jane Collyns, the wife of Edward West (top right).*

It is often assumed that most medieval armorial bearings have specific meaning. As many were no more than bands of contrasting colours or tinctures, much has been written to attribute qualities to each of these tinctures, and to arrange them in order of importance. This practice in England can be traced back to John de Bado Aureo who wrote his heraldic treatise, *Tractatus de Armis*, in the last years of the fourteenth century. De Bado Aureo and later writers distribute virtues to the tinctures in a variety of different ways. Gold, for example, shifts from being the tincture exclusively used by royalty to that associated with obedience. Faith was another attribute of gold and in this form it must have overlapped with blue as the tincture of loyalty. Blue varied as a tincture of war or of peace and friendship. There is nothing to suggest that medieval heraldry incorporated these ideas or that they have in any way affected post-medieval heralds in their task of creating and designing new armorial bearings. As Joseph Edmondson wrote in his *Complete Body of Heraldry*, in 1780, 'but as to such ridiculous fancies, the mere mention of them is fully sufficient'.

The numerous medieval arms featuring bands or stripes were greatly influenced by the twelfth-century Renaissance which awakened a love of decoration in the knightly classes. In addition, the structure of the shield was ideal for those who wished to decorate it in contrasting tinctures.

Any attempt to analyse early heraldry and the physical nature of the shield must take into account the Bayeux Tapestry, which depicts the Norman invasion of England in 1066. It shows knights armed with shields adorned with wavy geometrical designs and indeterminate dragon-like creatures. Twenty years later, in her eye-witness account of the First Crusade, the Byzantine princess Anna Comnena noted that the shields of Western European knights were plain with polished metal bosses and plates. Clearly, it is difficult to reconcile these two sources of evidence as it seems unlikely that the style and nature of shields would have altered so dramatically within 20 years. The Bayeux Tapestry designs almost certainly did not contribute to the heraldic designs which emerged approximately a century later. The centrifugal wavy patterns emanating from the centre of many shields on the Tapestry was not a formation found in early heraldry, which also had no place for dragon-like figures. Recently doubts have been cast on details found in

BELOW: *The Bayeux Tapestry – although not considered heraldic, the geometric configurations of the shields of knights have never been satisfactorily explained.*

LEFT: *Simple geometric forms of bars, bends and crosses in early medieval heraldry, seen in the College of Arms' Mowbray's Roll, painted c.1365-70.*

RIGHT: *Some forms of cross may have evolved from a central boss and small scattered crosses from weapon deflectors; both types are manifest in the arms of Knowles, painted 1616.*

the Tapestry, pointing out that some of the eating habits and items of dress depicted did not exist in Western Europe in 1066. There is a growing school of thought that later custodians of the Tapestry effected doodles and infillings; but until its threads are subjected to scientific examination, these doubts will remain unanswered. Given the possibility of later infillings, these shield decorations should be treated with a measure of suspicion.

Anna Comnena's account of plain shields with polished bosses and plates agrees with the general supposition that early twelfth-century shields were made of wood and covered on both sides with leather to which extra defences of metal were added. Exuberance of spirit and love of colour manifest in the twelfth-century Renaissance would allow for these bands of metal to be painted in contrasting tinctures. Similarly, studs and bosses, when painted in different colours would give rise to distinctive forms, which may have been the origin of many roundels or circles, the escarbuncle (a boss-like formation with decorated spokes) and some forms of heraldic cross which can be seen as a simpler form of the escarbuncle. Later theories often attribute the cross to the presence of the original user of the arms on a crusade. However, a shield strengthened with one vertical metal band and one horizontal one would provide a cross formation, and a decoratively-treated stud or boss could account for the variety of smaller crosses as individual heraldic charges.

The incidence of simple charges in early heraldry is manifested by the crescent. An analysis of *Smith's Ordinary*, a collation of medieval armorial bearings made in the sixteenth century, demonstrates the importance of the crescent. Out of the 9000 shields of arms depicted, 168 are listed under crescents – nearly one in 50 shields therefore bore this charge. It seems doubtful whether the medieval knights were inspired to adopt an Islamic device, as their later descendants have so often claimed, overlooking the fact that their ancestor often never partook in a crusade. Cognate heraldry may have played a part, that is to say the adoption of the crescent from the existing arms of a family connected by blood or feudal tenure. However, the frequency of the crescent suggests that its use had a more practical origin. The addition of a simple sliver of metal to a shield would serve to deflect an antagonist's weaponry; practicality in the twelfth century may have meant that the crescent was no more that a glancing device used to drive off a sword or an arrow at an oblique angle and a vital part of self-preservation in warfare.

The evidence that pieces of metal were used as deflecting devices on shields is given further credence by the mullet, shaped like a

ABOVE: *Crescents may have originated with pieces of metal hammered onto the shield to deflect weapons, as seen in the College of Arms'* Jenyn's Ordinary*; painted c.1380.*

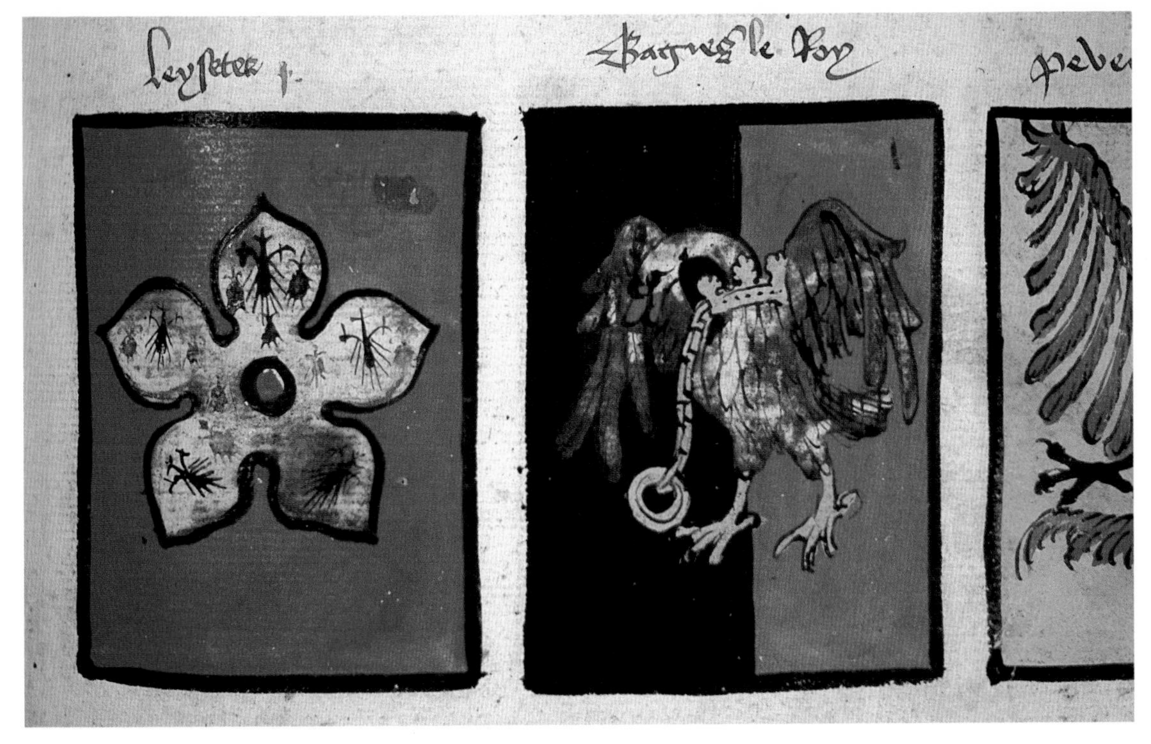

LEFT: *The swan badge of Bohun, inherited by Henry V through his mother, Mary Bohun, adjacent to the Leicester cinquefoil; painted c.1480.*

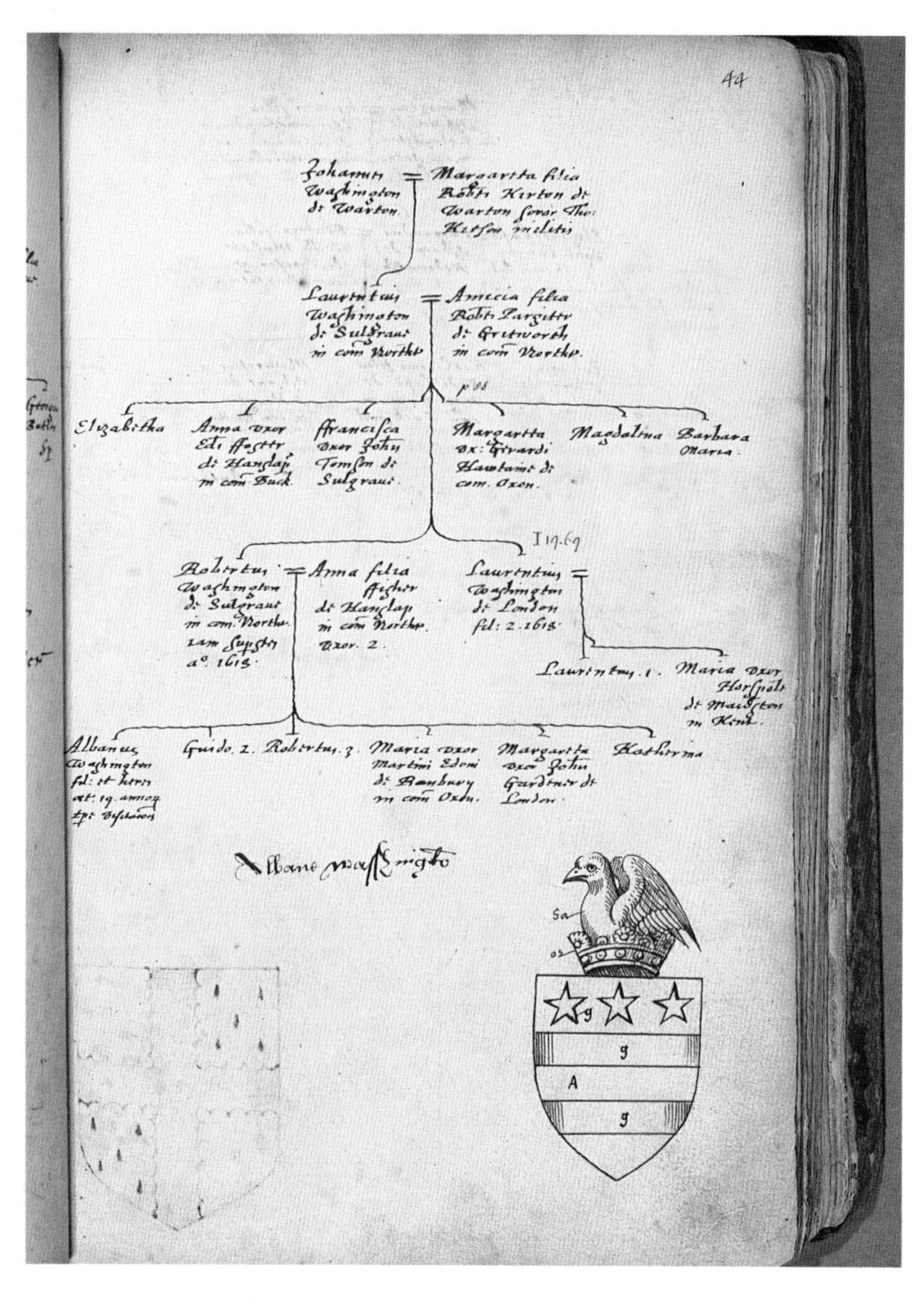

ABOVE: *The Washington pedigree and armorial bearings entered at the Heralds' Visitation of Northamptonshire, 1619. The arms may have inspired the American flag.*

FACING PAGE: *Martlets in the arms of Valence: tomb of Aylmer de Valence, Earl of Pembroke (died 1323) at Westminster Abbey.*

five-pointed star and frequently pierced in the centre. The term 'mullet' means 'little mill' or 'wheel', referring to the spur rowel. As a small, sharp piece of metal, it may have been hammered onto the shield for protective purposes and subsequently painted in contrasting tinctures to the background of the shield. *Smith's Ordinary* lists 280 shields charged with mullets. If mullets were used in this way, it is possible that charges such as annulets or rings, and billets or rectangles, may also have originated with pieces of metal employed as shield deflectors. Smith lists 93 and 73 shields for these charges respectively.

The practical nature of much early heraldry dictated by the structure of the shield can, to some extent, be seen in the choice of tinctures. Although these were seldom, if ever, chosen for symbolic reasons, a desire for recognition on the field of battle or tournament, and a love of bright colour gave rise to the principle of never placing colour (*Sable, Azure, Gules* or *Vert*) on colour, nor metal (*Argent* or Gold/*Or*) on metal. The limited use of green in early shields of arms is thus explained: it simply did not show up against the natural colours of the countryside.

In addition to permitting the structure of the shield to dictate the nature of much early heraldry, the medieval knight drew heavily upon fauna, exercising a subjective desire to be associated with the masculine and warlike characteristics of certain animal species. Many also wished to demonstrate a blood or feudal link with other families and the resultant grouping of families bearing similar arms is known as cognate heraldry.

The research of Sir Anthony Wagner, Clarenceux King of Arms, has admirably demonstrated the importance of the swan in cognate heraldry and in so doing has demonstrated that pre-heraldic legends may have provided the inspiration for certain heraldic charges. One eleventh-century legend tells of an unknown knight who disembarked from a river boat towed by a white swan in order to protect the widowed Duchess of Bouillon and her daughter Beatrice. His subsequent marriage to Beatrice imposed on her an oath never to question him as to his birth. A daughter, Ida, was born to the couple before Beatrice ultimately asked the fatal question. The Swan Knight departed as he came, never to be heard of again. Ida subsequently married Eustace, Count of Boulogne, and many of their descendants adopted the swan as their heraldic charge. Other versions relate that the Swan Knight rescued and married the widowed Duchess of Brabant, from whom sprang the ducal line of Cleves and other noble families, who also adopted the swan as a heraldic device.

The heraldry of the Washington family also exemplifies the cognate and the choice of a charge based on allegiance to another family. It is known that in 1182 one William de Hertburn purchased the manor of Wessyngton in County Durham, from which he and his descendants subsequently derived their surname, Washington. There is a plausible suggestion that the original William was the son of Patrick of Dunbar, the second son of Earl Gospatric of Dunbar. Certainly his thirteenth-century Washington descendants featured on their shield a lion similar to that of the Dunbar family. In 1278 Robert de Washington held the manor of Routhworth from the Barony of Kendal. The Barons of Kendal bore arms, *Argent two bars Gules*; and

Robert de Washington and his descendants exchanged their lion for the well-known arms, *Argent two bars Gules in chief three mullets also Gules*. It is thought that these arms may have inspired the armorial bearings of the United States adopted by Congress in 1782, and the stars and stripes of the American flag.

A constantly recurring charge in medieval heraldry is the cinquefoil. This combines the cognate with the pun. Puns have always provided inspiration for the choice of charges from the inception of heraldry down to the present day. Some cinquefoils are now believed to have originated with the pimpernel flower adopted as a punning charge by Robert FitzPernell, Earl of Leicester. The earldom and the pimpernel flower, stylised into the cinquefoil, subsequently passed to Simon de Montfort, Earl of Leicester, in the thirteenth century. In the baronial wars which split England during the reign of Henry III, it seems likely that many of de Montfort's supporters incorporated the cinquefoil in their arms to demonstrate their allegiance.

This combination of punning and cognate heraldry can be discerned with many charges. It explains much of the popularity of the martlet (ie the swift, swallow or martin). Although the speed of the martlet probably had an attraction in its own right, other families such as Valence, Earls of Pembroke, and Arundel adopted it as a punning device. *Volans* means flying, and *hirondelle* is the French for swallow. Both these families were linked to other families who thereby chose the martlet to feature in their arms.

The pun explains the use of many inanimate charges which might otherwise have had limited or no appeal. Many inanimate charges fall into this category. Leaky is said to have borne water bougets or goatskin containers; Seffington bore scythes and Shakerley and Shuttleworth bore shuttles. Spades were adopted by the families of Standelf, Gardner and Swettenham: a *delf* is that which is delved or dug, and vigorous digging usually produces sweat. Inanimate charges such as bugle horns and horseshoes are also frequent in medieval heraldry. Horseshoes were borne by the families of Ferrers, Ferounes and Shoyswell; horns by the families of Horne, Horner, Forrester, and hence Foster and Forster.

Over the centuries a number of romantic tales have emerged to account for charges appearing in some medieval armorial achievements. Most of these tales are apocry-

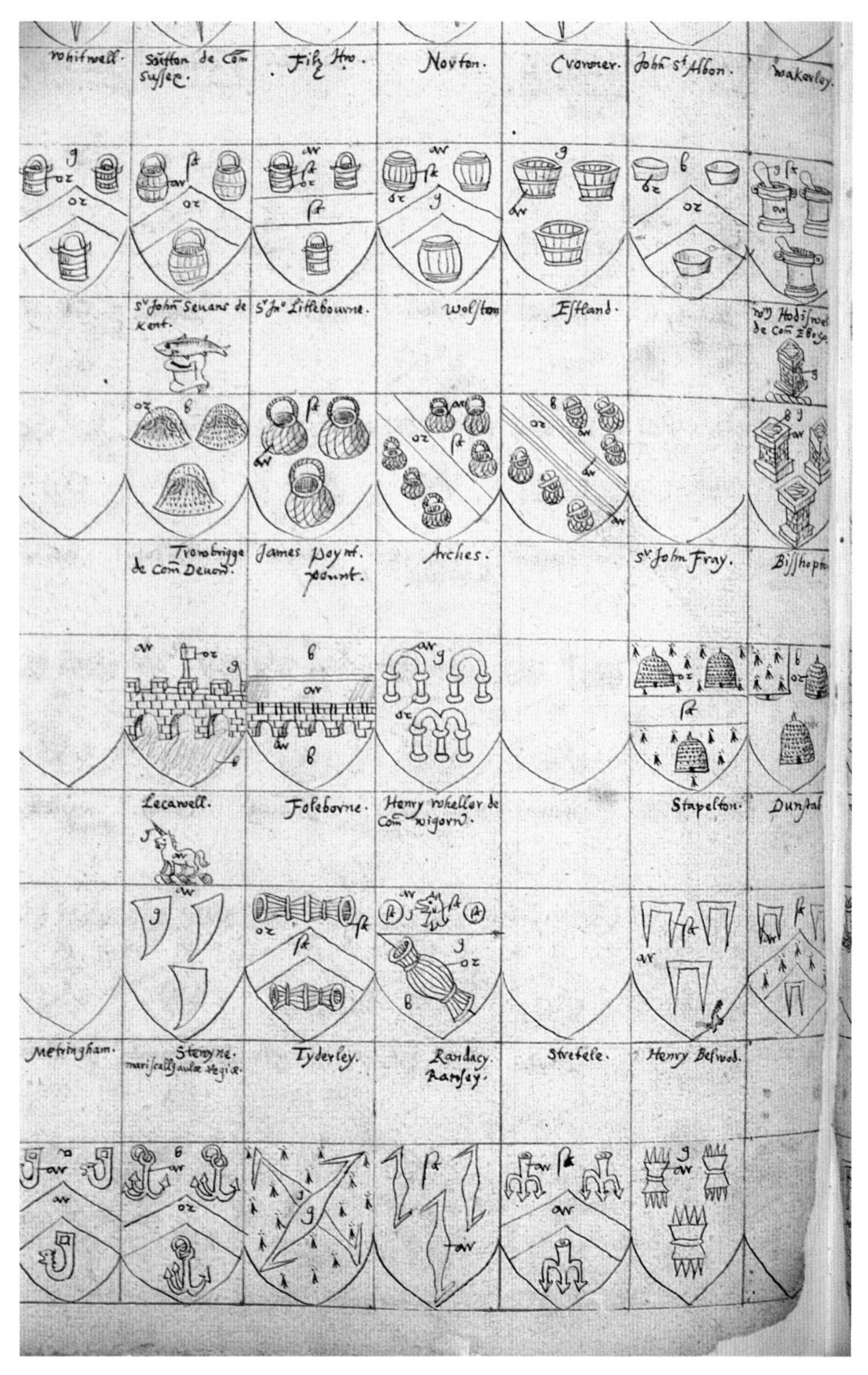

ABOVE: *A page from the sixteenth-century* Smith's Ordinary *showing inanimate objects in medieval arms; many were used as a punning allusion to the surname.*

phal and do not stand the test of critical enquiry. Traditionally, the Prince of Wales' badge of feathers was adopted by Edward, the Black Prince, from the crest of the blind King John of Bohemia who was slain at the battle of Crécy. This story ignores two facts: the crest of King John consisted of two eagles' wings scattered with linden leaves, and the ostrich feathers are known to have been used by some of the Black Prince's brothers. It is now recognised that the feathers were introduced into English regal heraldry by Philippa of Hainault, the mother of the Black Prince, and the feathers are likely to be a punning allusion to Ostrevans, a county held by her family.

However, in dismissing fanciful tales, the sceptic must be wary, for a few medieval heraldic charges may owe their origin to unusual events. The heart in the arms of Douglas is one such example. In 1330 Sir James Douglas undertook to convey the heart of Robert Bruce to the Holy Sepulchre at Jerusalem in accordance with the latter's dying wish. Sir James was killed on the journey, and both his body and the heart of Bruce were brought back to Scotland, where the heart was incorporated into the arms of the Douglas family. Another legend which may be based on fact concerns the FitzGerald monkey. A tale is told of Thomas FitzMoric, the thirteenth-century ancestor of the FitzGerald Earls of Desmond. On the news of his father's death, 'Suddainly the nurses running forth cryeing and lamenting the childe was left all alone, when a monkey that was kept in the house tooke him out of the cradle, carried him to the topp of the castle, there unwrapped him out of swaddling clothes, licked and lapped the childe and folded ye child up in cloathes againe and . . . brought him downe againe in safety, and left the sayed child where first he found him, and finding the nurse settled by the cradle gave her a sound boxe on the eares, as it is thought thereby warneing and admonishing her to looke better hereafter to her charge'. The crest of the Earls of Desmond, however, is a boar, but another branch of the family, the Earls of Kildare, bear a monkey. This suggests that it may have been John FitzThomas FitzGerald, 1st Earl of Kildare, an exact contemporary of Thomas FitzMoric, who was

RIGHT: *Although many families of Forester, Forster and Foster used stags or hunting horns as a punning allusion, one medieval family of Forster was more direct and used a forester himself, equipped with bow, arrows and horn.*

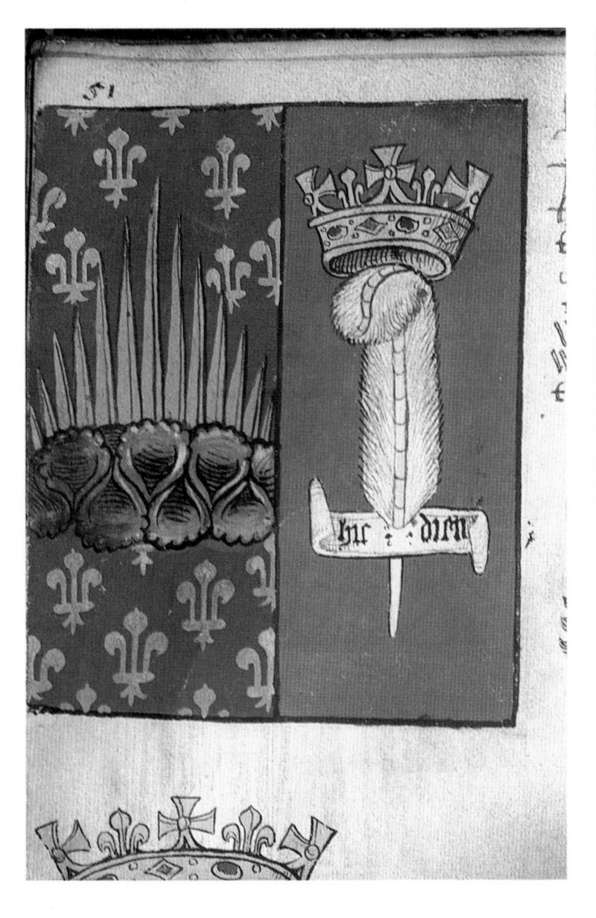

FAR LEFT: *An ostrich feather and the motto* HIC DIEN [Ich Dien] *shown as a badge of Edward III and now accepted as being derived from his wife Philippa of Hainault. Painted in the studio of Sir Thomas Wriothesley, Garter King of Arms, early sixteenth century.*

LEFT: *The heart of Robert Bruce in the arms of Sir James Douglas, Earl of Douglas and Avondale, c.1461. The crest is a dog-like salamander breathing fire (see chapter on heraldic monsters).*

carried off by the monkey. Here the legend recites that the infant was rescued by the castle monkey during a fire.

Moreiddig Warwyn was a twelfth-century Welsh chieftain who ruled over a territory roughly covered by Breconshire and North Carmarthenshire. Warwyn means 'fair neck' and may refer to a birthmark. Medieval superstition attributed this to an adder which frightened his mother while she was resting in a garden during her pregnancy. The mark of the snake was laid upon the neck of the child, his place of birth was named Lle-Dychrynllyd, the place of horror; and his descendants thereafter bore a boy's head with a snake entwined about the neck.

Towards the end of the Middle Ages several developments become apparent which were to influence the nature of future heraldry. Design began to break through the

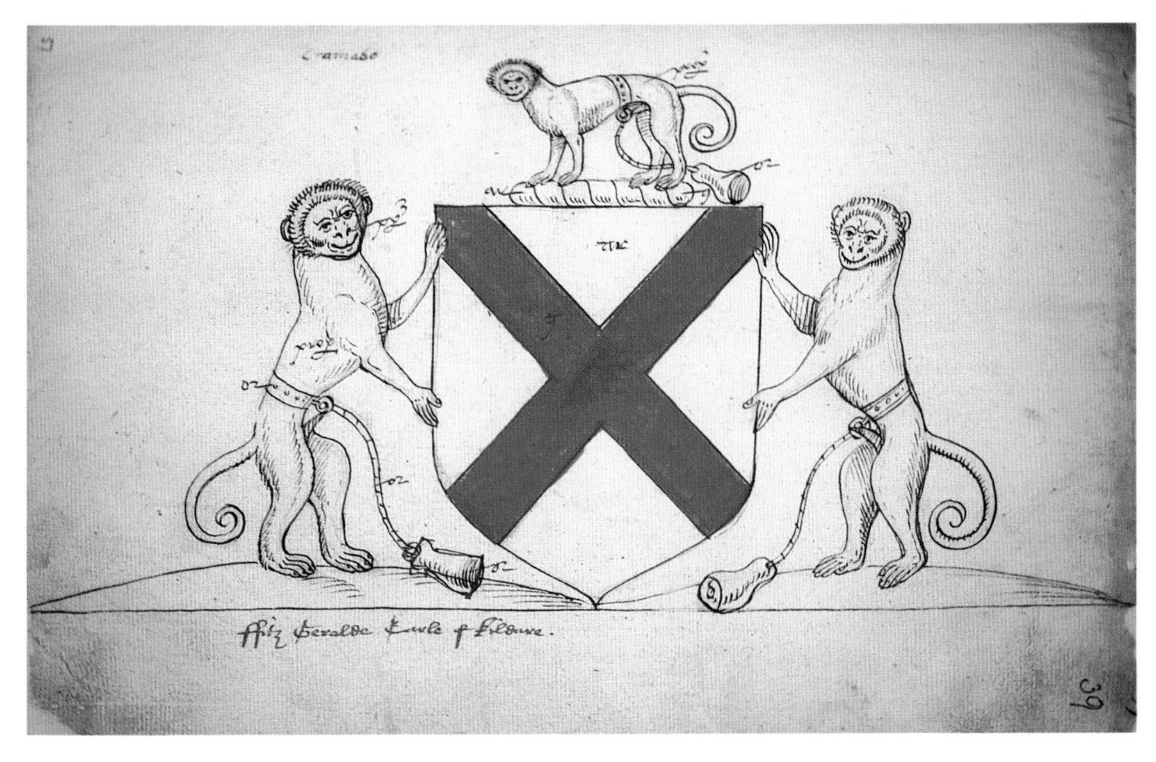

LEFT: *The FitzGerald monkey, supporters and crest of Gerald FitzGerald, Earl of Kildare, drawn c.1601.*

RIGHT: *Salters in the arms of the Company of Salters (granted 1530, although this drawing is contemporary). Both Companies subsequently received grants of crests and supporters at the end of the sixteenth century.*

FAR RIGHT: *Havettes and teasel in the arms of the Company of Clothworkers (granted 1530).*

medieval reluctance to place one charge upon another. Invariably a fess or a chevron had been placed between three devices of similar nature. Gradually these devices were placed on the fess or chevron, making it possible to set three other charges in the blank areas of the shield. This new arrangement was to be exploited by the early Tudor heralds to provide a style of heraldic design far removed from anything known to their medieval predecessors.

A second development stems from the granting of arms to corporate bodies such as the mercantile companies of London, beginning with the Drapers Company in 1438. These grants incorporated charges which reflected the craft or trade of the grantee and thus introduced a number of inanimate objects unknown to early heraldry. Charges long used as puns now acquired a new meaning as occupational heraldry. The arms of the Clothworkers Company granted in 1530, for example, featured the teasel, havettes and the ram. These charges recall the ancient crafts of fulling and shearing. New cloth was trampled in water for cleansing and thickening in a process known as fulling. Thereafter the fuller scoured the cloth with teasels or thistle

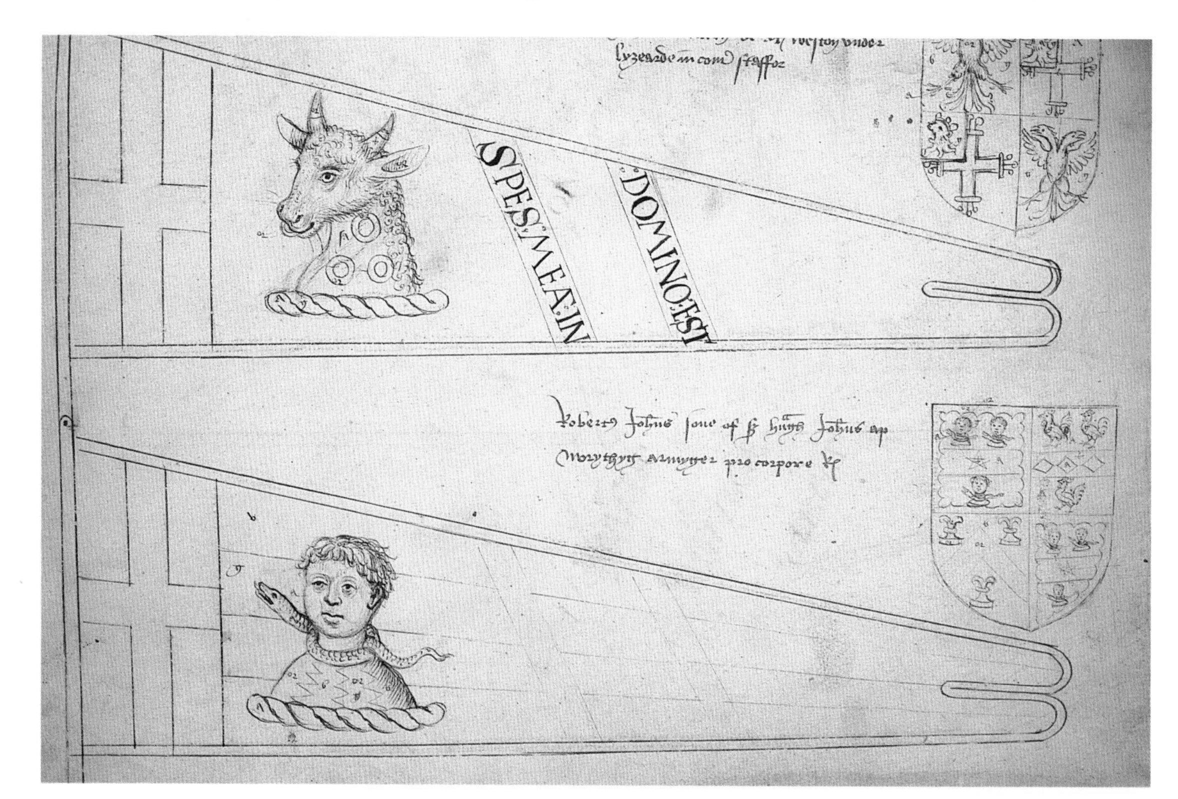

RIGHT: *The crest of Robert Johns indicates his descent from Moreiddig Warwyn, whose supposed birthmark on the neck was attributed to a snake, drawn c.1530.*

LEFT: *In later medieval heraldry devices appear charged on the Ordinaries. Examples from the Fenwick Roll, painted during the reign of Henry VI, include escallops on a bend, a lion on a chief, estoiles on a saltire, and lozenges on a bend.*

heads to remove loose particles and raise a nap before it was passed to the shearman, who stretched the material over a padded bench with the aid of a havette, a form of double hook. The crest of a ram is a clear allusion to the source of the raw material, but may also imply the shearman's stretching frame which in France was known as a *rame*. The choice of charges reflecting the grantee's career or occupation was increasingly to influence the nature of heraldry.

With the incorporation of the royal heralds in 1484, and the subsequent growth of Tudor bureaucracy, a better system of record-keeping came into existence. It therefore becomes gradually easier to ascertain the original grantee or bearer of the arms, to know more about him and the reasons why particular charges were chosen. At the same time the granting King of Arms can be identified and his particular preferences in design can be discerned.

In 1484 John Writhe was Garter King of Arms, a position which he held from 1478 to 1504. New grants of armorial bearings made by John Writhe and his fellow Kings of Arms during the two-year reign of Richard III numbered five, namely Whiting, Rede, Gough, Horton and the Company of the Wax Chandlers. Of the personal grants, only Rede included a crest, that of a duck, possibly a shoveller, *bendy Or and Argent*; his arms may be blazoned as *Gules on a bend wavy Argent three ducks Sable beaked and legged Gules*. The ducks, being birds frequenting reeds, are clearly a straightforward pun, showing that the pun as an inspiration of design was still in use. Of the remaining

ABOVE: *Typical grants of armorial bearings made by Sir Thomas Wriothesley, Garter King of Arms, 1505-34. Crests are made pale, bendy or checky and hold, or are placed between, sprigs of foliage, and arms are heavily charged with different devices.*

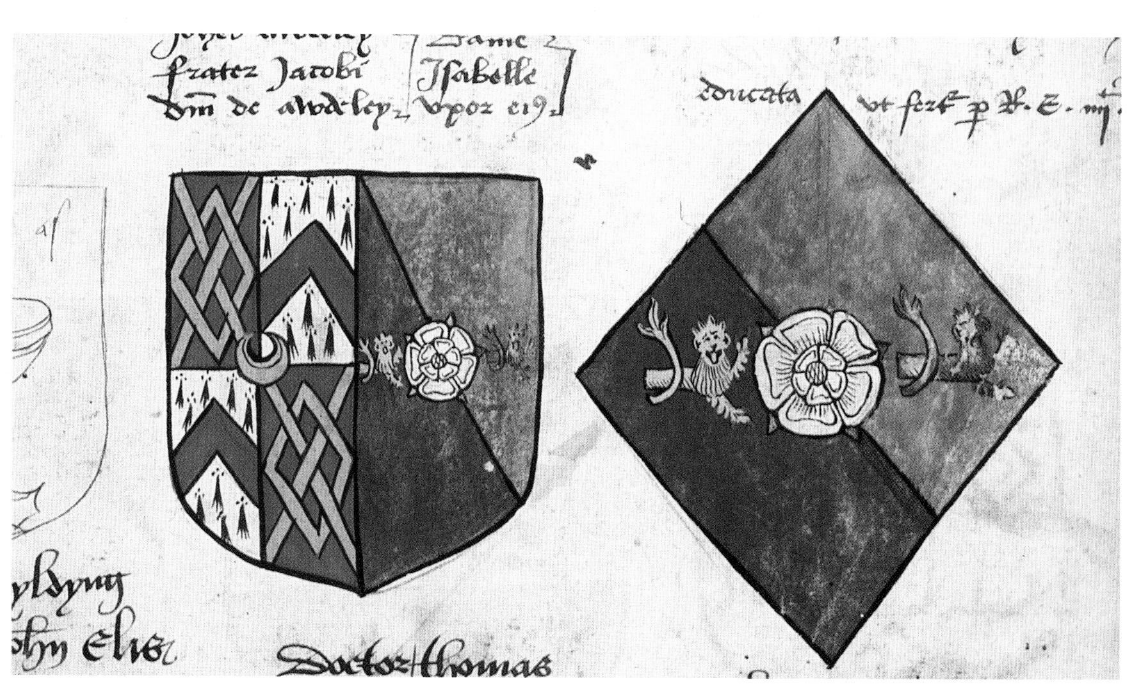

RIGHT: *Blue and murrey, the livery colours of the house of York in the arms granted to Isabella Mylberry, illegitimate daughter of Edward IV (right); the same marshalled with those of her husband, John Awdeley (left).*

personal grants, Horton is notable for including a *fess company countercompony between three crossbows*. The reason behind the crossbows may be elusive; but the compony or chequered fess was granted with the chequers in blue and murrey, the livery colours of the house of York. This inclusion of royal livery colours is a feature of several fifteenth-century grants and extends also to the blue and white of the house of Lancaster. Cognate heraldry, like punning heraldry, had survived the Middle Ages.

The apparent paucity of grants of armorial bearings that can be attributed to John Writhe and his colleagues at the end of the fifteenth century is misleading. It was a period enormously rich in heraldic creation, but the records of the College of Arms giving details of specific grants are sparse. Badges and supporters proliferate, yet documentary Letters Patent issued by the Kings of Arms granting them seem non-existent. The power to grant and confirm all armorial bearings had been vested in the Kings of Arms since the early fifteenth century, when this could have been interpreted as applying only to the shield of arms. Badges and supporters were therefore not considered to come under royal jurisdiction, and Letters Patent would have been unnecessary. Another reason for the lack of documentary evidence may have been that it was only the upper echelons of armigerous society who assumed badges and supporters: people whose gentility was never in doubt, and who required no authority to prove their social status. The style of heraldic designs in this period, however, suggests a common designing source, and it seems unlikely that many people would have assumed arms without recourse to the heralds. The monster supporters of the late fifteenth century, such as the pantheon, bagwyn and enfield, appear to come from the imagination of one man or group of men, presumably the heralds. The Kings of Arms were therefore probably far more active in granting arms than the surviving documents would imply, only issuing Letters Patent to those whose right to bear arms might be challenged. Discussion and informal sketches rather than formal documentation may also have been sufficient to produce arms. This may explain the absence of any documentation for the grant of the College of Arms itself; none would query the right of the Kings of Arms to grant armorial bearings to their own corporation.

Writhe's son, Thomas Wriothesley, succeeded his father as Garter King of Arms in

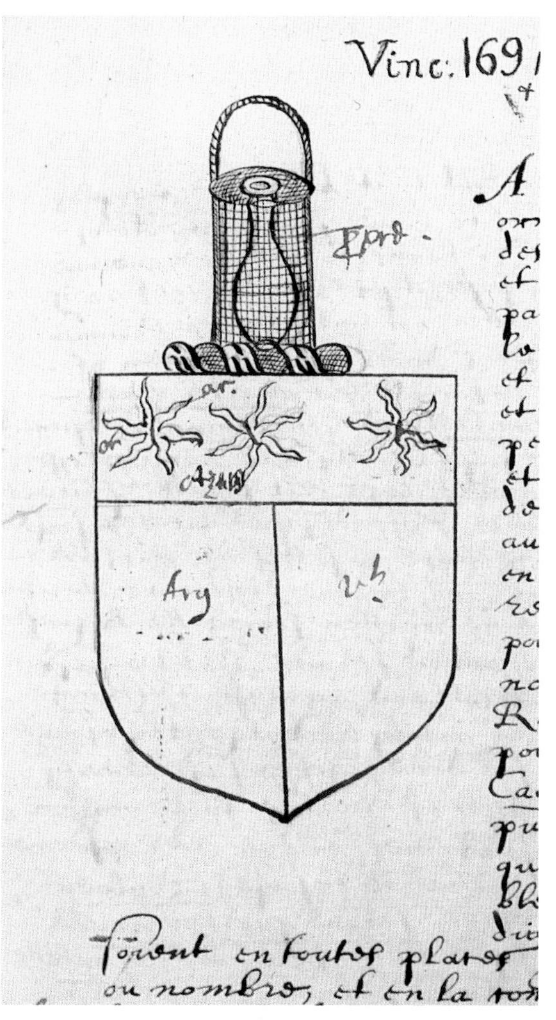

LEFT: Ung orynall dedens son case en leurs propres coleurs, *a urinal in its basket, granted as a crest by John Writhe, Garter King of Arms, to Louis Caerlion, 1493.*

BELOW: *Typical of puns used by Sir Thomas Wriothesley, Garter King of Arms, is the rabbit within a warren, the crest in the grant of armorial bearings made to Ralph Warren of London, c.1528, who subsequently became Lord Mayor in 1536.*

RIGHT: *Woodpecker 'chopping' in the crest in the grant of armorial bearings made to Richard Chopping, alderman of London, c.1532.*

1505, an office he held until 1534. Wriothesley and his contemporary Thomas Benolt, Clarenceux King of Arms, 1511-34, were responsible for a period of heraldry unique in its creativity and distinctiveness. Approximately 500 Wriothesley/Benolt arms have been identified. With the exception of those made to women and clergymen, all include a crest, which was a major break with medieval practice. Until the early sixteenth century, crests were borne by the limited few of tournament rank, whose attributes in the fifteenth century also included supporters. Wriothesley and Benolt now allowed crests to be granted with all arms, while restricting the use of supporters; and this practice has continued to the present day. A typical Wriothesley/Benolt crest was subject to an exaggerated form of the art and science of heraldry previously found in the shield. Crests of animals were therefore divided by a paly, barry, quarterly or bendy formation charged with additional devices, and were frequently provided with a sprig of foliage to hold in beak or claw. The shield itself drew heavily upon the late fifteenth-century practice of charging Ordinaries with a further device; typical arms of the Wriothesley period contained two or three charges in combination with an Ordinary such as a chevron or fess, in stark contrast to medieval heraldry where only one such charge would have been used. The result is arguably cluttered and lacking in control; but it is nonetheless exciting and allowed English heraldry to break away from its medieval restrictions, providing for future freedom of design.

The reasoning behind Wriothesley's choice of charges is too often obscure. Cognate heraldry accounts for the frequent use of blue and murrey, the livery colours of the house of York, which had been adopted by the Tudors in addition to their more familiar colours of green and white. Similarly, association with the Crown doubtless accounts for the many Wriothesley grants incorporating the greyhound which was, *par excellence*, the royal beast of the Tudors. (Henry VII used two greyhounds as his supporters.) Occupational heraldry, as found in the arms of fifteenth-century mercantile companies, is not immediately obvious. In 1493 John Writhe had granted Louis Caerlion, Doctor of Medicine, the crest of a urinal in a basket. During the Wriothesley period such an obvious allusion to the grantee's occupation seems to have been confined to simple charges, for example, bezants or gold roundels for a goldsmith.

In contrast, the heraldry of Wriothesley and Benolt is liberally sprinkled with puns; Edmund Haselwood's crest is typical: *a squirrel sejant Azure collared and charged with three roundels in pale Or and grasping a branch of hazel Vert fructed Or.* Ralph Warren was granted the crest of: *a mount Vert environed of a palisade Or thereon a rabbit statant Sable eared and footed Or about the neck a collar compony Argent and Gules cottised Or.* The crest of Richard Chopping was: *an oak tree Vert fructed Or the trunk bendy wavy of four Argent and Gules thereon a green woodpecker proper.* (The woodpecker is, of course, the ornithological chopper.) The crest of John Chrystmas sports a cubit arm grasping a branch of holly, as do the crests of William Hollys and William Grene. John Pasmere was granted the crest of: *a demi sea hare Azure scaled Argent the ears and forefeet Gold.* 'Puss' is a term still used by beaglers for the hare and *mare* is Latin for sea.

The mid-sixteenth century witnessed a return to simplicity in design for which Thomas Hawley, Clarenceux King of Arms from 1536 to 1557, would appear to be largely responsible. Hawley favoured engrailed crosses or chevrons, placing these between animals or animals' heads. His grants demon-

LEFT: *A page of crests granted by Sir Thomas Wriothesley, in which three arms hold bunches of holly as a pun on the surnames of Chrystmas, Hollys and Grene.*

strate that the personal whims and tastes of individual heralds have played a major part in heraldic design and the choice of charges. At times these seem to have dominated, to the near exclusion of any wishes or preferences of the grantee.

There was also a large increase in the number of grants of arms, and recent evidence suggests it may have been by as much as tenfold. It is now known that Hawley's successor, William Hervey, Clarenceux King of Arms from 1557 to 1567, was responsible for approximately 80 grants a year. Many of these relate to the growing number of Court officials and members of the professional and mercantile classes. A typical page of Hervey grants in the official records of the College of Arms contains 23 entries, with grants to the Queen's physician, a skinner of London, a sergeant at law, an alderman of London, a doctor of the arches, a knight, a Londoner, a gentleman of unspecified location or occupation, a gentleman of Devon, a Londoner, a water bailey of London, another Londoner, a gentleman of Warwickshire, a gentleman of Norfolk, another of unspecified residence, another of Cornwall, two master cooks to the Queen's Majesty, the Lord Mayor of London, the latter's wife, a gentleman of Kingston in Surrey, and two goldsmiths of London.

By 1584, the centenary of the College of Arms, the simplification of heraldic design first seen under Hawley as a reaction to the Wriothesley period had intensified, and was being applied to a growing number of new grantees. The heraldry of 1584 was largely the responsibility of the industrious Robert Cooke, Clarenceux King of Arms.

William Segar, Garter King of Arms from 1604 to 1633, wrote of Cooke that he 'confirmed and gave Armes and Crests without number to base and unworthy persons for his private gaine onely, without the knowledge

LEFT: *Sea hare crest of John Pasmere, granted c.1520. 'Puss' is a term used for a hare, and* mare *is Latin for sea.*

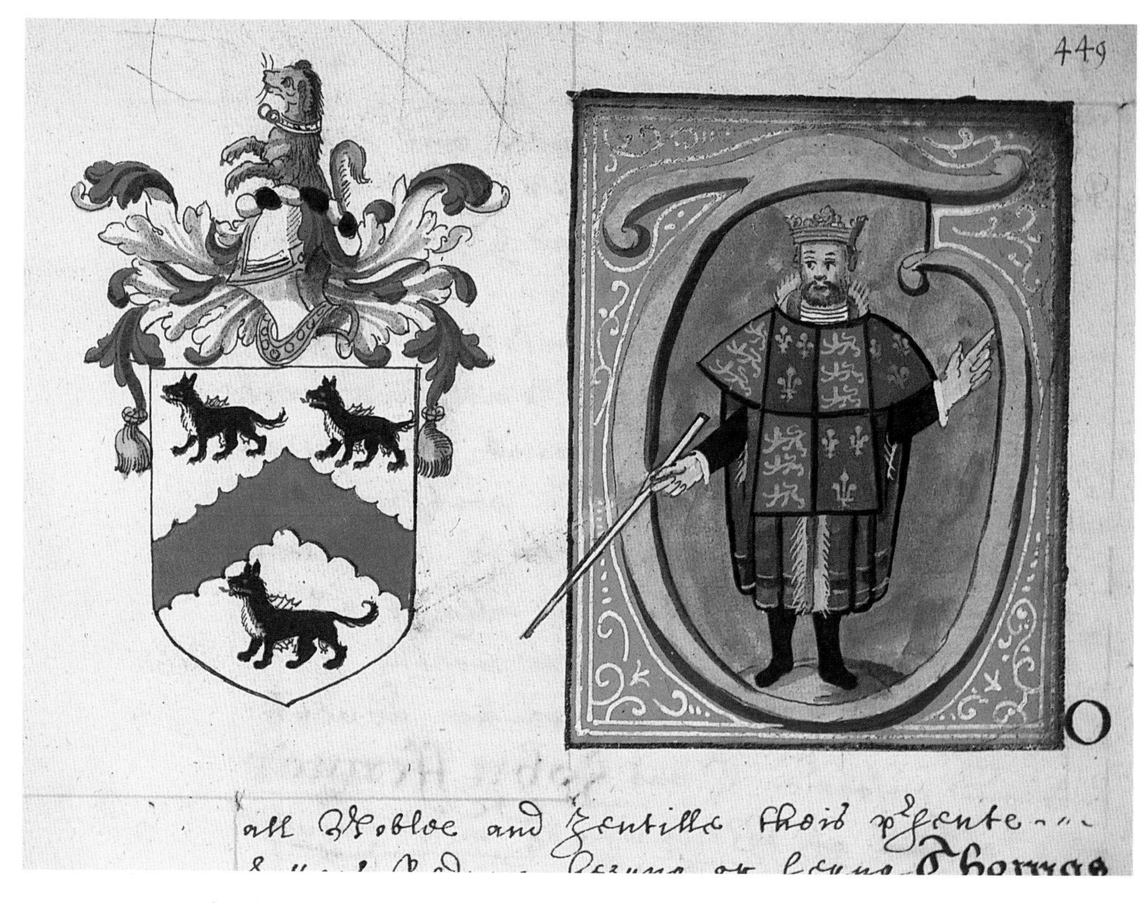

RIGHT: *Thomas Hawley, Clarenceux King of Arms, granting arms to John Fennar in 1556. Hawley favoured a greater simplicity in design than that found in the early sixteenth century. The animals in the arms are 'wolffs maryn' (black sea wolves with white fins).*

of the Erle Marshall'. 1584 was certainly a year of activity in Cooke's office. *Hare's Ordinary* lists 25 Cooke grants specifically for that year. Of other undated grants from this same source, between 14 and 21 are likely to have fallen within the same period, which suggests that Cooke was approaching something in the region of a new grant each week. However, this is misleading. It is now known that Cooke's predecessor, William Hervey, granted approximately 80 new grants a year. There is every reason to suppose that Cooke accelerated this rate. The troublemaker Ralph Brooke, York Herald, accused Cooke of making nearly 500 grants over 30 years, a figure long accepted as reflecting the late Tudor situation. An analysis, however, considerably exceeds this figure. Furthermore, there are late Tudor armorials in the College which would seem to relate exclusively to contemporary grants. Taking these factors into account, it seems that Brooke's statement is missing a nought – the figure intended was 5000 and not 500. For genealogists, this sheds new light on the Heralds' Visitations, which are not so much a record of old arms-bearing families, but of new Tudor grantees; current research is showing that in mid- to late Tudor Visitations, it is usually the man who heads the pedigree who was the original recipient of the armorial bearings. Cooke may therefore have granted as many as 150 new armorial bearings in 1584 alone.

Cooke's style is in stark contrast to the complexity of Wriothesley/Benolt heraldry. He made full use of the Ordinaries, generally leaving these plain. When he departed from this, it was usually to adopt the engrailed line, although other varied lines were avoided. Twelve examples of engrailing occur in 100 consecutive grants made around 1584. The Ordinaries were then combined with an additional charge, repeated three times when fess or chevron were used, or five when placed between or on a cross or saltire. In only seven out of these same 100 grants is a further additional charge to be found. These charges were essentially traditional: lions, lions' heads, faces and gambs, boars' heads, mullets and escallops abound in Cooke's heraldry. The result is neat and well-composed, but arguably it remains somewhat dull. Gone is the exuberance of early Tudor heraldry which, for all its lack of balance and control in design, possessed excitement and a sense of innovation.

As with Cooke's arms, so his crests relied heavily on traditional charges. In 25 consecutive Cooke crests granted in 1584 there feature two human arms, two lions, two eagles, a phoenix, a dove, a fox, a talbot, a bull, a swan, a gryphon, an ermine, an ounce, a tyger, an ostrich and a fleur-de-lis.

These crests are then differenced in a simple way; issuing from, or gorged with, a coronet being a much favoured expedient. The more exotic creatures found a hundred years before, such as the pantheon, bagwyn and enfield, were generally eschewed, and the heraldry of 1584 provided nothing new to take their place. It may be thought that this conservatism was to Cooke's own taste, but perhaps it reflected a wider and popular sentiment that new heraldry should be traditional. This view was to become increasingly apparent during the next hundred years.

By 1684 the conservatism of heraldry was such that its survival seemed in question. Linked with the increasingly unpopular Heralds' Visitations, soon to be terminated with the final Visitation of London in 1687, heraldry appeared ill-suited to adapt to the changing times. On the one hand there was a failure to innovate which might otherwise have provided an outlet for creative heraldic design. On the other hand there was the apparent inability, perhaps excusable under the existing circumstances, to check the growing number of 'new men', the product of increasing economic and social changes, from quietly appropriating or self-assuming armorial bearings to which they had no entitlement. This situation was to reach its nadir in the first decade of the eighteenth century, but a measure of its seriousness was already apparent at the bicentenary of the College of Arms in 1684. The number of grants made in

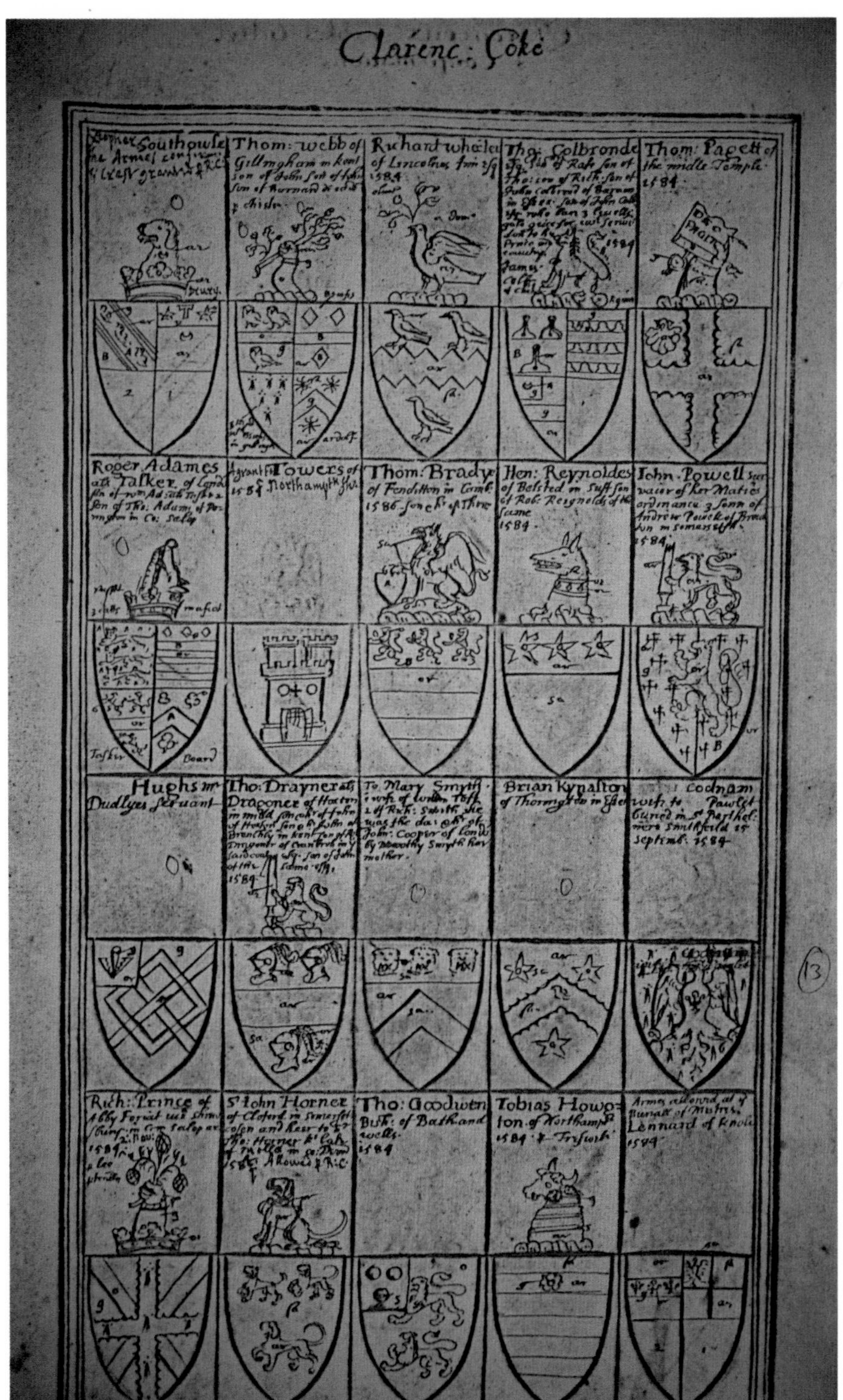

ABOVE: *Grants of Robert Cooke, Clarenceux King of Arms, made in 1584 and contained in* Hare's Ordinary.

LEFT: *The armorial bearings of the Corporation of Clergymen's Sons, granted 1684.*

that year was only eight. Of these eight, one was to a corporate body, the Corporation of Clergymen's Sons, a charity established for the relief of the widows and children of clergymen. A gloomy grant made at a gloomy time in the history of heraldry, it was blazoned as *lozengy Argent and Sable on a chief Purpure a cross paty Or between two books opened Argent the leaves cover and clasps Gold*; and for the crest: *the Efigies of Charitie standing on a wreath of the colours of the field habited in a loose Garment Sable, her face, breast, hands and feet proper, her hair dishevelled Or, accompanied with three naked boys, vis one on her dexter side*

RIGHT: *The armorial bearings granted in 1784 to the brothers Charles and William Smith suggest that good composition and design were not always of importance in late eighteenth-century heraldry.*

BELOW: *The armorial bearings of John Zephaniah Holwell, Governor of Bengal, and survivor of the Black Hole of Calcutta, granted in 1762.*

and the other in her arms all proper and crined Gold. If the depressing nature of this design is anything of a guide, it is perhaps as well that heraldry found no major outlet in new corporate grants at this time. Such was not to happen for many years to come.

Of the remaining seven grants made in 1684, one was to John Dugdale, Windsor Herald, being arms for his wife, Elizabeth, the daughter and heir of Thomas Pigeon: *Azure a chevron between three pigeons' heads erased Argent.* Presumably a grant to a herald is a good indication of the taste prevailing at the time. That taste would not appear to have changed from the days of Robert Cooke. Six grants remained for other individuals: a Doctor of Physick from Norwich, the Recorder of the City of London, one of the chaplains-in-ordinary to the king, an ex-High Sheriff of Hertfordshire, an alderman and sometime mayor of Cambridge, and a would-be gentleman from St Albans. The design of these 1684 grants is notable in that it differs little from that of the Cooke era. Only the pegasus crest of the Doctor of Physick provides a little interest among otherwise plain-lined Ordinaries, lions, eagles, roses and other familiar and conservative charges. Much has been written praising the qualities of late seventeenth- and early eighteenth-century heralds. Dugdale and Anstis are famous names, and none doubts their ability as scholars, administrators and genealogists, but as heralds creating new heraldry their record is nothing less than abysmal.

By 1784 the position had improved, with 40 new grants being made. Of these, many were based on earlier armorial bearings which had hitherto been used by the grantee without proper authority. Some families were at least being made aware that appropriating the arms of another family of the same surname with whom there was no known connection was not a proper way to behave, and were proceeding to have grants of armorial bearings in their own right.

Other grants of 1784 exemplify a groping for new ideas. Typical of this is the grant to Charles Smith, an officer in the Royal Artillery, and to his brother William Smith, a captain in the East India Company. The arms manifest the use of dissimilar charges scattered with Ordinaries and Sub-Ordinaries with little sense of design. The charges are obvious, relating as they do to the careers of the two grantees with a different crest for each brother. However, it can be argued that this choice of the obvious in late eighteenth-century heraldry was too often made at the expense of the aesthetic.

The importance attached to the meaning of charges during this period, at the apparent expense of design and good composition, is demonstrated by a number of grants which recite a specific event in the grantee's life which subsequently inspired the choice of a particular device. In 1762 a grant of armorial bearings was made to John Zephaniah Holwell, sometime Governor of Bengal. His armorial bearings are blazoned as: *Or on a bend Gules three goats passant Argent attired and unguled of the field on a canton sinister Sable a human skull proper, with this motto* MISERRIMA VIDI; *and for the crest a demi-man representing Surajud Dowla, Subah of Bengal in his complete dress, the left hand resting on the head of a tiger inspired with fury the right hand grasping a scimitar in attitude of striking the blade broken all proper and over it this motto* SCUTO DIVINO. The Letters Patent to John Zephaniah Holwell then recites at some length the events leading up to 'the dreadful Confinement and Suffocation in the Black Hole Prison in Fort William at Calcutta in the East Indies in the nights preceding the 20th day of June one thousand seven hundred and fifty six', during which 'One Hundred and Forty Six being crammed into a Dungeon at Eight o'clock in the Evening from whence the said John Zephaniah Holwell and Twenty Two more only survived at Six in the Morning . . .'

In the same grant book is that made in 1758 to John Garmston of the City of Lincoln, whose gruesome crest is blazoned as *a shark's head regardent and couped Argent swallowing a negro man proper* with the motto OPERA DEI MIRIFICA. Regrettably the recital does not tell the tale which must lie behind this choice of crest, and one is left to wonder whether the unfortunate victim survived his ordeal.

The tiger in the crest granted to Robert Adams in 1732 was not so lucky. The recital of the Letters Patent states that Adams, when Governor of the Coast of Malabar in 1729, was 'attacked by a tiger who seized him by the left Arm the marks whereof are Still to be seen, but through Providence he had the good fortune to destroy that furious Beast by ripping open his Belly with a Lance that his Guts fell out and immediately died on the spot . . .'

John Hockin, Vicar of Oakhampton and Rector of Lydford in Devonshire, received a grant of armorial bearings in 1764, which recited that 'in Time of War with France, at the Beginning of Queen Anne's reign a large

ABOVE: *Voracious shark in the crest granted to John Garmston of Lincoln, 1758.*

LEFT: *The tiger killed by Robert Adams, Governor of the Coast of Malabar, was granted in his arms and crest, 1732.*

RIGHT: *The arms granted to John Hockin in 1764 commemorate his father's single-handed repulsion of a French raiding party.*

French privateer cruising in the Bristol Channel, came to Anchor off an Estate called Godrevey then in the possession of John Hockin his Grandfather before mentioned who was one of the principal Inhabitants of the Parish, and it being conjectured that the Privateer's Intent was to send in her Boat to plunder the House which stood alone, and carry off the Cattle from the Estate, The said John Hockin and his Family were alarmed and collected their Friends and Neighbours to keep Watch that Night on the Cliff or Beach. At Daybreak they all dispersed, thinking the Danger over but just as Thomas Hockin, His father aforesaid, a young Man was getting into Bed, another person whose Fears had led him out more than once to take a View, came in a great hurry and told him that a Boat full of Men was making for the Shore as fast as they could row, on which the said Thomas Hockin slipped on his Clothes and catching up a Gun and a Pole to feign the appearance of another ran out and down a steep hill to the Sea in sight of the Boat from whence he was fired at several Times, and then got behind a Rock which served him as a Breastwork and from thence with his one Gun only fired on the Boat with so much vigour and Effect as to prevent the Crews Landing, and at last make them turn about and row back again to their Ship as fast as they could . . .' The Arms of Hockin commemorate this event by depicting the English lion with gun and scattered French fleurs-de-lis in the sea.

Another marine episode is celebrated in the grant of 1828 to Thomas Stott of the City of Quebec, sometime Paymaster of the 29th Regiment of Foot, and in 1828 Paymaster of the 4th Royal Veteran Battalion. His Letters Patent recite that 'in the night of 10th November 1816, being on board the Harpooner Transport on his Voyage from Canada to England, the Ship struck on a Rock off the Island of Newfoundland where the Memorialist and two hundred and six other Persons only out of a Crew of three hundred and eight four Souls were most providentially saved by means of a Rope conveyed by an English Bull Dog which swam to an uninhabited part of the Island previously reached by some Sailors from the wreck . . .' The crest granted for Stott was blazoned as *issuant out of waves of the sea a demi bull dog proper around his neck and reflexed over the back a Log line Or holding between the paws a Wreath of Oak fructed also proper*.

LEFT: *The bulldog swimming with rope in the crest of Thomas Stott, granted 1828.*

It is perhaps regrettable that the practice of reciting events which dictated the choice of charges was discontinued, leaving the observer of heraldic design to guess as to the reasoning behind the choice. However, this loss was more than compensated by the refreshing developments in heraldic design which had occurred by 1884. The number of new grantees had more than doubled and numbered 82 in 1884. Of these, three were impersonal: the Borough of Harrogate, the Borough of Ramsgate, and the newly-constituted Diocese of Southwell. Although only a small number, it marked the beginning of a resurgence in corporate heraldry.

Of personal grants, supporters for new peers numbered only three and included those to Lord Tennyson: *two leopards guardant Gules ducally crowned and semi of fleurs de lis Gold*. There was also the grant of supporters by Royal Licence to a baronet, Sir Henry William Dashwood: *two male gryphons Argent gorged with a collar flory counter flory*. This exemplifies something of the new spirit in heraldry with the reintroduction of a fifteenth-century creature so untypical of the conservative heraldry of the intervening centuries. The grants of 1884 included one to a single woman, Sophy Felicite de Rodes. Grants to women have never been numerous, but they have been consistent and may today be poised to take a greater percentage of the total.

LEFT: *Typical heraldry of 1884; the arms of Crisp exemplify the use of varied line (ie the invected chevron) cotises (ie the smaller chevronels). The crest is a cameleopard, derived from the giraffe.*

RIGHT: *The arms of Pring, granted 1884, use the varied line (ie the dovetailed pale) and place this between four annulets, an arrangement characteristic of the period.*

BELOW: *One of the first badges to be granted after their revival in 1906 was the crowned catamountain's face of Sir Alfred Scott-Gatty, Garter King of Arms.*

The number of grantees from overseas in 1884 had risen, which reflects the imperial expansion of the age. There were six, among them being Sir John Hall, the Prime Minister of New Zealand, the Rajah Oodai Pertab Sing of Bhinga, and James Matthew Taylor, vice-consul in Corfu. Grants to the administrative and professional classes also increased. Those in the Commission of the Peace in 1884 accounted for 16 grantees, suggesting that a concerted effort was being made to approach Justices of the Peace to ensure that they became properly armigerous. The Church, the Law, the Army and medicine account for four, three, three and two respectively. There is also an officer of Arms, Arthur Staunton Larken, Richmond Herald.

No attempt was made in 1884 to introduce new charges. Even the unusual, such as the snail, cameleopard and the Dashwood male gryphons were reintroductions rather than creatures making their first appearance in heraldry. The lion accounts for 15 crests, the human arm for ten, the stag six and the eagle five, showing that long-used charges were still preferred.

Nonetheless, in contrast to 1784, the heraldry of 1884 is refreshing. It manifests a new and frequently successful approach to design. There is a spirited treatment and rearrangement of charges, particularly in arms. The segmented heraldry, that is to say the placing of different and frequently discordant charges above and below fess or chevron, is largely absent. Good design suggested that two identical charges above a chevron should be repeated by a third identical charge beneath. Varied lines are used to cover the more unusual forms, such as flory, counterflory, dovetailed, and rayonny. Ordinaries are frequently cotised; crosses are parted and fretted, made formy or botonny; and there is a liberal use of gouttes, ermine spots and party divisions.

By 1884 it is also clear that the traditional arrangements were beginning to break down. No longer was it necessary to place three charges on a bend, fess or chevron. Two greyhounds are courant on a bend and five horseshoes are charged on a chevron. A fess is set between two talbots' heads, and there is a cross couped charged with four bombs all between two anchors; the heraldry of earlier centuries would have used three talbots' heads, two above the fess and one below, and five bombs with four anchors.

The heraldry of 1884 is simple, neat and interesting, with a unity in its design and none

LEFT: *The arms of Culham of New Zealand bring together a crowned hammer (a culling implement) and a boar's head (a further allusion to ham), to create a badge-like device. This is then used as a single charge to be repeated three times in the shield, demonstrating the influence of badge formations in the arms of twentieth-century heraldry.*

of the segmented clutter with which this period is so often wrongly credited. Two names stand out as designers, and any history of heraldry must give them due credit. They are Alfred Scott-Gatty, Rouge Dragon Pursuivant, and Henry Farnham Burke, Rouge Croix Pursuivant. Both of them were destined to become Garter King of Arms.

In 1984, the quincentennial year of the College of Arms, the number of grantees had risen to 191. Of these, 28 were impersonal, demonstrating an upsurge in corporate heraldry. Twelve came from overseas, including a grant to the University of Hong Kong. Local authorities accounted for 11 of these 28 grants. The remainder were diverse: the Australian Shipping Commission, the Chartered Institute of Building, the Roman Catholic Diocese of Toronto and the Engineering Council.

Grants from overseas may have constituted a high percentage of corporate grants, but personal grants from overseas were surprisingly low, only 23 out of a total of 191. Ten were honorary grants to Americans, an enigmatic source which may develop in the future, seven were Canadian and there were three each from Australia and New Zealand. The small number of personal grants from Australia in 1984 is in contrast to greater numbers in previous years. The five grants to Australian corporate bodies in 1984 do, however, show that heraldry is thriving in that country.

The year 1906 saw the revival of the badge; and its use and development is characteristic of twentieth-century heraldry. There were no known grants of badges between the sixteenth century and 1906, but in 1984 there were 73. In the Middle Ages badges were borne by followers and retainers of armigerous individuals. Today they are used by bodies or people associated with a corporate body, or by members of the grantee's family, such as non-armigerous sons-in-law, and grandchildren in the female line, who are not entitled to bear and use the arms and crest.

The reappearance of the badge has been a major factor influencing design in arms where styles have become increasingly diverse and ingenious. As the badge is free-standing and not enclosed within the restricted area of a shield, it has encouraged the combining of charges to provide a single new device which has then been introduced into the arms. Typical examples of this are fleurs-de-lis with the petals terminating in animals' heads, or with the outer petals extending into wings; a harp terminating in a stag's head; martlets flying through coronets; pickaxes enfiling mullets; and a variety of charges encircled by annulets, frequently treated with a compound outer edge, such as embattled or potenty. The medieval leopard's face, *jessant de lis*, now has many successors, following its tradition of combining separate charges to form a single device. The badge may also be influencing the positioning of charges. As badges are often circular or symmetrical in design, this has encouraged a realignment of charges in arms so that they no longer all point upwards or face to the dexter. Heraldry

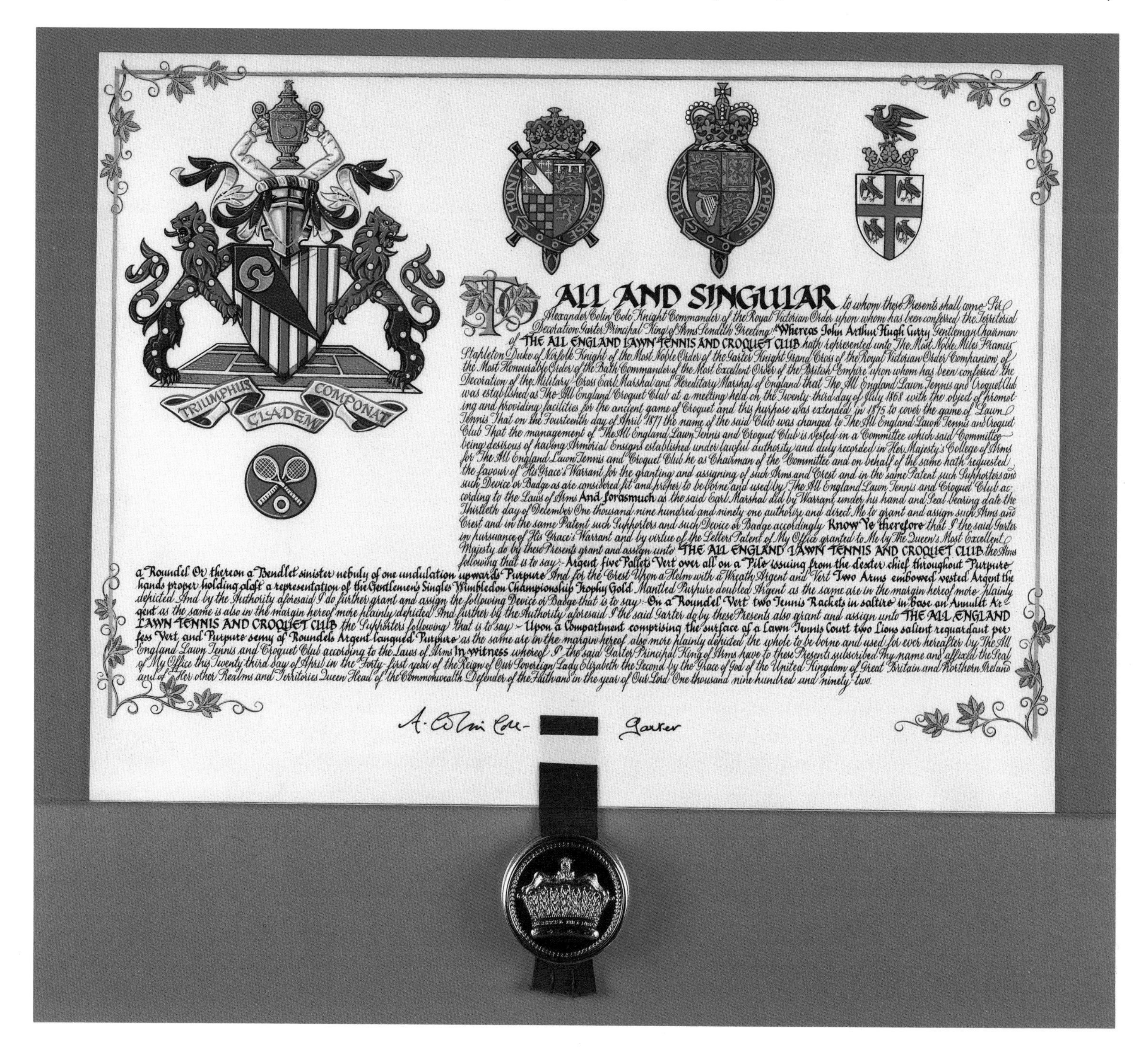

TO ALL AND SINGULAR to whom these Presents shall come Sir Alexander Colin Cole Knight Commander of the Royal Victorian Order upon whom has been conferred the Territorial Decoration Garter Principal King of Arms Sendeth Greeting! Whereas John Arthur Hugh Curry Gentleman Chairman of THE ALL ENGLAND LAWN TENNIS AND CROQUET CLUB hath represented unto The Most Noble Miles Francis Stapleton Duke of Norfolk Knight of the Most Noble Order of the Garter Knight Grand Cross of the Royal Victorian Order Companion of the Most Honourable Order of the Bath Commander of the Most Excellent Order of the British Empire upon whom has been conferred the Decoration of the Military Cross Earl Marshal and Hereditary Marshal of England that The All England Lawn Tennis and Croquet Club was established as The All England Croquet Club at a meeting held on the Twenty-third day of July 1868 with the object of promoting and providing facilities for the ancient game of Croquet and this purpose was extended in 1875 to cover the game of Lawn Tennis That on the Fourteenth day of April 1877 the name of the said Club was changed to The All England Lawn Tennis and Croquet Club That the management of The All England Lawn Tennis and Croquet Club is vested in a Committee which said Committee being desirous of having Armorial Ensigns established under lawful authority and duly recorded in Her Majesty's College of Arms for The All England Lawn Tennis and Croquet Club he as Chairman of the Committee and on behalf of the same hath requested the favour of His Grace's Warrant for the granting and assigning of such Arms and Crest and in the same Patent such Supporters and such Device or Badge as are considered fit and proper to be borne and used by The All England Lawn Tennis and Croquet Club according to the Laws of Arms And forasmuch as the said Earl Marshal did by Warrant under his hand and Seal bearing date the Thirtieth day of December One thousand nine hundred and ninety-one authorize and direct Me to grant and assign such Arms and Crest and in the same Patent such Supporters and such Device or Badge accordingly Know Ye therefore that I the said Garter in pursuance of His Grace's Warrant and by virtue of the Letters Patent of My Office granted to Me by The Queen's Most Excellent Majesty do by these Presents grant and assign unto THE ALL ENGLAND LAWN TENNIS AND CROQUET CLUB the Arms following that is to say:- Argent five Pallets Vert over all on a Pile issuing from the dexter chief throughout Purpure a Roundel Or thereon a Bendlet sinister nebuly of one undulation upwards Purpure And for the Crest Upon a Helm with a Wreath Argent and Vert Two Arms embowed vested Argent the hands proper holding aloft a representation of the Gentlemen's Singles Wimbledon Championship Trophy Gold Mantled Purpure doubled Argent as the same are in the margin hereof more plainly depicted And by the Authority aforesaid I do further grant and assign the following Device or Badge that is to say:- On a Roundel Vert two Tennis Rackets in saltire in base an Annulet Argent as the same is also in the margin hereof more plainly depicted And further by the Authority aforesaid I the said Garter do by these Presents also grant and assign unto THE ALL ENGLAND LAWN TENNIS AND CROQUET CLUB the Supporters following that is to say:- Upon a Compartment comprising the surface of a Lawn Tennis Court two Lions salient reguardant per fess Vert and Purpure semy of Roundels Argent langued Purpure as the same are in the margin hereof also more plainly depicted the whole to be borne and used for ever hereafter by The All England Lawn Tennis and Croquet Club according to the Laws of Arms In witness whereof I the said Garter Principal King of Arms have to these Presents subscribed My name and affixed the Seal of My Office this Twenty-third day of April in the Forty-first year of the Reign of Our Sovereign Lady Elizabeth the Second by the Grace of God of the United Kingdom of Great Britain and Northern Ireland and of Her other Realms and Territories Queen Head of the Commonwealth Defender of the Faith and in the year of Our Lord One thousand nine hundred and ninety-two.

A. Colin Cole – Garter

BELOW: *The armorial bearings of the All England Lawn Tennis and Croquet Club (Wimbledon); sport and the arts are major factors in twentieth-century heraldry, with grants of arms made to corporate bodies and leisure allusions contained in the arms of individuals.*

is now rich in examples of animals respecting (facing) each other, and flora and inanimate objects with stalks or apexes pointing inwards or outwards. With this has come a further move away from the traditional two-one arrangement of upright charges. The positioning of the Sclater bees and the Tesco cloves provide examples (see illustrations in the chapter on fauna and flora).

A less rigid attitude to heraldic design during the twentieth century has manifest itself in several ways, particularly with the wider use of unusual Ordinaries and Sub-Ordinaries; the flaunch, for example, is now much favoured. Curiously this is not true of the varied lines, where only embattled and wavy have held their own. Similarly gouttes and ermine spots are much less apparent. There is no doubt that this freedom of design in modern heraldry has allowed for the continuous rearrangement of traditional charges, rather than a search for new ones. The principal exception to this is found with the use of flora and fauna from around the world, although many such charges are rapidly becoming, or have become, traditional. The maple leaf and the wattle are obvious examples of this, as are the lyrebird and the Australian magpie. All were absent in 1884, but are familiar charges in current heraldry.

Novel inanimate charges in the 1980s were rare. There was some oriental weaponry, a cream-skimmer, a pair of swivels and the prow of a Viking ship in 1982-83, and the following year produced a ko (a Maori digging stick) and a koruru (a Maori carved head), a tuning cone, and a reed hook. There were also signs that chemical symbols had begun to establish themselves in heraldry, with the appearance of the DNA chain, the benzene ring and conventional representations of a neutron and an atom. There is no doubt that the benzene ring in particular will become increasingly popular as a simple and distinctive heraldic charge.

The choice of charges in the second half of the twentieth century frequently reflects the occupation and career of the grantee or his ancestors. The pun is still apparent, and cognate heraldry is widely used in the sense of taking charges from the arms of a county or school with which the grantee has been associated. A new and important source of design inspiration is provided by the leisure pursuits of the grantee, which have provided scope for subtle use of the Ordinaries and Sub-Ordinaries. Pily arms can suggest a backgammon board; and when piles Argent are voided and engrailed on a blue field, they suggest coral and are suitable for those with snorkelling interests in tropical waters. Similarly, mountaineering, camping and sailing need not be represented by realistic crampons, tents or sailing boats. A lozengy or checky field can be effective. If each lozenge is divided per fess Argent and Azure, a series of snow-capped mountain peaks against the sky is suggested. Similarly, if the Azure is rendered Vert, the effect of tents in the countryside is obtained. Chequers divided per bend Argent and Azure provide white sails on a blue sea. Those interested in the theatre have recently made use of papillonny, a rare field used during the Middle Ages which is reputed to be derived from scales of a butterfly's wing. Papillonny can suggest the seats in an auditorium. It has recently spread

ABOVE: *The armorial bearings of the Royal Philharmonic Orchestra incorporate violin bridges in arms and badge, an example of a new inanimate charge in heraldry.*

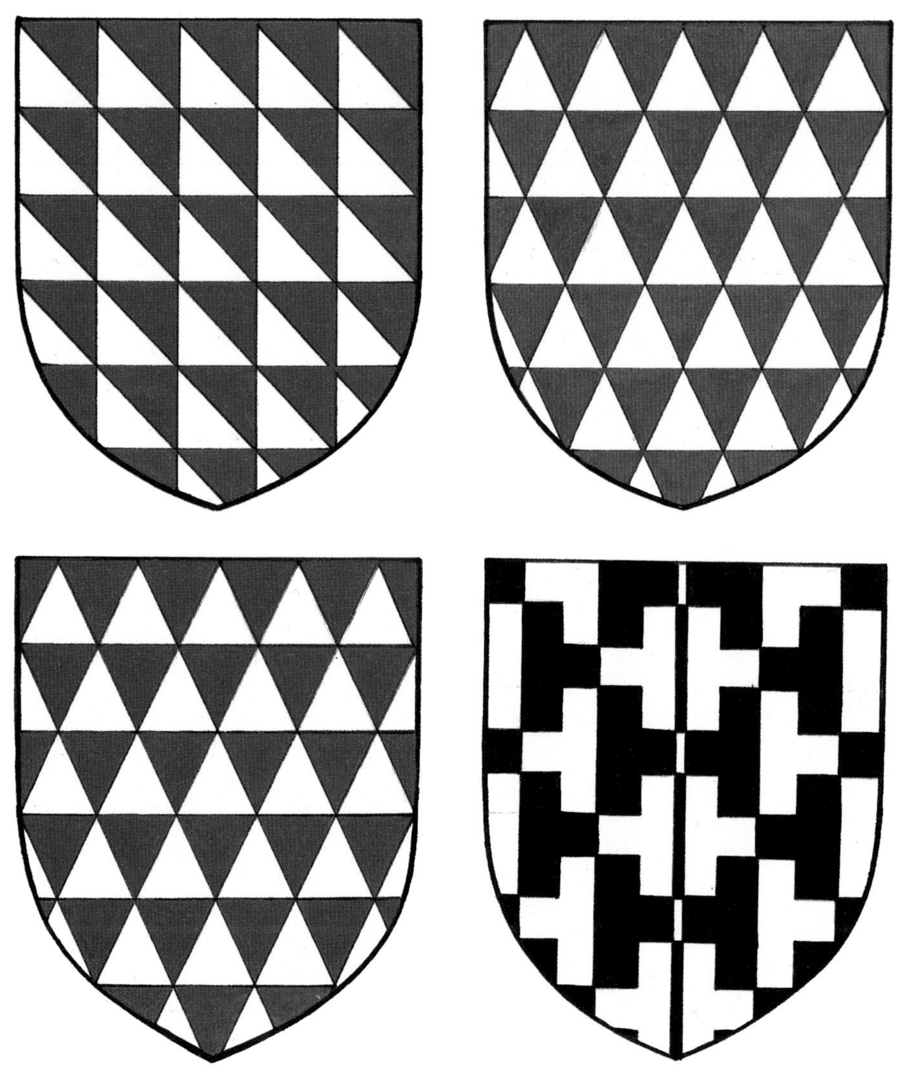

ABOVE: *The use of simple field divisions can suggest leisure pursuits, for example, sailing (top left), camping (top right), mountaineering (bottom left) and photography, with a vairy potenty field providing a series of black camera formations (bottom right).*

from leisure heraldry into educational heraldry, where it can also represent seats, as in the arms of the Holborn Law Tutors, and into occupational heraldry where it implies roof tiles.

The means by which heralds arrive at a suitable design has probably altered very little since the fifteenth or sixteenth century. It therefore serves to describe the process as it operates today. An approach is made by the would-be grantee to the College of Arms, the Court of Lord Lyon (in Scotland), or the requisite authority under whose jurisdiction he or she comes. At the College of Arms such approaches are either made to a herald known to the grantee or to the College in general. If the latter is the case, then the grantee becomes the responsibility of the herald-in-waiting (ie on duty) at the time. The first job of a herald is to ensure that the grantee is eligible for a grant of arms to be made by the Kings of Arms, who are empowered to grant only to 'eminent' men and women. In practice, anyone who holds a civil or military commission, a university degree or professional qualification, or who has achieved a measure of distinction in a field beneficial to society as a whole is eligible to bear arms. Similarly, grants of armorial bearings are made to corporate bodies such as local authorities, places of education, professional bodies and leading commercial companies. The herald, acting as agent to the Kings of Arms, will then draft the relevant petition or memorial, addressed to the Earl Marshal. If the latter approves the application, he issues his Warrant to the Kings of Arms to grant such armorial bearings as they deem suitable.

The herald and grantee draw up an acceptable design together. For the herald's part, he must ensure that the design is distinctive in its own right; and that being different from anything already on the register, it constitutes in the full sense a new coat of arms. It is also his job to uphold the principles of good heraldry, and to be the guardian of good heraldic taste. Within this limitation, however, it is right and proper that the grantee should be allowed whatever charges he wishes. In practice, few grantees come forward with firm proposals for a design, and leave the herald to use his own ideas and methods to produce suitable arms. Individual allusions and charges are perhaps less important than the ultimate visual effect of the design; they are simply a means to achieve a distinctive and pleasing result. The process has provided rich and varied results in the past and should ensure that heraldry has an exciting future.

RIGHT: *The armorial bearings of Mead, granted 1975, show that simple yet distinctive heraldry can still be obtained in the twentieth century. The arms combine the pun of green and yellow fields for meads or meadows, with an allusion to the grantee's ancestry, which had connections with America. The two flaunches suggest the continents of North America and Europe.*

FACING PAGE: *Papillonny field in the arms of Holborn Law Tutors suggesting seats in an auditorium; the nuts are the fruit of the hazel, the ancient tree of wisdom.*

Exd

C.S
Y+R
P'tg

Lancaster

POTESTAS EX VOLUNTATE

POTESTAS·EX·VOLUNTATE

TO ALL and SINGULAR to whom these Presents shall come, Sir Alexander Colin Cole, Knight Commander of the Royal Victorian Order, upon whom has been conferred the Territorial Decoration, Garter Principal King of Arms, Sir Anthony Richard Wagner, Knight Commander of the Most Honourable Order of the Bath, Knight Commander of the Royal Victorian Order, Clarenceux King of Arms, and John Philip Brooke Brooke-Little, Esquire, Commander of the Royal Victorian Order, Norroy and Ulster King of Arms Send Greeting! Whereas Valerie Aggett Feme Sole, Bachelor of Laws of the University of Durham, Solicitor of the Supreme Court of England & Wales, Principal of Holborn Law Tutors Limited hath represented unto The Most Noble Miles Francis Stapleton

Le Roy edward

5
HERALDIC MONSTERS

Peter Gwynn-Jones

LEFT: *Dragon supporter to the attributed arms of King Cadwalader, painted in the early sixteenth century.*

Popular belief has a tendency to credit heraldry with the invention of gryphon, unicorn, cockatrice and other fabulous monsters. Such a belief, though flattering to past heralds, is far from the truth. Any understanding of heraldic monsters must take into account the medieval bestiary, that curious compilation based on the work of Physiologus who, at some unknown date between the second and fifth centuries AD, wrote his book of beasts. This book later grew with the factual and fanciful additions of many writers, until it finally evolved into a kind of zoological scrapbook, proving one of the most popular and avidly read works of the Middle Ages. No attempt was made to differentiate between fact and fancy, the medieval mind happily accepting that the gryphon or unicorn were as real as the familiar animals of the domestic farmyard.

BELOW: *Gryphon supporter to the arms of Cardinal Wolsey.*

Although the occasional monster of the bestiary found its way into early heraldry, it was not until the fifteenth century that heraldry turned its attention in earnest to this source, and began that steady recruitment of the fabulous which was to reach a climax during the Tudor period. The zoologist, meanwhile, turned to science and, following the sixteenth-century Swiss naturalist Conrad Gesner, began collecting specimens at first hand and noting the finds of the new explorers and discoverers of the wider world. The process of discarding the monster in favour of real, though less exotic, creatures had begun and, but for its preservation by the heralds, it might have been destined for complete obscurity.

The gryphon was probably the first of these bestiary monsters to find its way into heraldry. As early as 1167 it features on the seal of Richard de Redvers, Earl of Essex. Bestiary accounts state that the gryphon had the size and strength of over 100 eagles and the ability to seize and carry off an ox in each foot. It was guardian of mines of gold, hidden in the high mountains where it built its nest which was lined with the precious metal. There are accounts of a feud between gryphons and a race of horseborne Scythians who attempted to steal this gold. Bitter antipathy arose between gryphons and horses, which suggests that the charging of a gryphon on a shield of arms may have been a deliberate attempt by the medieval knight to instil fear into the horses of his opponents. Goblets in the shape of gryphons' claws or eggs were highly prized in the courts of medieval Europe, and were usually made from antelope horns and ostrich eggs. The gryphons' gold can be traced back to Aristeas, a Greek of the seventh century BC. This remarkable traveller reached the mountains of central Asia and returned to report of a people who stole gold from fearsome creatures which he called gryphons. There is much here to suggest that the creature was the bearded vulture or lammergeyer, a huge bird with a wingspan of nearly ten feet, which nests in inaccessible cliffs in the Asiatic mountains. In spite of sceptical zoologists, the lammergeyer is still held to be able to seize and carry off sheep. The gold of the region is real enough and is still mined today.

Aristeas seems to have confused these gryphons with gryphons already known to him in his domestic Greek culture. The Greek gryphons, upon which Aristeas grafted the lammergeyer, and the latter's association with gold, appear from seals to have had a Middle Eastern origin. They are probably nothing more than a composite creature, the symbolic combination of the eagle, the king of the birds, with the lion, the king of the beasts. If not an eagle, the bird may have been the gryphon vulture, sacred to the Egyptian god Osiris and other deities. Its characteristic ruff may account for the gryphon's stylised ears, which certainly predate the Aristean merger. It is these ears which distinguish the head of the gryphon in heraldry from the otherwise identical head of an eagle.

The dragon was another early arrival in heraldry and continues to enjoy widespread popularity, frequently appearing in grants of new armorial bearings to Welshmen. It is also popular with grantees associated with the City of London, two dragons featuring as supporters in the city's armorial bearings. Like the gryphon, the dragon has remained largely unaltered by heraldry, except perhaps for the extra pair of legs which it acquired in the fifteenth century, for which the heralds seem largely responsible. Earlier dragons have two legs, and are known as wyverns, and the four-legged simply as dragons.

The dragon is thought to have been brought to Britain by the Romans who used it as the badge of the Roman cohort. They were inspired by the Dacian tribesmen from north of the Danube, who used long windsock banners, in the mouths of which they placed lighted tapers or torches. These banners were called *dracones* and would seem to be responsible for the wings of the dragon of heraldry, and also for its fire-breathing qualities. These characteristics were merged with the earlier dragon of the classical bestiaries, which is described as the largest of the snakes and one that lassoes its prey in a knot with its tail and suffocates it; this is a very passable description of a python. In Britain, the Romano-Britons retained the dragon in their iconography. The Welsh word *draig* or dragon is also used for 'leader' and the attributed arms of Uther Pendragon (the reputed father of King Arthur) are *Or two dragons addorsed Vert crowned Gules.*

The heraldic dragon of the West is not to be confused with oriental dragons. These wingless and bewhiskered monsters are closely associated with water, and their origin may owe something to the crocodile. Such dragons are relative latecomers to heraldry, and are chiefly associated with the armorial bearings granted to persons associated with the Far East.

ABOVE: *Wyvern crest of Sir William Fitzwaryn, created Knight of the Garter c.1360.*

Like the python, the cobra also played its part in the creation of a fearsome heraldic monster: the cockatrice or basilisk. Although the basilisk is now depicted in heraldry with an additional dragon's head at the end of its tail, the cockatrice and basilisk have a common origin. It was never the size of a dragon; the bestiaries give it a length as small as six inches. It was regarded as the king of the snakes, the name basilisk being derived from *basileus*, the Greek for 'king'. Its venom was so deadly that even birds flying over it could be overwhelmed and would drop dead from the sky. Nonetheless, the cockatrice or basilisk could be conquered by weasels. This emphatic statement in the bestiaries clearly refers to the mongoose; and the cobra fits, its head being responsible for the cockscomb

ABOVE: *Cockatrice in the arms and crest granted to John Langley, 1632.*

and wattles. Once the head had been associated with a cock, this element was fancified until the creature was believed to be half-cock and half-snake, and reptilian wings were therefore introduced. A later addition can be traced to the English so-called naturalist, Alexander Neckham, who in about 1180 stated that the cockatrice was hatched from the egg of an aged cock incubated by a toad; other versions give the incubator as a snake. Intriguingly, so great was the fear instilled by the cockatrice that in the fifteenth century a cock was put on trial in Basle on the charge of having been found laying an egg. It is not known how the trial went except that the cock was found guilty in spite of having his own defence counsel. It is to be wondered how the cock and his counsel communicated.

Although popular in the heraldry of recent centuries, the unicorn was rare in the Middle Ages. As bestiary writers likened Christ to the unicorn, its use in heraldry was regarded as blasphemous. The fabulous and miraculous horn of the creature was considered the most valuable of all charms against poison and sickness. So prized was it, that the horn belonging to Queen Elizabeth I was valued at £100,000. This and other such horns can now be identified as the spiral horn of the narwhal, a species of small whale found in northern seas and sporting a tusk of fine ivory that can develop to the length of seven or eight feet.

There are two generally-held theories on the origin of the unicorn: firstly, it is thought that the animal might be the Arabian oryx (a species of antelope); the second theory favours the single-horned Indian rhino. Neither of these takes into account the medieval legend of the unicorn, which held that the only way to catch the creature was to send a virgin, preferably nude, into the forest. The unicorn would then come and lay its head trustingly in her lap and follow her faithfully wherever she went. This legend, together with the horn – an obvious phallic symbol – have strong pagan and sexual undertones. Again, oryx and rhino do not explain the old nursery rhyme, 'The lion and the unicorn were fighting for the crown; the lion beat the unicorn all around the town'. This enmity between lion and unicorn is one of the oldest concepts found in mythology. Frequently the unicorn was chased across the sky by the lion and was slain by it. It is known that the lion was a solar symbol, and the sun in turn was sacred to the ancient gods of the Indo-European peoples. By inference the unicorn was a lunar symbol; this is borne out by its frequent appearance on ancient seals and coins in conjunction with a crescent moon. The moon was sacred to the goddesses of the Indo-Europeans, who were governed by matriarchal systems until they were replaced by male-dominated societies several thousand years before Christ. The unicorn's goddesses thus linger on in the medieval virgin legend and the unicorn itself has taken refuge in heraldry. The legend enabled Christ to be associated with the unicorn, the virgin being identified with the Virgin Mary.

The unicorn may have originated as a calendar creature, one that is composed of parts of several animals each sacred to a particular season of the year, with the horn as a fertility symbol, the symbol of life. Unreliable though he is, it may be significant that Ctesias, writing in about 400 BC, states that the unicorn's horn was white, red and black, the colours of womanhood: white for the virgin, red for the sexually-active woman and black for the aged hag. On the other hand, the unicorn may after all have a natural origin. It is known that the white bull was also sacred to many of the ancient goddesses. It is just possible that one or more tribes learnt to graft the horn buds of a young calf into the centre of its forehead. This is physically possible and results in a single massive horn.

Gryphon, dragon, cockatrice and unicorn were familiar monsters of the bestiaries and as such have remained largely unchanged by their use in heraldry. Less familiar creatures underwent a process of heraldic evolution. The use of three-dimensional crests from the fourteenth century and appearance of supporters in the fifteenth century brought a need for new heraldic source material. Supporters in particular required beasts with claws and feet to support arms – geometrical or inanimate objects were no good for this. So the heralds turned in earnest to the bestiaries as well as to the natural world around them. During the sixteenth century heralds became bolder and more imaginative; and, by the end of the Tudor period, remarkable changes had taken place. The results can therefore be regarded as heraldic monsters in their own right. One of the new arrivals, dating from the beginning of the fifteenth century, is the yale. Bestiary accounts provided it with the remarkable ability of being able to swivel its horns at will, laying one back in battle, keeping it in reserve in case the forward attacking horn was damaged. Apparently it also enjoyed wallowing in water. Although some tend to favour the wildebeest as the origin of the yale, medieval mapmakers consistently depict it as an animal of the East. Its physical characteristics point to the water buffalo, which attacks with sudden swipes of the horn, and this possibly accounts for the swivelling characteristics.

Although comparatively slight, the evolution of the yale in heraldry can be discerned in the treatment of the animal's horns in the fifteenth century. It first appears as a supporter to the arms of John, Duke of Bedford, who intended it to be a punning allusion to his earldom of Kendal, or Kend-eale. The Bedford yale had straight horns and a long tail. It subsequently passed with the earldom to Sir John Beaufort, Duke of Somerset; and two yales were used by the latter's daughter and heir Margaret, Countess of Richmond, the mother of Henry VII. The Beaufort yale is slightly different, with convoluted horns and a short tail.

ABOVE: *Unicorn supporters of Robert Monckton Arundel, Viscount Galway, who died in 1810.*

More noticeable changes are apparent with the heraldic antelope. This originated with the antelope of the bestiary, which was essen-

LEFT: *Yale supporter to the arms of John Beaufort, Duke of Somerset and Earl of Kendal, c.1440.*

RIGHT: *Heraldic antelope, the dexter supporter to the arms of Henry VI. It is not clear whether he used supporters, or whether these were attributed to him shortly after his death; painted in the early sixteenth century.*

tially a gentle creature and can be identified with the black buck, an animal which was then widely distributed in the Middle East before it retreated to its present limited range in India. Heraldry evolved the black buck into a monster of ferocious countenance, with tufts of hair, a tusked nose and serrated horns. The serrated horns may be an exaggerated and stylised rendering of the spirals found in the natural animal.

The heraldic tyger was a particularly popular charge at the beginning of the sixteenth century. It too originated with the bestiary where it was placed correctly between lion and leopard. The bestiary writers stated that the tyger was exceedingly fierce and swift and that the only way to escape it was to throw down mirrors or looking-glasses. The tyger was then distracted by its own image, believing itself to be one of its cubs. Curiously, the bestiaries do not mention the tyger's stripes; but these were Persian tigers which were rather less pronounced in their striping than their Bengal counterparts. So the tyger came into heraldry as a cat-like creature, albeit unstriped. Developments at this stage enhanced its ferocity by making its face wolf-like, adding serrated ears and a horn or tusk to the end of its nose. The heraldic tyger in its fully-evolved form is essentially a creation of heraldry, and bears little resemblance to the tiger of nature or to the tyger of the bestiaries. The former has since been introduced into heraldry in its own right.

RIGHT: *Male gryphon, the sinister supporter to the arms of Sayntleger (St Leger), confirmed in 1531. This transitional creature retains the horns and hairy mane of its bison origins.*

An extreme case of heraldic evolution is the male gryphon, which should not be confused with the gryphon described previously; the male gryphon has a spiky, wingless body. A clue to the origin of the male gryphon is in a supporter to the arms of St Leger, painted in 1530, showing a creature with a hairy mane, two horns, and sparks of fire emanating from various points of its anatomy. Eventually the hairy mane was depicted in feathery form and the horns discarded. The only

LEFT: *Heraldic tyger in the arms and crest of Thomas Sybell, confirmed in 1531.*

maned and horned creature in the bestiaries is the bonacon. Interestingly, the bestiaries report that the bonacon defended itself by means of a fiery emission from its backside, which was capable of setting fire to everything contained in several acres behind it. It seems that the heralds found descriptions which were not precise in stating from which part of the anatomy the fire came, and therefore placed fiery emissions at random.

RIGHT: *Male gryphon supporters granted in 1884 to Sir Henry William Dashwood, baronet. A special Royal Licence was required to allow supporters to be borne by a baronet. In this evolved state the male gryphon has lost its horns and hairy mane. The latter is now normally replaced by feathers, as with the more familiar winged gryphon which features in the Dashwood crest.*

Such an emission from the mouth may subsequently have been mistaken for a beak.

With the bonacon, identification with a natural animal is possible. Some bestiaries state that its horns curled back on themselves so that if you bumped into it 'you did yourself no harm'. It was reddish in colour, with a woolly mane. All this points directly to the European bison, *Bison bonasus*, which was adapted and evolved in heraldic use to the male gryphon found in heraldry today.

At the high point of bestial heraldic evolution, the early Tudor period, there is some indication that monsters reverted to their original bestiary form, suggesting that earlier changes were not always deliberate, but were instead misinterpretations. The salamander evolved into a fire-breathing dog-like monster with a lion's tail before reverting to its bestiary origin as an amphibian (see the illustration of the arms of Douglas in the chapter on the art of heraldry). Salamanders of any form were held to be so cold that they sought the hottest flames as their haunts, where they survived unscathed. This fabulous characteristic has rendered it a popular heraldic charge for fire-fighting organisations. There is no good reason to associate the natural salamander with fire. However, the bestiary account received lingering credence from no less than Benvenuto Cellini, the Renaissance artist and silversmith, who recalled that in 1505 his father 'saw in the midst of the hottest flames a little animal like a lizard which was sporting about in midst of the most scorching blaze'.

The panther provides further indication that heraldic evolution was somewhat haphazard. The supporter to the arms of Queen Jane Seymour shows a creature with a striped skin of multicolours. Doubtless this was based on a bestiary which referred to the colours, but omitted to describe how they were arranged. That a mistake had been made would seem to have been accepted by later members of the Seymour family, who reverted to the more familiar spotted creature. However, the panther was subjected to another change. Sir William Segar, Garter King of Arms, wrote of the panther at the beginning of the seventeenth century, 'this beast . . . is admired of all other beasts for the beauty of his skyn being spotted of variable colours; and beloved and followed of them for the sweetness of his breath that streameth forth of his nostrils and ears like smoke, wch our paynters mistaking, corruptly do make fire'. In this form it is known as the 'panther incensed', and it is significant that 'incensed' can mean either enraged or sweetly smelling. The kindly-disposed panther of the bestiary was thus transformed by heraldic painters into a monster characterised by fire, flames and ferocity. The original panther, or pard, is likely to have been a cheetah, for the leopard was held to be the bastard offspring of lion (ie leo) and pard. The natural leopard is more akin to the lion in shape, but is spotted like the cheetah, thus inheriting characteristics from both of its supposed parents.

Birds as well as mammals were the subject of heraldic evolution, a good example during the Tudor period being the heathcock or moorcock. A study of contemporary renderings of the bird show clearly how it originated with the blackcock, which was then abundant in southern England and the Midland counties. The first stage in the evolution was to exaggerate the wattles of the blackcock, which are prominent in the mating season, into something resembling those of the domestic farmyard cock. This was soon followed by the elongation of the tail feathers. At first the elongation retained the distinctive lyre-like formation of the natural bird, but in a later stage the tail feathers were

LEFT: *Salamander crest and badge of Baron Sterling of Plaistow.*

LEFT: *Panther supporter to the arms of Jane Seymour, third wife of Henry VIII, painted c.1536.*

RIGHT: *Panther 'incensed' crest of Japan Tobacco (UK) Limited.*

straightened and swept upwards in two sharp points. In this way heraldry created its own monstrous bird; only the retention of the black plumage provides a tenuous link with its natural origin. In time, this may also be discarded.

In addition to drawing on the bestiaries, Tudor heralds introduced new monsters of their own imagination. Into this group fall a number of composite monsters such as the bagwyn, a roebuck with a wolf's tail, and the more complicated enfield with the head of a fox, the chest of a greyhound, the talons of an eagle, the body of a lion and the hind legs and tail of a wolf. One such creature is the alphyn, which is similar to the heraldic tyger. Combining the body of an existing heraldic monster (the tyger) with the forelegs of an eagle, it also possesses an unexplained knot in its tail; it has recently enjoyed a revival of popularity.

Perhaps more successful was a monster that did not combine parts of existing creatures, but sprang from outright imagination: the pantheon. Held to be an inhabitant of the skies, it is hence usually depicted

ABOVE: *The heathcock or moorcock evolved from the blackcock.*

BELOW: *The alphyn crest of Roberts.*

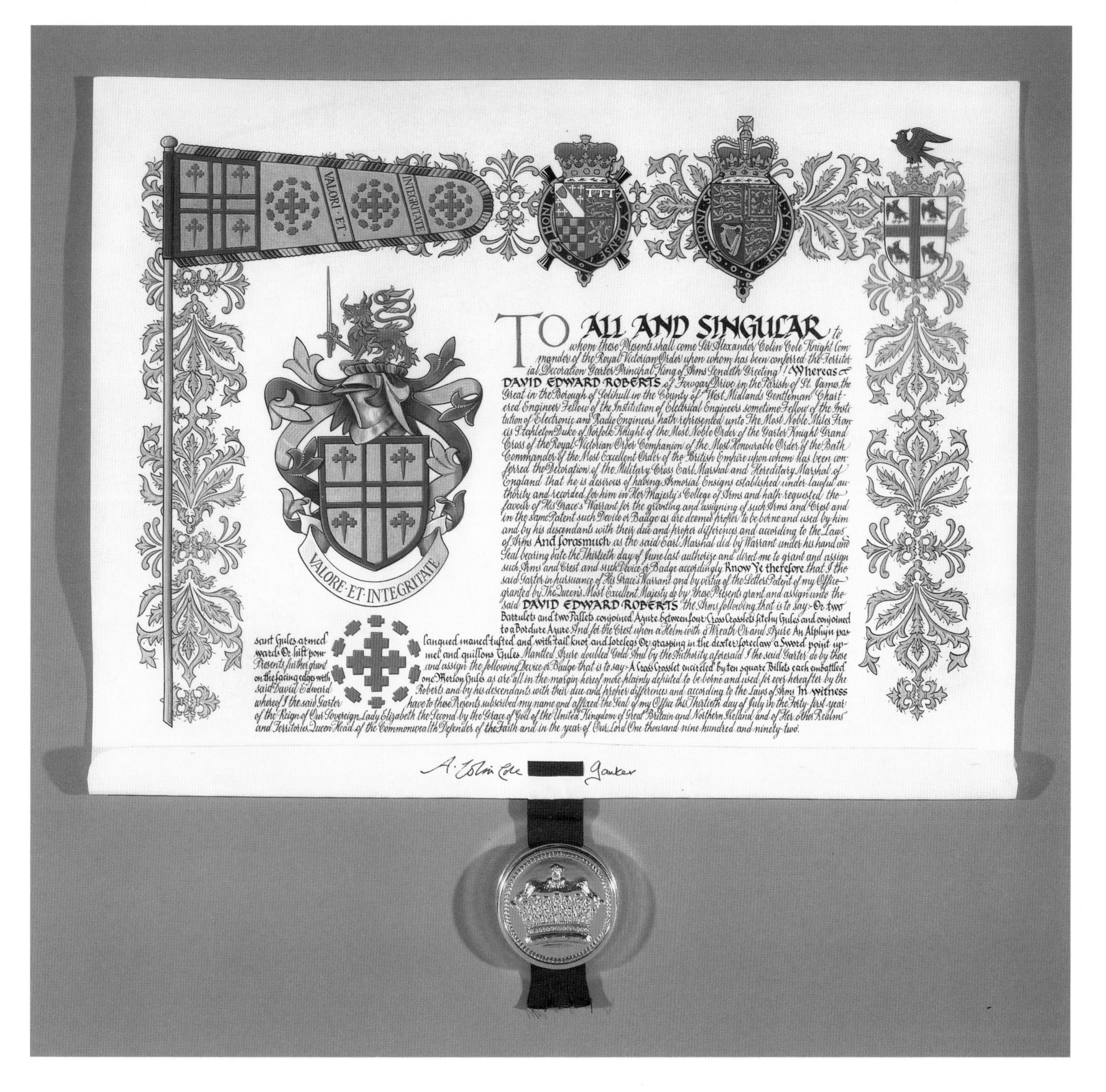

TO ALL AND SINGULAR to whom these Presents shall come Sir Alexander Colin Cole Knight Commander of the Royal Victorian Order upon whom has been conferred the Territorial Decoration Garter Principal King of Arms Sendeth Greeting! Whereas DAVID EDWARD ROBERTS of Fougay Drive in the Parish of St. James the Great in the Borough of Solihull in the County of West Midlands Gentleman Chartered Engineer Fellow of the Institution of Electrical Engineers sometime Fellow of the Institution of Electronic and Radio Engineers hath represented unto The Most Noble Miles Francis Stapleton Duke of Norfolk Knight of the Most Noble Order of the Garter Knight Grand Cross of the Royal Victorian Order Companion of the Most Honourable Order of the Bath Commander of the Most Excellent Order of the British Empire upon whom has been conferred the Decoration of the Military Cross Earl Marshal and Hereditary Marshal of England that he is desirous of having Armorial Ensigns established under lawful authority and recorded for him in Her Majesty's College of Arms and hath requested the favour of His Grace's Warrant for the granting and assigning of such Arms and Crest and in the same Patent such Device or Badge as are deemed proper to be borne and used by him and by his descendants with their due and proper differences and according to the Laws of Arms And forasmuch as the said Earl Marshal did by Warrant under his hand and Seal bearing date the Thirtieth day of June last authorize and direct me to grant and assign such Arms and Crest and such Device or Badge accordingly Know Ye therefore that I the said Garter in pursuance of His Grace's Warrant and by virtue of the Letters Patent of my Office granted by The Queen's Most Excellent Majesty do by these Presents grant and assign unto the said DAVID EDWARD ROBERTS the Arms following that is to say:- Or two Barrulets and two Pallets conjoined Azure between four Cross Crosslets fitchy Gules and conjoined to a Bordure Azure And for the Crest upon a Helm with a Wreath Or and Azure An Alphyn passant Gules armed langued maned tufted and with tail knot and forelegs Or grasping in the dexter foreclaw a Sword point upwards Or hilt pommel and quillons Gules Mantled Azure doubled Gold And by the Authority aforesaid I the said Garter do by these Presents further grant and assign the following Device or Badge that is to say:- A Cross Crosslet encircled by ten square Billets each embattled on the facing edges with one Merlon Gules as are all in the margin hereof more plainly depicted to be borne and used for ever hereafter by the said David Edward Roberts and by his descendants with their due and proper differences and according to the Laws of Arms In witness whereof I the said Garter have to these Presents subscribed my name and affixed the Seal of my Office this Thirtieth day of July in the Forty-first year of the Reign of Our Sovereign Lady Elizabeth the Second by the Grace of God of the United Kingdom of Great Britain and Northern Ireland and of Her other Realms and Territories Queen Head of the Commonwealth Defender of the Faith and in the year of Our Lord One thousand nine hundred and ninety-two.

A. Colin Cole Garter

FACING PAGE: *A Chinese phoenix derived from the argus pheasant, and blazoned as a* fynye in ys pper collers *(ie a phoenix proper). The crest of the Company of Painter Stainers with three Chinese phoenix heads in the arms, granted in 1486.*

RIGHT: *Pantheon supporters of Charles Powlett, Duke of Bolton, who died in 1699.*

BELOW: *A sea monster, generally believed to be a sea calf, granted* c.*1520 to George Witwang of Northumberland.*

in purple or black and liberally sprinkled with stars. It is increasing in popularity as a charge or heraldic device suitable for this age of space travel and developing technology.

Closely allied to the composite monster are the monsters of sea and air. They were not strictly a Tudor invention, since there lurked a medieval belief that everything on land had its counterpart in the sea, and extreme belief sometimes extended this to the air. Tudor heralds made good use of these ideas and placed wings, scales, fins and fishtails on a variety of land animals. This practice has been revived in recent years, and many such marine and airborne monsters occur in modern grants of arms.

Renaissance heraldry showed a surprising reluctance to adopt the new discoveries made by contemporary travellers and explorers as charges, and this attitude continued well into the nineteenth century. One exception to this was the Chinese phoenix, which was adopted by two city livery companies in the fifteenth century. This is a clear indication of the City of London's immediate interest in foreign trade and shows a growing awareness of the importance of the Orient.

RIGHT: *Classical phoenixes based on the eagle; supporters to the arms of West Midland County Council.*

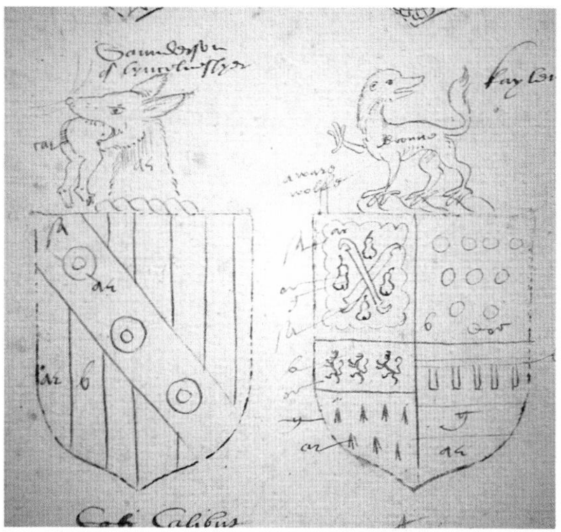

RIGHT: *The werewolf crest of Kaylewaye, one of the few new monsters to enter heraldry in the late sixteenth century.*

The argus pheasant native to China had evolved in Chinese culture into the *feng huang*, which was confused by travellers from the West with the legendary European phoenix. Further alterations by English heraldry turned it into an exotic fowl, now known as the Chinese phoenix. The more familiar European phoenix was, in fact, derived from a real eagle with painted wings, which was burnt with spices in a nest of palm branches by the ancient Egyptians. This took place at Heliopolis every 160 years as a sacrifice to the sun and to celebrate the leap year. This practice had been recorded in garbled form in the bestiary, and had given rise to the belief in a fabulous bird separated from its aquiline origin.

The apparent failure to make use of the zoological findings of explorers and adventurers marked the beginning of a new and conservative age in heraldry. From the late Tudor period for some 250 years, heraldry was essentially retrospective, preferring to rearrange the old rather than adopt the new. Virtually the only novelty was in the use of human beings or bits of human beings. Heralds seemed mesmerised by the human arm as crest material, giving it every sort of object to grasp. For supporters there are endless military and naval figures, as well as natives of conquered territories, a clear reflection of Britain's preoccupation with the developing empire.

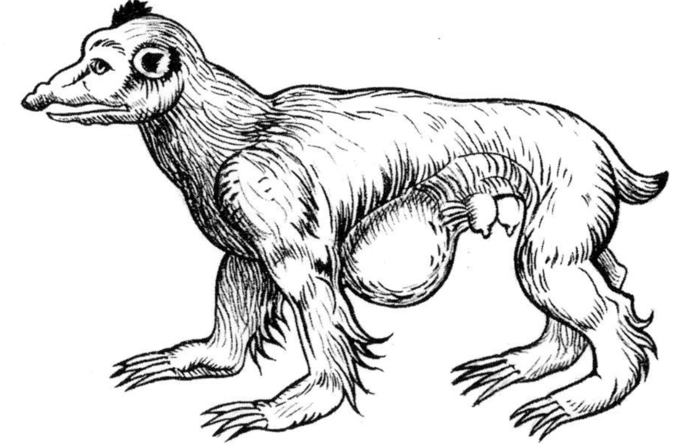

LEFT: *A missed opportunity: a drawing of an explorer's first impression of an opossum with a bulging pouch from South America (1516). Sixteenth-century heraldry failed to utilise such discoveries, which might otherwise have evolved further into the monstrous.*

LEFT: *Winged lynx supporters to the arms of the College of Ophthalmologists.*

RIGHT: *Catoblepas crest of Ward.*

But heraldry did not remain static, and the nineteenth century saw a reawakened interest in monsters. The medieval bestiaries again provided a useful source. The lynx of the bestiary, credited with remarkable eyesight and capable of seeing through solid objects, has become increasingly popular. The addition of wings symbolises the speedy dissemination of its visual services, and introduces a new monster to heraldry. Another recent addition, also endowed with useful qualities, is the caladrius. Bestiary writers reported that this bird drew the sickness out of an invalid with its eyesight, then flew up to the sun where the heat consumed the disease and restored the patient to health. The bird of the bestiaries is drawn like a gannet; but it may have evolved from the calandra lark which has a high, soaring flight, explaining its association with the sun.

The catoblepas has also been recently drawn from the bestiaries. Originally described as a native of Africa south of the Sahara, it was an animal of moderate size with a remarkably heavy head bent downwards towards the earth. Other bestiary writers state that the catoblepas was like a bull. All of this suggests the wildebeest. Again, a process of evolution would seem to have taken place; but this time without the help of the heralds, as the catoblepas is not found in heraldry before the twentieth century. The wildebeest evolved into a monster to which Edward Topsell refers in his bestiary writings in 1607 as 'a beast all set over with scales like a dragon, having no hair except on its head, great teeth like swine and having wings to fly and hands to handle'.

ABOVE: *Caladrii crest of the Isle of Wight Health Authority.*

New monsters, the product of the imagination of modern heralds, continue to appear. Composite creatures in the tradition of the gryphon, and land animals with wings, or fishes' scales and tails, are increasing in number. Similarly, like the Chinese phoenix, evolved zoology from other cultures is again being used, particularly from the Indians of North America and from the Orient.

LEFT: Chi Lin *or Chinese unicorns, supporters to the arms of the Chinese University of Hong Kong.*

Willm Welhowe de
Richat Surrey
John Carylle de Warnhm
de Sussex
John Hartstrane
Lincoln
Richard Bakehm de Colehm
Barkshire
Robert Barow de Flokerbroke
en la contee de Chestre
James Spencer

6
FAUNA AND FLORA

Peter Gwynn-Jones

LEFT: *Squirrel crests granted by Sir Thomas Wriothesley, Garter King of Arms, 1505-34, exemplifying the use of smaller indigenous mammals* *(see chapter on the art of heraldry)*.

The connection of heraldry with natural history leads back to the beginning, to the twelfth-century shield of Geoffrey Plantagenet which was charged with little lions of gold.

The lion's position in heraldry is unrivalled. Numerically, it has proved the most popular of all charges. Artistically, it has provided the heraldic painter with enormous scope for stylisation and interpretation. Zoologically, it holds the interesting position of being the only non-indigenous animal to feature significantly, or indeed at all, as an early medieval heraldic device. The idea that thirteenth- or fourteenth-century man combed the bestiary, the medieval book of beasts, and thus brought in a variety of Asian and African animals is simply untrue.

Although the lion roamed over the greater part of Europe during the Pleistocene age, by the twelfth century its European habitation was confined to the menageries of royal courts. Henry I's menagerie at Woodstock boasted the lion, and its presence probably influenced the choice of the lion for Geoffrey Plantagenet's shield, and later for the Royal Arms of England. This physical presence, combined with its frequent mention in the Bible and the classics, as well as its age-old reputation as the king of beasts, ensured that the lion became much more than an obscure entry in the bestiary; it enabled it to compete heraldically in a spectacular and successful fashion with the native animals of Europe.

One of the oldest and finest extant rolls of arms is the thirteenth-century Heralds' Roll. Of its 195 shields, 43 contain the lion.

ABOVE RIGHT: *Thirteenth-century Heralds' Roll showing luces or pike (second row) and lions.*

RIGHT: *Lions in medieval arms, painted c.1530.*

LEFT: *Bull crests painted in the early sixteenth century, but mainly of medieval origin.*

Zoology then features on ten other shields, a meagre number in comparison. Of these, one is charged with a bear, one with a crow or raven, three with luces or pike, three with eagles and one with a crane. Since the thirteenth century the lion's popularity has fluctuated, but its place as the pre-eminent zoological charge has never been challenged; from 1952 to 1972 it featured in nearly 20 per cent of all supporters granted. Its use has now surpassed that of the human being, which was in wider use during the last century.

The lion apart, any study of early heraldry will reveal only a sprinkling of animal species. Inevitably these reflected the nature of the bearers of coat armour. The medieval barons and knights were crude, rough men, preoccupied with war and self-advancement. When not pitting their strength against each other, it was directed towards the baiting and chasing of animal life. This unsophisticated and martial masculinity is reflected in the heraldry of the age, where stag, bull, bear, wolf and boar represent the pursued, and the horse, greyhound, talbot (the original hunting hound) and birds of prey represent the pursuers. Speed was signified by the martlet which loosely covered the swift, swallow and species of martin. These characteristics became so deeply engrained in the system that even today there are many who would regard the foxhound as more heraldic than the poodle or Pekinese, and the stag beetle to be preferred to the more effeminate butterfly. It is debatable whether it is right to maintain this attitude.

The pun was exceptional in breaking through this barrier and accounts, for example, for species of fish borne on the shields of families such as Tench, Breame and Herring. Again, the Lucys bore luces or pike, the Roches bore roach, the Ellises bore eels and the family of Gournay bore a gournard.

It was not until the fifteenth century that heraldry turned its attention in earnest to the animal world and began recruiting the non-indigenous, a process stimulated by the new practice of adorning the helmet with a crest and the subsequent use of supporters. Once again, the medieval bestiary was a rich source of inspiration. Two popular additions entering heraldry in this way were the elephant and the ostrich, the former often bearing a castle on its back as a derivative of the Indian howdah, and the latter holding in its beak a key, horseshoe or other metal object as an exaggerated reference to its liking for roughage to assist the gizzard. More frequently, heraldry turned to the indigenous, adding to the small number of those mammals and birds found in the heraldry of earlier centuries, and embracing such humble species as

RIGHT: *Snake crest of Watson, showing the young snakes bursting from their mother's belly, granted 1580.*

FAR RIGHT: *Hedgehog crest of Claxton, showing roundels presumed to be grapes stuck on its spines, confirmed 1561.*

the hedgehog, rabbit, and squirrel. No attempt was made to study animal life at first hand, and curious medieval accounts of nature passed unverified into heraldic use. Baby adders burst to life from their mother's belly, cranes held rocks in their raised claws to prevent them falling asleep, and hedgehogs caught falling grapes on their spines to carry away to their young.

The use of zoology in heraldry had reached and passed a climax well before 1600. The Tudor heralds never showed any real inclination to move beyond the bestiary or the native European species. In the meantime zoological knowledge had increased immensely as explorers pushed back the frontiers of the known world. Heraldry was left behind, and it was not until the nineteenth century that any attempt was made to catch up. Of the 182 grants of crests made by the Kings of Arms between 1674 and 1700, only seven feature non-indigenous animals: three cranes, two peacocks, one camel and one vulture.

RIGHT: *Tragopan crest of Laward, alias Lord, of London, early sixteenth century.*

In any generalisation there are bound to be exceptions, and sixteenth-century heraldic ornithology provides three interesting examples. At the beginning of Henry VIII's reign, Sir Thomas Wriothesley, Garter King of Arms and Thomas Benolt, Clarenceux King of Arms, granted a tragopan as a crest to Robert Lord, alias Laward, of London. Improbable though the bird may seem, it is not, as previously thought, a product of Tudor imagination. It is a species of pheasant which displays with horn-like wattles, which are clearly depicted in the Laward grant.

In the mid-sixteenth century the turkey made its appearance in a grant by Thomas Hawley, Clarenceux King of Arms, to Robert Cooke. The turkey's name is, of course, misleading. The turkey is a native of North America, and its introduction to Europe in the sixteenth century as a domestic fowl brought it to the attention of the heralds who used it to provide a suitable pun on the grantee's surname.

Towards the end of the sixteenth century Robert Cooke, Clarenceux King of Arms (not to be confused with the turkey grantee) introduced the bird of paradise as a crest for John Browne of Spexall in Suffolk. First knowledge of the species, now known as the great bird of paradise, was obtained by Western explorers, who found skins which had been stripped from the body, leaving behind the legs. Cooks's grant is therefore accurate in its depiction of a legless bird.

LEFT: *Thomas Hawley, Clarenceux King of Arms, granting the crest of a turkey to Robert Cooke of Mildham in the county of Norfolk, 1556.*

The conservatism of seventeenth- and eighteenth-century heraldry is manifested by the fox, an animal regarded as vermin in the Middle Ages and thus generally excluded from heraldry except as a pun for such families as Todd ('todd' being an ancient synonym for the fox). There was a reassessment of its reputation with the newly instituted sport of fox-hunting, a pastime enthusiastically adopted by a large proportion of recently armigerous families. However, these families preferred traditional charges for their heraldry, such as the wolf, bear, falcon or stag, which represented the field sports of the Middle Ages. They were thus trying to infer a medieval gentility, which could not be sug-

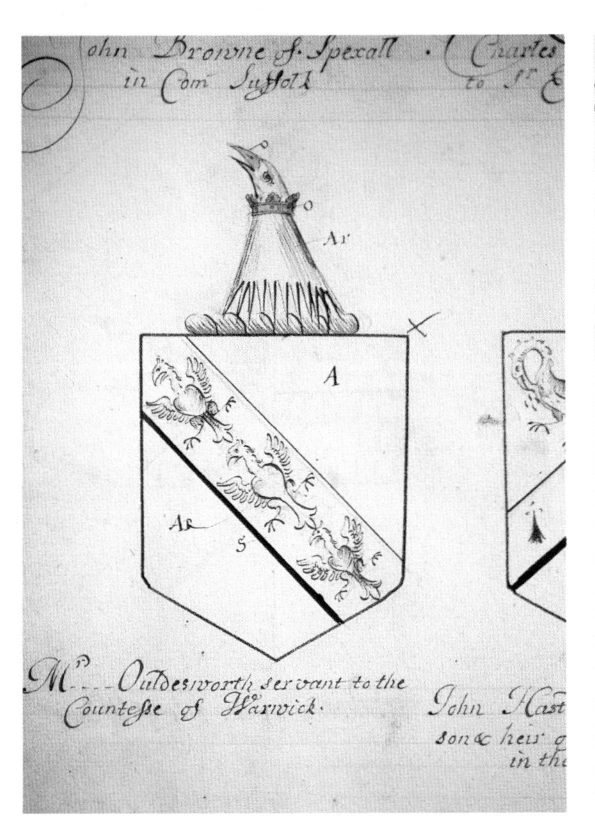

FAR LEFT: *Bird of paradise crest of John Browne, granted 1591.*

LEFT: *Fox supporter and sea fox crest of the Alliance and Leicester Building Society. The fox features in the arms of the County Council of Leicestershire, alluding to the fox-hunting tradition of that county.*

gested by the use of newly appraised fox.

The nineteenth century witnessed an awakened interest in zoology. Today this interest continues to increase. For example, of the 1254 supporters granted by the Kings of Arms between 1950 and 1970, 17 incorporate the kangaroo, compared with three between 1820 and 1920. Animals such as the zebra, giraffe, okapi and many species of antelope from the African continent; the bison, moose and beaver from North America, and the koala bear and duck-billed platypus from Australia, have also made an impact on heraldic design. In addition, more obscure animals like the armadillo, coati, species of opossum and marmosets from Latin America, are no longer unknown in heraldry. This is an encouraging trend; the very different outlines of these animals provide excellent and exciting design material. It is to be hoped that new grantees will realise that possessing a giant anteater as a crest is far more distinctive than opting for yet another lion device.

While mammals were attracting new interest in the last century, species of non-indigenous birds were not so popular. Grants of supporters between 1820 and 1920 provide instances of new arrivals from the crane, stork, and ibis group; beyond this only the emu, kiwi and tjarder were granted. Since 1950, however, a far wider use has been made of English birds, and non-European species have been recruited in increasing quantities, the weaverbird, kookaburra, penguin, secretary bird and the tui bird of New Zealand being numerically the most conspicuous. The supporters to the arms of the Textile Institute are blazoned as weaverbirds, but are, in fact, red bishop birds, members of the false weaverbird family. It is to be hoped that future blazoning will be more specific, as the weaverbirds cover many species of distinctive colouring. The sudden spurt in ornithological interest may be explained by the natural colouring of a bird's plumage, which is generally brighter and better suited to heraldry than the drabber, duller colours of

RIGHT: *Coati crest of Gwynn-Jones, exemplifying the wider range of animals which have been used in heraldry since 1800.*

LEFT: *'Weaverbirds', more precisely red bishops* (euplectes orix), *supporters to the arms of the Textile Institute.*

the mammal. Once the current preference of depicting the mammal in its natural colours ceases to be an important factor in the system, and it becomes more acceptable to colour it in heraldic tinctures, then perhaps it will match the present popularity of the bird. There is no sound heraldic reason why an armadillo, for example, should be preferred in natural pinkish brown. A green armadillo plated in gold, the crest of Oliver, stands in the good heraldic tradition of the Middle Ages, when mammals were invariably rendered in primary colours.

The new interest in mammal and bird may soon be extended to fish and insect. The dolphin, long regarded as the king of fishes, and the marine equivalent of the lion on land and the eagle in the air, was the only 'fish' regularly used in heraldry, the use of others being generally restricted to the pun. However, game fishing has recently encouraged the use of the salmon, trout and other more exotic species. Even the fishing fly is now found as a heraldic charge. The recent appearance of such as sunfish, flying fish, parrotfish and angelfish reflect interests in sailing and snorkelling in tropical climes.

A small number of insects, arachnids and crustaceans featured during the Renaissance and Tudor periods. The grasshopper, or greshop, of Gresham, and the stag beetle of Hartwell are two punning examples. The bee is also popular as a symbol of industry, and more recently the octagonal cell formation of the honeycomb has been introduced as a field for the shield. Twentieth-century heraldry has increased the range of invertebrates. The slater (a long-antennaed relative of the wood louse) is a punning crest for Sclater, and a water boatman displayed gold is the crest for Hammond, alluding to the rowing interests of that grantee. Combining the pun and career is the elephant hawkmoth of Lord Delfont. This insect provides not only a pun on his title, but moths are associated with bright lights at night and are hence appropriate for a notable impresario.

Less popular as heraldic charges are reptiles and amphibians, except for a number of snakes which feature in various knotted formations in late Tudor grants subsequently. Snakes have remained frequent as a component part in the Rod of Aesculapius, the classical god of medicine, and in the caduceus

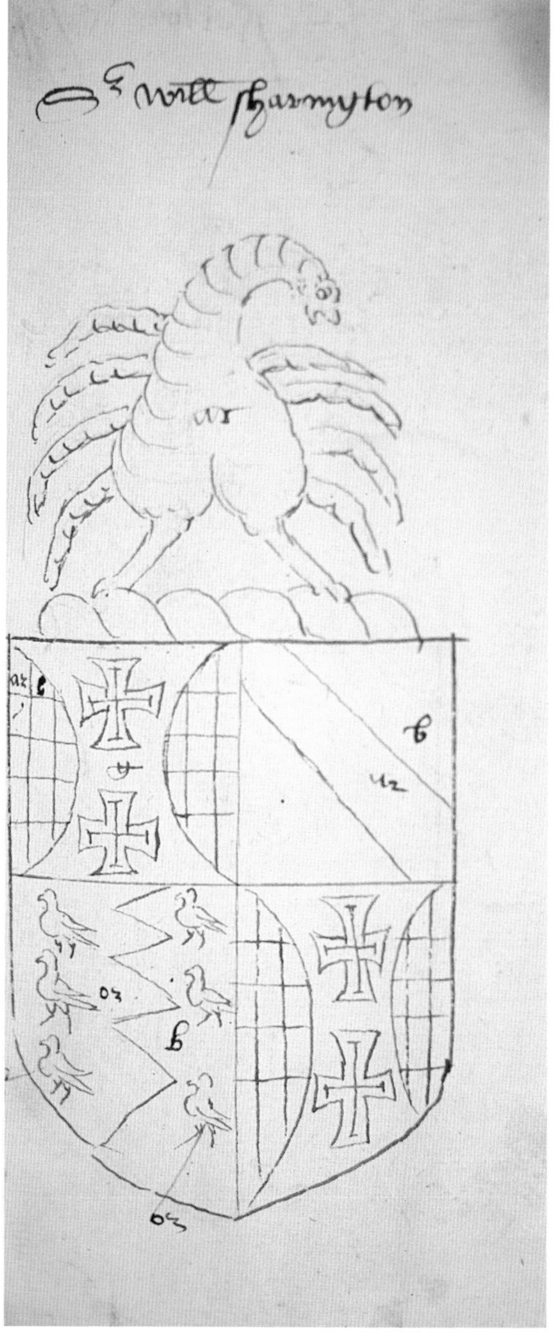

ABOVE LEFT: *Stag beetle crest granted in the early sixteenth century to William Hartwell.*

ABOVE RIGHT: *A curious interpretation of a scorpion, the crest of Sir William Sharington (Sherrington), c.1547.*

RIGHT: *Bees and a slater in the arms and crest of Sclater.*

or wand of Mercury, a charge suitable for those connected with the media of communication. The chameleon is a recent arrival, and its ability to change colour offers considerable scope for grantees involved with the theatre. There are several species of chameleon which, with their various horns and facial embellishments, make for excellent and distinctive crests.

For the amphibians, the frog remains a rarity; but a notable exception is a sixteenth-century crest which shows a leaping frog as a delightful pun for the family of Dryland. The increasing interest in wildlife conservation and ecology may now help the heraldic position of frog and toad. The East Hampshire District Council, for example, was recently granted the natterjack toad, thus helping to cement the link between twentieth-century heraldry and wildlife conservation.

The mollusc has a long heraldic history. As a pun for families such as Shelley, its use is obvious. More difficult to ascertain is to what extent its common use in heraldry derives from its adoption as a pilgrim's badge. Whelks provide a pun for names such as Wilkinson. Cowrie shells, hitherto used as a currency in tropical regions of the world, have featured in the arms of bankers; and there is much scope in mollusc charges for persons concerned with the building industry, or insurance, with its emphasis on protection.

Two types of animal fur have been widely used since the inception of heraldry in the twelfth century, reflecting the sartorial fashion of the time. Ermine is a white fur covered with black spots representing the tail tips of the natural animal. Vair is composed of the grey-blue back skins of a type of squirrel, stitched alternately with its white belly skins. Originally both ermine and vair were probably stitched over shields, but paint was soon substituted, allowing their forms to be represented in different colours. A misunderstanding of the French word 'vair' led to translators confusing this with the word *verre* meaning glass, and so Cinderella was given

LEFT: *The natterjack toad crest of East Hampshire District Council; beechnuts feature in the arms.*

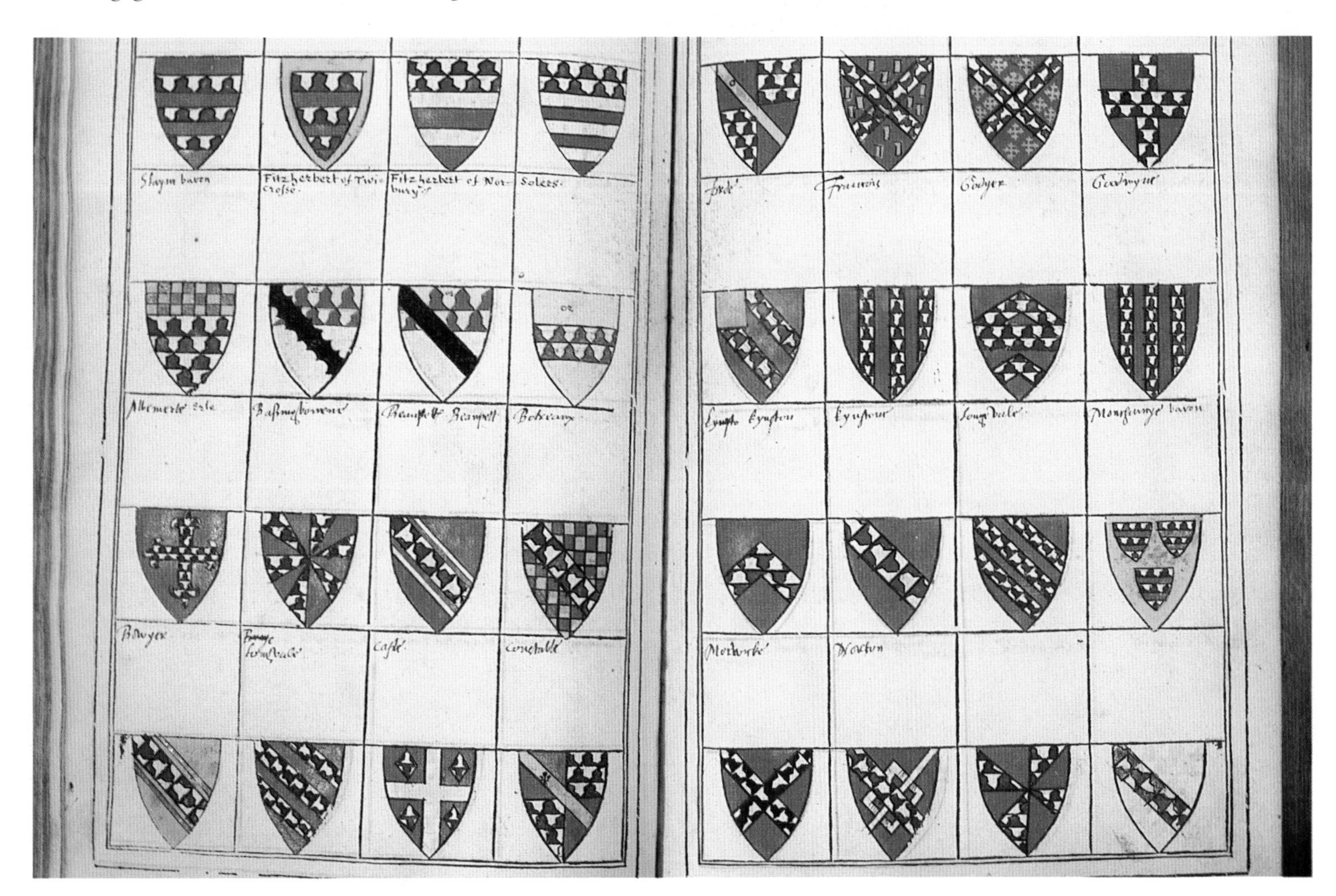

BELOW: *Examples of vair in the* Holles Ordinary.

slippers of an impossible material instead of fashionable squirrel skin.

Heraldic botany has invariably come a poor second to zoology. The rose and fleur-de-lis, the garb or sheaf of corn, (particularly associated with the earldom of Chester) and the simple devices of cinquefoil, quatrefoil and trefoil, these alone made any real impact on medieval heraldry. Trees, fruit and leaves appeared rarely as charges, usually as punning allusions to surnames. Other forms of flora were negligible or non-existent. Tudor heraldry made some attempt to rectify this, but in general its botanical charges played a secondary role. More often than not they featured as a simple sprig held in the feet or mouth of a zoological charge to render this more distinctive from existing devices featuring the same animal, or as a pun.

The rose is particular, and is the botanical counterpart to the zoological lion. The plucking of red and white roses in the Temple gardens by John Beaufort, Duke of Somerset, and Richard Plantagenet, Duke of York, is the traditional origin of their adoption as the badges of the rival houses of Lancaster and York. The truth is different. Eleanor of Provence introduced a golden rose into English heraldry which was subsequently adopted, as a badge, by her eldest son Edward I. Her second son, Edmund Crouchback, Earl of Lancaster, changed his rose to red in order to distinguish himself from his brother. Thereafter, this red rose adhered to the title of Lancaster. Meanwhile, the white rose had anciently been a Mortimer badge, and features in arms from the area of the Welsh Marches, the Mortimer stronghold. For example, the town of Ludlow in Shropshire bore *Azure a lion couchant between three roses Argent*. It was through his Mortimer descent that Richard Plantagenet, Duke of York, laid claim to the English throne and thus linked the white rose to the Yorkist cause. Some cinquefoils and even quatrefoils may have a rose origin, being simplified and

BELOW: *Sprigs, twigs and flowers feature as secondary charges in the crests of many Tudor grants.*

stylised versions of that flower. Others may reflect an ancient loyalty to Simon de Montfort in the baronial wars of the thirteenth century.

The fleur-de-lis is one of the more controversial charges in heraldry. Although it is found in the arms of seemingly unconnected families throughout Europe, it is most familiar in the Royal Arms of France. As such, it was appropriated by Edward III and remained a feature in British regal heraldry until discarded in 1801. French legend asserts that Clovis, King of the Franks, received the fleur-de-lis as a divine gift in return for his conversion to Christianity in 496. It is possible that Clovis, trapped between an army of heathen Goths and the river Rhine may have noticed the water iris growing far out into the river. Recognising the possibility of fording at that point, he managed to lead his army to safety and subsequently adopted the iris, in the form of the fleur-de-lis, as his emblem.

The first definite association of the fleur-de-lis with the heraldry of the French monarchy dates from the reign of the twelfth-century King Louis VII, hence the suggestion that the fleur-de-lis is a pun on the name Louis. It is also known that a fleur-de-lis formation was a Moslem motif and there is speculation that Louis VII was attracted to it while taking part in the Third Crusade. However, this may be coincidence, as such a formation is aesthetically obvious and might easily be reached by different civilisations without outside influence. Furthermore the fleur-de-lis has a pre-heraldic history as a royal device in France, where it featured on crowns and sceptres. At the beginning of the eleventh century Robert II decorated the rim of his crown with fleurs-de-lis; and 200 years earlier a fleur-de-lis formed the finial of the Emperor Charlemagne's sceptre.

More intriguing are the attributed arms of King Pharamund – *Sable three frogs gold*. King Pharamund was reputedly the great-grandfather of King Clovis, and was said to have been descended from a river god. There is some indication that the Merovingian dynasty of France founded by Clovis paid special attention to the frog, either mystical or emblematic, and this may account for many ancient fairy stories where frogs turned

These are the Armes and Seales of Ludlowe in ye countie of Salop, incorporated by king Edward the Fourth in the first yeare of his reigne, by the name of Bailiffes Burgesses and Communaltie of the towne of Ludlow: the said King in consideration of the laudable and voluntary services performed by the said Burgesses and Communaltie in assisting him in the acquiring and obtayning of his right (the Crowne of England long time from him and his ancestors withholden) and the great danger of life, calamities, robberies, thefts oppressions, losse of goods and other greevances which they for his

ABOVE: *White roses in the arms of Ludlow, confirmed at the Visitation of Shropshire, 1623.*

LEFT: *Fleurs-de-lis in the arms of Louis, Dauphin and later Louis XI of France. The dolphin in the arms and crest is a pun on his title of Dauphin; the Hyghalmen Roll, painted c.1450.*

RIGHT: *Three frogs in the attributed arms of King Pharamund, ancestor of the Merovingian kings of France.*

BELOW: *Christopher Barker, Garter King of Arms, granting armorial bearings to Thomas Bell in 1542. The decorative border includes the royal badges of Tudor rose and fleur-de-lis, together with native flowers and fruits.*

OPPOSITE PAGE, BELOW RIGHT: *Examples of flora and fauna, sometimes highly stylised, in the Fenwick Roll.*

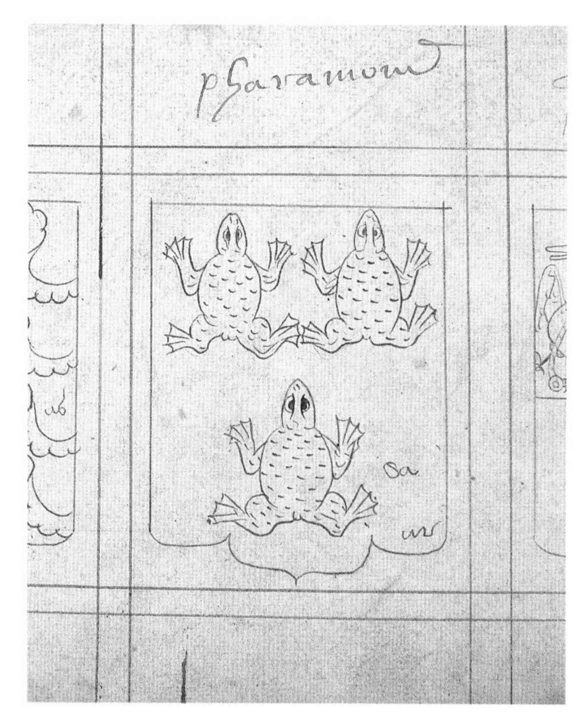

into princes and vice versa. This in turn may also have inspired the Flemings to call their French neighbours the nickname later revived by British sailors in the nineteenth century, translated as 'Froggy'. The golden water iris occupies the same habitat as the frog; and the one reflects the physical shape of the other. Whether this was recognised and the fleur-de-lis represents both the flower and a stylised frog, is a matter of speculation.

Before 1700, trees rarely appear in English heraldry. Of the 9000 shields in the sixteenth-century *Smith's Ordinary*, whole trees appear in only seven. Qualities of strength and endurance typified by the oak might, for example, have appealed, but clearly they did not. The tree was more often limited to a punning use until it obtained a new popularity in the eighteenth century, which was followed by a growing interest in flowers in the nineteenth. Heraldic use can therefore be seen as reflecting gardening tastes, from the period of Georgian landscape gardens to the herbaceous borders of the Victorians. Today, a wide range of flora is in use, particularly the non-European; the dogwood of North America, hibiscus, lotus and the Australian wattle and waratah flower are examples which are now well established in heraldry.

Nonetheless, if largely restricted to rose, fleur-de-lis and foils in pre-eighteenth-

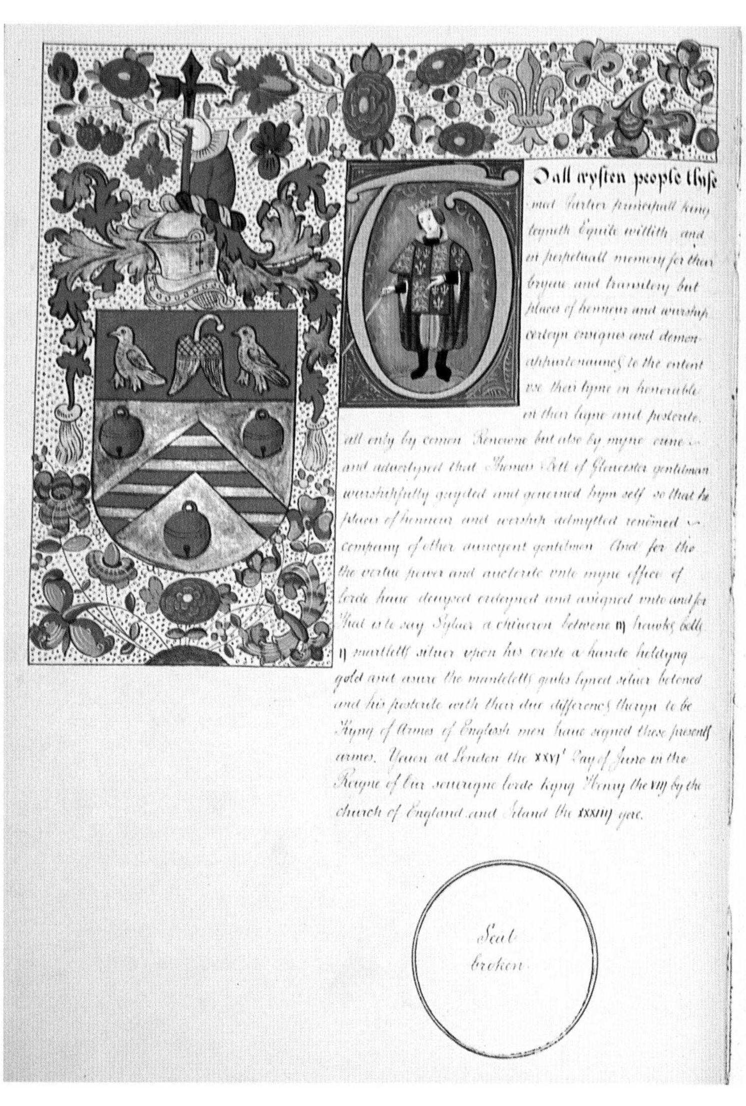

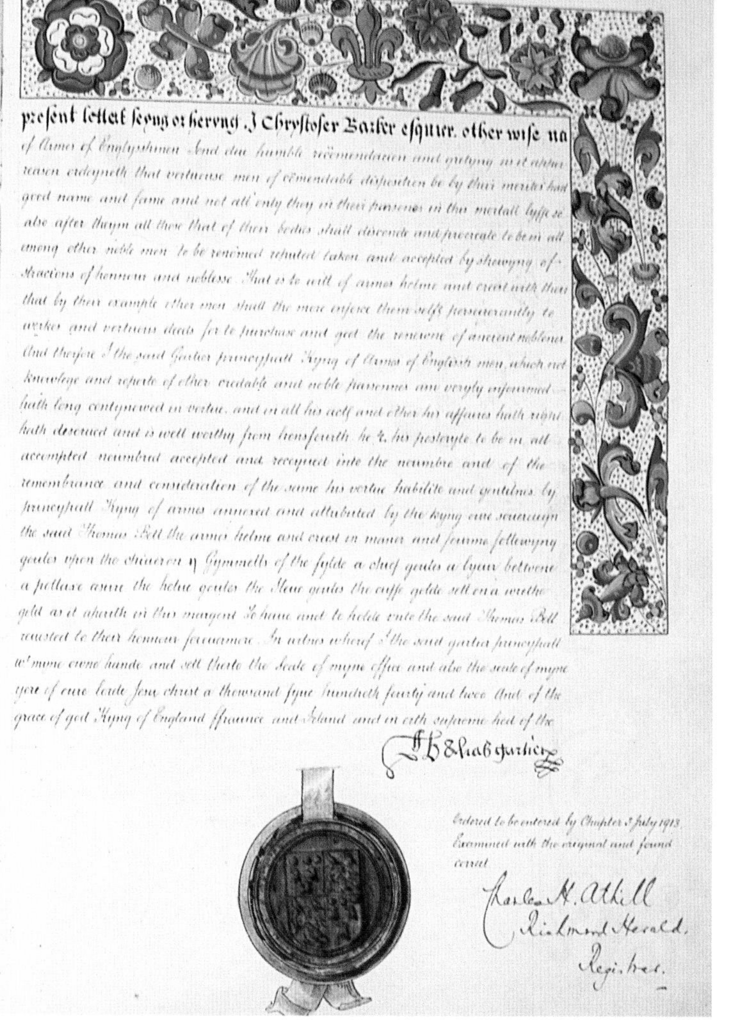

century shield and crest, the flower has featured on the periphery of heraldry as a decorative motif in the borders of Letters Patent issued by Kings of Arms when granting new armorial bearings. Floral borders to Letters Patent date back to the fifteenth century and feature the native flowers of the countryside, with campion, periwinkle, heartsease or wild pansy, honeysuckle, columbine and dog rose proving the most popular. Conspicuously absent are primrose, daffodil and cowslip. Heraldic principle precludes gold or yellow being used on silver or white, and vice versa, as they fail to stand out against each other and it seems to have extended to these non-heraldic borders. The columbine was one of the few native flowers to enter pre-eighteenth-century heraldry. Its use was limited to a handful of armorial bearings, including that granted in 1461 to the Company of Cooks. Its presence in this grant may result from a confusion with a type of ginger used for culinary purposes, known as 'colambyne' or 'columbyne', a native of Colombo. Alternatively, it may have been intended to act as a form of talisman or charm, the columbine flower being held 'to be very medicinable for dissolving impostumations and swellings in the throat'. If this is so, then it represents a rare example of herbal law in heraldry, two sciences which otherwise remained far apart.

ABOVE: *Columbine in the arms of the Company of Cooks, originally granted in 1461, as entered at the Visitation of London, 1687.*

ABOVE: *Cloves, representing grocery, and badgers, notable for their good house-keeping, are combined in the armorial bearings of Tesco Stores (Holdings) Limited.*

Leaves attracted little interest in the Middle Ages but since 1700 their use in heraldry has been widespread. The maple leaf of Canada must rank as one of the more spectacular successes. The *Quebec Gazette* first refers to it as an emblem in 1805, and soon after it was incorporated as a device in the regimental colours of the Prince of Wales' Royal Canadian Regiment. Today it features in the Royal Arms of Canada, in the Canadian national flag, and is requested as a device by the majority of Canadians petitioning for a grant of new armorial bearings.

Fruit are largely confined to punning use, with a few exceptions. One such exception is the pomegranate, where its numerous seeds provide an allusion to the seeds of learning. Similarly, the hazelnut is the fruit of the hazel, the pre-Christian tree of wisdom; both of these are useful botanical charges for places of education and a welcome relief from the over-used open book and torch of youth.

With the exception of the Welsh leek, vegetables have been largely ignored by heraldry. Tudor livery reflected the leek's colours of green and white, and there is a contemporary reference to the thirteenth-century Welsh prince, Llewellyn the Great 'clad in robes of royalty, a robe of green and white silk'. In the fourteenth century, Edward, the Black Prince, ordered cloth of 'green and white' to make short, particoloured coats and hats for his Welsh troops, the first soldiers to appear on the continental battlefields in a national uniform. Although no medieval source described the leek as a Welsh emblem, its wearing was an established custom in Tudor times. Some complain about the twentieth-century intrusion of the more aesthetically pleasing daffodil as a national emblem, forgetting that the daffodil was known as St David's leek.

Zoology and botany are frequently combined, with an animal holding a flower or sprig in foot or mouth. However, a more imaginative combination dates from the thirteenth century: a lion or leopard's face *jessant de lys*. The traditional belief that it represents the English lion swallowing the French lily has been challenged, as the device first appears in the thirteenth century, when it was used by the Cantelupe family. The Latin word, *lupus*, suggests that the original animal was intended to be a wolf, thus providing a pun on the Cantelupe surname. However, this overlooks early blazon which refers to the lion or leopard as 'Lupard', which also provides a pun. The fleur-de-lis has been combined with the animal in twentieth-century heraldry by terminating the upper petals in animal heads in several recent grants. This combination of the two branches of natural history, zoology and botany, has considerable scope for future heraldic design.

RIGHT: *Australian fauna and flora exemplified in the unusual supporters – brush-tailed possums and eucalyptus trees – of the Zoological Board of Victoria, Australia. A helmeted honey eater features in the crest.*

SEMPER · LIBERTAS

WE Sir Anthony Richard Wagner, Knight Commander of the Royal Victorian Order, Garter Principal King of Arms, John Riddell Bromhead Walker, Esquire, Member of the Royal Victorian Order, upon whom has been conferred the decoration of the Military Cross, Clarenceux King of Arms, and Walter John

LEFT: *Cardinals and dogwood flowers are popular charges in American heraldry, and are combined in the armorial bearings of Prince George County in the Commonwealth of Virginia, granted 1976.*

LEFT: *Recent fleurs-de-lis badges terminating in animal form.*

7
ROYAL HERALDRY

Henry Bedingfeld

LEFT: *Tomb effigy of Queen Eleanor of Castile at Westminster Abbey, 1291-93.*

The Royal Arms of England date back to about 1198. In that year, or perhaps a bit earlier, King Richard I Cœur de Lion had his second Great Seal made, showing three lions passant guardant in pale, and this device has been borne by English monarchs ever since. Before that date lions were certainly attributed to kings of England, but it is uncertain whether they were actually used in practice. Richard I's first Great Seal shows a lion rampant facing the sinister on the visible half of a curved shield; the invisible half is thought to have borne a similar lion facing the first. In these positions the lions are rearing up as though they are about to fight, the heraldic term for this being 'combatant'. The fact that King Richard did not continue with this design and changed it to the three lions makes it clear that heraldry was still in an experimental stage, and that designs were not strictly fixed.

We have seen that Geoffrey of Anjou bore six golden lions on a blue shield, but it is a curious fact that his father-in-law, Henry I of England, who apparently gave him the shield, did not, as far as we know, bear arms himself, although descendants of his illegitimate sons, Robert, Earl of Gloucester and Reginald, Earl of Cornwall bore lions. Geoffrey of Anjou's son, Henry II, the first Plantagenet king, is not known to have borne arms either, but he has been attributed with two lions passant. Henry II's sons, on the other hand, did bear arms: John, during his father's lifetime, may have borne two lions passant guardant, Richard I's we have mentioned, and William de Longespée, an illegitimate son, bore the same arms as his grandfather Geoffrey of Anjou. After Henry II's death in 1189 his queen, Eleanor of Aquitaine, who died in 1204, had a seal cut the reverse of which shows a shield bearing the three lions.

Ingenious heralds of the later Middle Ages attributed fictitious armorial bearings to pre-armorial monarchs, from King Arthur onwards. Those assigned to Edward the Confessor, based on the design on the reverse of a penny coin minted in his reign, were later used with the Royal Arms by Richard II (1377-99) in a personal rather than a formal capacity, as he had a particular devotion to him. All the Norman kings of England were

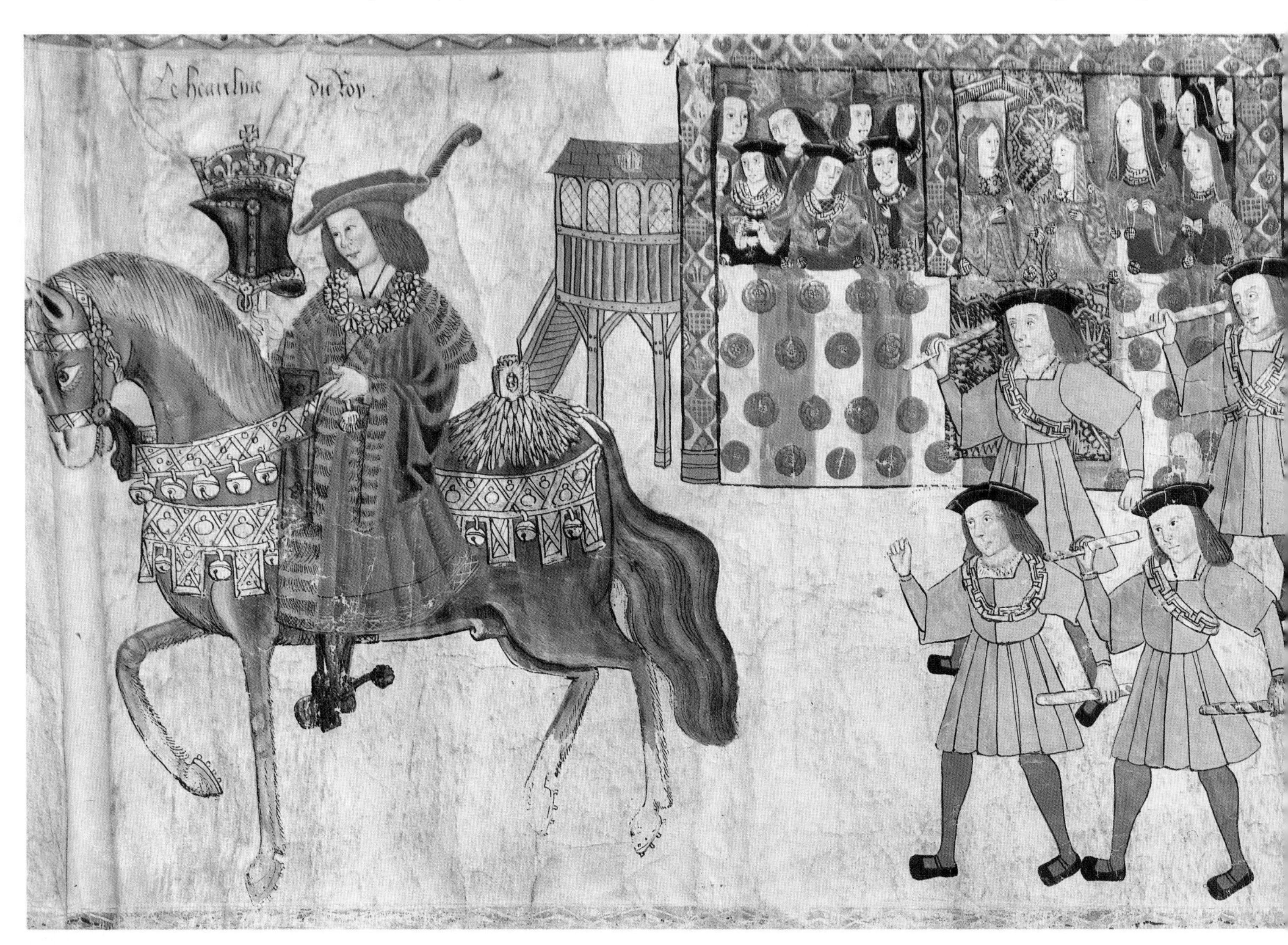

BELOW: *Henry VIII, from the Westminster Tournament Roll, 1511.*

attributed two gold lions passant guardant on a red field. King Stephen, not a male-line descendant of the Norman royal house, was attributed a single Sagittary and sometimes three Sagittaries. Matthew Paris, in his thirteenth-century *Historia Anglorum*, attributed the three lions passant guardant to all the Norman kings, including King Stephen. All these attributions were retrospective; there is no evidence that they were ever used by the kings in their own days.

The Royal Arms of the three lions of England were used on their own until the fourteenth century. In 1337 Edward III claimed the throne of France, styled himself King of England and France, and quartered the French Royal Arms with those of England to emphasise the point. The ancient French arms were blue with gold fleurs-de-lis scattered throughout, and they were placed in the first and fourth quarters, the superior position, as the French monarchy was older than the English. In about 1400 Henry V of England reduced the number of fleurs-de-lis to three, to copy the practice adopted by Charles V of France in 1376. This new version of the quartered arms continued unchanged until Queen Mary married Philip II of Spain in 1554.

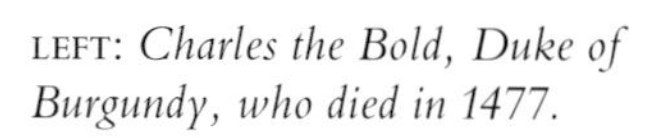

LEFT: *Charles the Bold, Duke of Burgundy, who died in 1477.*

In about 1300 crests first made their appearance in England. It became the fashion to place a modelled object, frequently an animal or animal's head, on top and pointing in the same direction as the helmet. From the top of the helmet flowed a cape of material thought to protect the wearer from the heat of the sun or to deflect blows to the neck. The crest, with a wreath of twisted material, or a coronet, held the cape or mantling, as it became known, in position. The third Great Seal of Edward III shows for the first time a crest of a gold lion wearing an ancient crown standing upon a chapeau or cap of maintenance, an ancient cap of dignity made of red velvet and turned-up ermine. Henry VII continued to use this crest, but it was not until the reign of Henry VIII that an arched crown of crosses formy alternating with fleurs-de-lis became continuously used with the chapeau inside the crown. This is very much like the present royal crest, though there have been variations in the style of the crown in the intervening centuries.

Animal supporters, holding and guarding the shield, have been consistently used in the display of Royal Arms since the reign of Edward IV, but they have varied. Supporters have been attributed to earlier kings of England, from Edward III to Henry V, but their authority is considered doubtful. The antelope supporters attributed to Henry VI only appear on buildings completed after his death, for example the Eton Gateway and St George's Chapel, Windsor. However, an interesting discovery was made in 1895 when a copper jug was found in the palace of King Prempeh at Kurnasi in Ghana. It is now in the British Museum and clearly shows the Royal Arms of King Richard II with two lions reguardant as supporters. It has been dated to about 1390 from the couchant hart badge that appears on it, together with other royal badges. Further evidence, however, will be needed before it can be established that Richard II and other kings prior to Henry VI consistently displayed supporters.

The origin of supporters to shields is still unclear. It is probable that it was just a question of artistry; seal engravers, carvers and sculptors merely added beasts from favourite badges or the arms of associated families as a form of decoration. Early seals include animal decoration in the void between the shape of the shield and the circular rim. The custom of adding this extra decoration proved popular with the higher nobility. Increasing numbers of them adorned their arms in this fashion, and the king was no exception. Henry VI displayed two white antelopes, sometimes a lion and a panther, or antelope or heraldic tyger; Edward IV a black bull and white lion, a gold lion and a black bull, or a white lion and hart, or two white lions; and Richard III a white lion and a white boar, or two white boars.

When Henry Tudor came to the throne in 1485 as Henry VII, he chose as supporters two greyhounds, animals associated with the house of Lancaster from which he was descended. A few years later, a red dragon was substituted for one greyhound, presumably to emphasise his links with Wales. His son, Henry VIII, changed them to the more regal gold lion and red dragon. These were also used by his children, Edward VI and Queen Mary until her marriage to Philip II of Spain in 1554. Queen Mary's marital arms were supported by a black eagle (from the Hapsburg arms) and a gold lion.

Royal Arms are arms of sovereignty, and are borne in order to show the territorial possessions of the king or queen. The French quartering, however, represented a claim rather than actual possession. They are not

FACING PAGE: *Portrait of King Richard II (1377-99) at Westminster Abbey.*

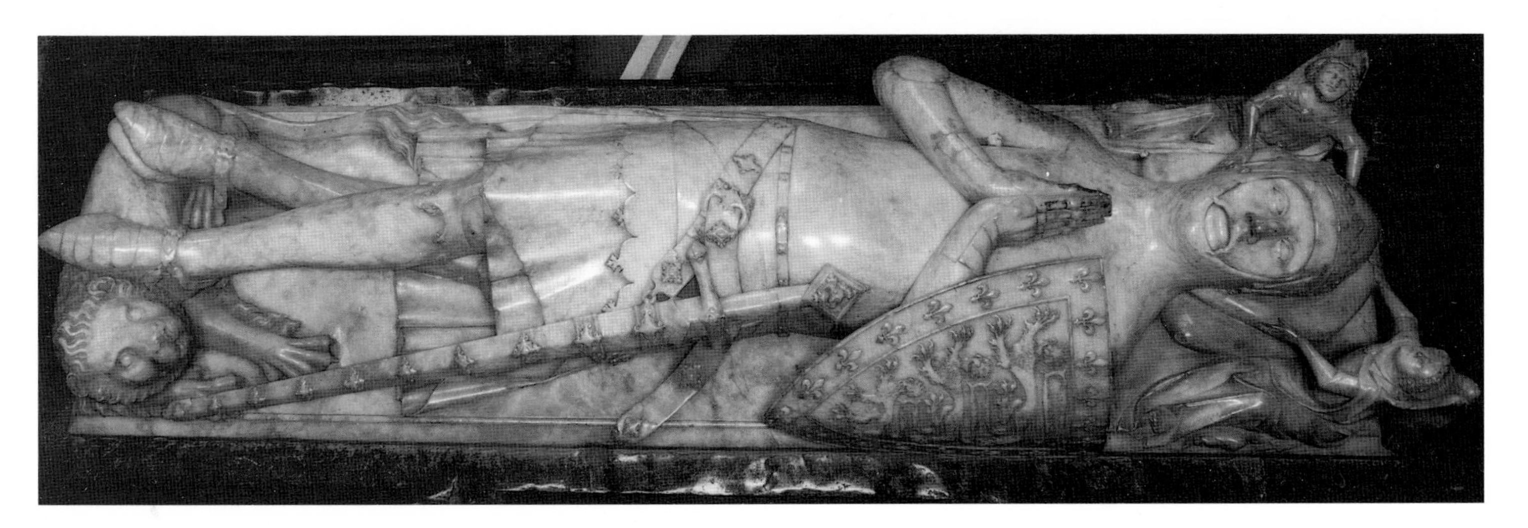

BELOW: *The effigy of John of Eltham, Earl of Cornwall (died 1336), at Westminster Abbey.*

RIGHT: *The phoenix and falcon badges of Elizabeth I.*

FACING PAGE: *The arms of James I, with the crests of England, Scotland, France and Ireland.*

Queene Elizabeth bare for her Badges the Phenyx Burninge with
this Motto SEMPER EADEM being a true type or figure of her -
Princely selfe wch whilest she lived was the only Phenix living in -
the whole world.
Her other Badge was a white Falcon Crowned houlding a Scepter and
standing on a stock or Roote of a Tree betwene 2 growing Branches of

BELOW: *Mary Queen of Scots married the Dauphin of France (later Francis II) in 1558.*

personal arms, which pass from father to son; upon a change of dynasty the new king gives up his personal arms to take on the symbols of his new sovereignty. This Henry Tudor, Earl of Richmond, did when he became king. Queen Mary Tudor, on the other hand, when she married King Philip II of Spain, bore the arms of her husband impaled with her own. This complicated piece of marshalling shows King Philip's sovereignty, through his wife, over England (and France) and Queen Mary's sovereignty, through her husband, over Castile, Leon, Aragon, Sicily, Granada, Austria, Burgundy (shown as ancient and modern), Brabant and with Flanders and Tyrol overall. Queen Mary was succeeded by her sister Elizabeth in 1558, who kept to the arms of France modern and England, but whose supporters became a royally-crowned gold lion and a red dragon; her adopted motto was *Semper Eadem* ('Always the Same'). When Elizabeth died in 1603 another dynastic change occurred when her Stuart cousin, James VI of Scotland, succeeded to the throne of England as James I. As King of England James bore in the first and fourth grand-quarters the arms of his predecessors, France modern and England; the Royal Arms of Scotland – *Or a lion rampant and a double tressure flory counter flory*

England

Scotland

France

Ireland

p.105 & 168

RIGHT: *The Royal Arms of Great Britain and Hanover 1816-37, borne by George III, George IV and William IV.*

Gules in the second quarter, with Ireland in the third quarter – *Azure a harp stringed Argent*. The harp as a badge had previously been associated with Ireland when that lordship had been raised to a kingdom by Henry VIII, but when James I became king the harp was formally included as a part of the whole achievement to show King James' full sovereignty. James I retained the golden lion supporter of England and substituted his own unicorn supporter for Elizabeth's dragon. The unicorn first appears as a supporter to the arms of the kings of Scotland on the coinage of James III in the fifteenth century, but it is a single unicorn, sitting and holding the shield from behind; two unicorns on each side of the shield date from 1503, during the reign of James IV. Scottish sovereigns continued to use these supporters for the next century until James VI became King of England. The lion and unicorn are Queen Elizabeth II's supporters today, and they are blazoned, *a Lion guardant Or royally crowned proper and a Unicorn Argent armed tufted crined and unguled gorged with a coronet composed of crosses formy and fleurs-de-lis thereto a chain affixed and reflexed over the back all Or.*

The Royal Arms remained the same until 1688, although they were not used during the Commonwealth when Oliver Cromwell ruled England as Lord Protector and the royal family were in exile after the Civil War. The Stuart arms have survived in the arms of the descendants of Charles II's illegitimate sons. The Duke of Grafton bears them, *debruised by a baton sinister compony of six pieces Argent and Azure*; the Duke of St Albans *debruised by a baton sinister Gules charged with three Roses Argent*; and the Duke of Richmond's arms have, instead of a baton sinister, *a bordure company Argent and Gules charged with eight Roses of the second barbed and seeded proper.*

When Mary Stuart came to the throne in 1688, she reigned jointly with her husband William of Orange. The arms of William III and Mary II were the same as those of James I, with the addition of the arms of Nassau on a shield in the centre. This still exists today as the arms of the kingdom of the Netherlands and is blazoned, *Azure billety and a Lion rampant Or*. When Mary's sister, Anne, succeeded in 1702, she bore the Stuart Royal Arms (without the Nassau shield) until the Act of Union in 1707, which created the kingdom of Great Britain, necessitated another armorial change. The first quarter of the shield became England impaling (side by side with) Scotland, but the double tressure counter flory was dimidiated, that is, cut off, or omitted along the palar line; this coat was repeated in the fourth quarter. In the new scheme France was placed in the second quarter and Ireland remained in the third.

Anne was the last of the Stuart monarchs when she died in 1714, and was succeeded by George, the Elector of Hanover, Duke of Brunswick and Lüneburg and Arch Treasurer of the Holy Roman Empire, who became king as George I under the terms of the Act of Settlement of 1701. This again necessitated another change; the repeated fourth quarter in Queen Anne's arms were removed and replaced by the Hanoverian arms. The new quartering symbolised King George's German possessions: Brunswick (*Gules two Lions passant guardant in pale Or*), Lüneburg (*Or semy of hearts Gules and a Lion rampant Azure*), and Westphalia (*Gules a Horse courant Argent*) and, in the centre, the augmentation of the Arch Treasurer of the Holy Roman Empire (*an inescutcheon Gules charged with the golden crown of Charlemagne*). The latter augmentation was only borne by the king, not by other members of the royal family. (Curiously enough *The Times* still carries George I's arms on its masthead.)

Another change was necessary under the Act of Union with Ireland, and in 1801 the Royal Arms were rearranged. After nearly 500 years the opportunity was now taken to drop the French Royal Arms, and the quarterings now became (1) England (2) Scotland (3) Ireland and (4) England repeated; an

FACING PAGE: *Attributed and actual Royal Arms from William the Conqueror until George III (1816).*

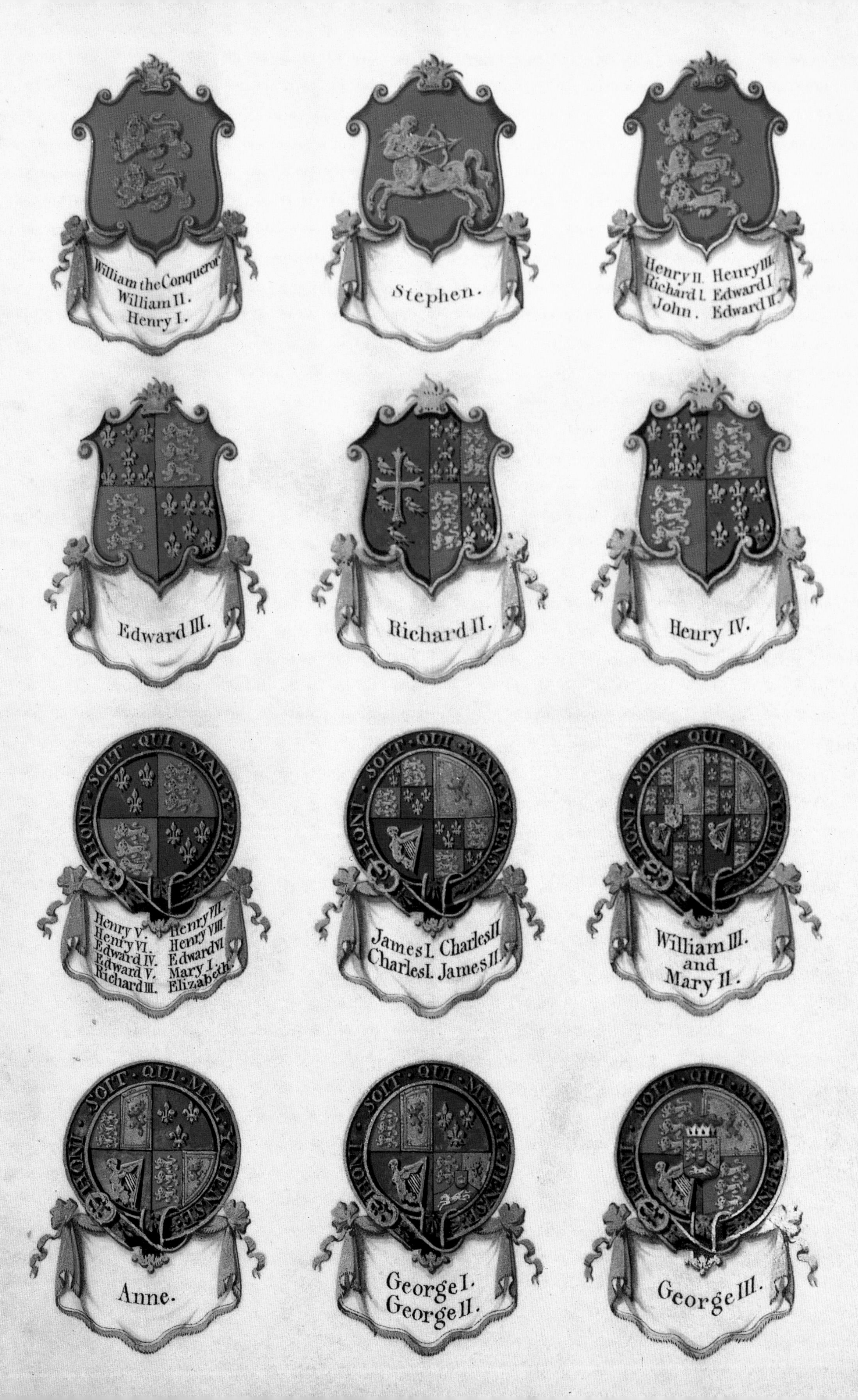
William the Conqueror
William II.
Henry I.
Stephen.
Henry II. Henry III.
Richard I. Edward I.
John. Edward II.
Edward III.
Richard II.
Henry IV.
HONI SOIT QUI MAL Y PENSE
Henry V. Henry VII.
Henry VI. Henry VIII.
Edward IV. Edward VI.
Edward V. Mary I.
Richard III. Elizabeth.
HONI SOIT QUI MAL Y PENSE
James I. Charles II.
Charles I. James II.
HONI SOIT QUI MAL Y PENSE
William III.
and
Mary II.
HONI SOIT QUI MAL Y PENSE
Anne.
HONI SOIT QUI MAL Y PENSE
George I.
George II.
HONI SOIT QUI MAL Y PENSE
George III.

additional shield was placed in the centre with the arms of Brunswick, Lüneburg and Westphalia with the augmentation of the Arch Treasurer in the centre. As George III was also the Elector of Hanover, the central shield was surmounted by the Electoral bonnet. When, a few years later, Napoleon overthrew the Empire, and under the terms of the 1815 Congress of Vienna the Electorate became the kingdom of Hanover, a crown replaced the Electoral bonnet in 1816. The Hanoverian version of the Royal Arms exists today in the arms of the Earl of Munster, a descendant of an illegitimate son of William IV, though the crown has been removed and the whole is *debruised by a baton sinister Azure charged with three anchors Or.* The Royal Arms remained unaltered until William IV died and was succeeded by Queen Victoria in 1837. As Queen Victoria, as a woman, was prevented by Salic law from succeeding to the kingdom of Hanover, the Hanoverian shield and crown were removed from the Royal Arms. The resulting arms, quarterly England, Scotland, Ireland and England, have been borne by Queen Victoria and every succeeding monarch until the present day.

In the chapter on the science of heraldry mention was made of cadency marks placed on shields to distinguish one son from another. Royal heraldry, however, has different rules and for many centuries the label of three points for sons of the monarch, each suitably differenced, has been employed. Originally, however, the Royal Arms were differenced with a bordure as well as the label. Of Edward III's sons Edward, Prince of Wales (the Black Prince) bore quarterly France ancient and England with a label of three points Argent; Lionel of Antwerp, Duke of Clarence (died 1386) bore the same shield with a label of three points Argent each point charged with a canton Gules; John of Gaunt, Duke of Lancaster (died 1399) bore France ancient and England with a label of three points Argent the points Ermine; Edmund of Langley, Duke of York (died 1402) bore a label of three points each charged with three torteaux (red roundels); and Thomas of Woodstock, Duke of Gloucester

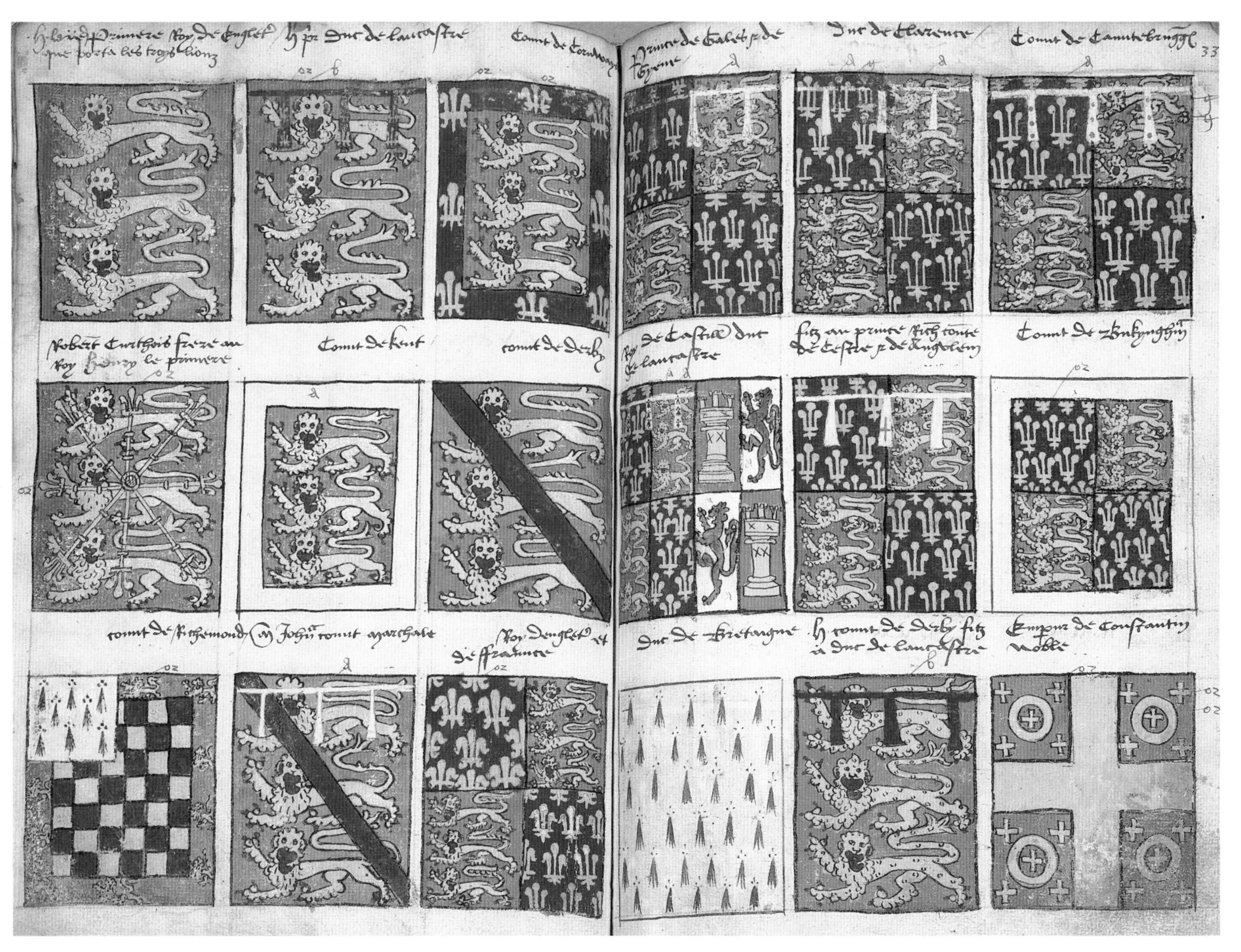

BELOW: *English Royal Arms before 1400,* Flower's Ordinary, *1520.*

(murdered 1397) bore the Royal Arms with a bordure Argent.

John of Gaunt's illegitimate Beaufort children by Catherine Swynford, daughter of Sir Payn Roet, Guienne King of Arms, when later legitimated, bore the Royal Arms with a bordure company Argent and Azure. The Somerset Dukes of Beaufort, illegitimately descended from the Beaufort Dukes of Somerset, bore the same arms, and the present duke continues to do so. Margaret Beaufort, daughter of John, Duke of Somerset and great-granddaughter of John of Gaunt, married Edmund Tudor, Earl of Richmond, and it is probable that this alliance induced Edmund Tudor to adopt the Royal Arms with a bordure Azure charged with alternating martlets and fleurs-de-lis Or. The son of this marriage was Henry Tudor, and the few drops of royal blood brought to him by his mother gave him his claim to the throne, which he successfully pursued in 1485.

The modern system of royal cadency relies entirely upon the label, children of a monarch having a label of three points, and grandchildren a label of five points, assigned only by Royal Warrant. King George V had four sons, and he issued a Royal Warrant in 1921 specifying the labels to be borne by them. His eldest son became Edward VIII (and upon his abdication in 1936 Duke of Windsor), his second son became George VI, his third son Henry became Duke of Gloucester and his fourth, George, Duke of Kent. The Duke of Gloucester was assigned a label of *three points Argent bearing a lion passant guardant Gules on the central point between a cross of St George on the outer points*; the Duke of Kent was assigned a white label of *three points each point charged with a blue anchor*. Their sons were later assigned white labels of five points; that of the present Duke of Gloucester bears *three St George's Crosses and two lions passant guardant Gules*, while that of the present Duke of Kent bears a label *charged alternately with three blue anchors and two St George's crosses*. The sons and daughters of the Dukes of Gloucester and Kent are not styled 'Royal Highness', and bear their fathers' arms. Queen Elizabeth, the Queen Mother bears the undifferenced Royal Arms impaling the arms of Bowes-Lyon, and the supporters are a *lion guardant Or imperially crowned proper* and a *lion per fess Or and Gules*. Her Majesty does not use a crest or motto.

King George VI ceased to be styled 'Emperor of India' upon India's independence in 1947, and when Elizabeth II succeeded to the throne in 1952 the opportunity was taken to alter the heraldic royal crown. The imperial crown's high semi-circular arches were slightly depressed in the middle, reverting to the design used in the reign of Charles II.

The sovereign's arms are arms of sovereignty or dominion and cannot be quartered or impaled with those of his or her consort. The Duke of Edinburgh has borne since 1949: quarterly, (1) *Or semy of hearts Gules three lions passant in pale Azure crowned Gold* (the arms of Denmark); (2) *Azure, a cross Argent* (the arms of Greece); (3) *Argent two*

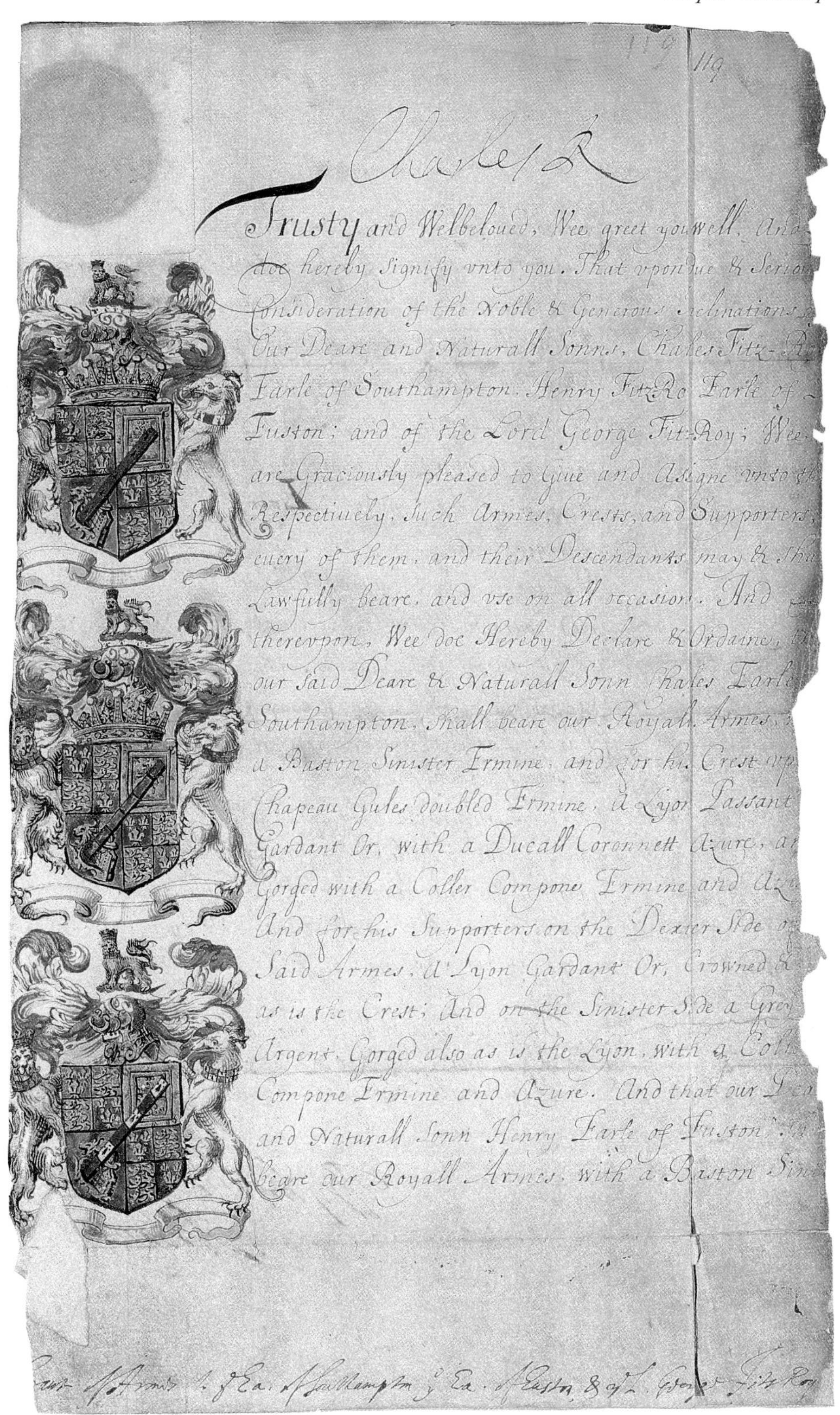

119 119

Charles R

Trusty and Welbeloued, Wee greet you well. And doe hereby Signify vnto you, That vpon due & Serio[us] Consideration of the Noble & Generous Inclinations [of] Our Deare and Naturall Sonns, Charles Fitz-R[oy] Earle of Southampton, Henry FitzRo Earle of Euston; and of the Lord George FitzRoy; Wee are Graciously pleased to Giue and Assigne vnto th[em] Respectiuely, such Armes, Crests, and Supporters, [as] euery of them, and their Descendants may & sha[ll] Lawfully beare, and vse on all occasions. And therevpon, Wee doe Hereby Declare & Ordaine, th[at] our said Deare & Naturall Sonn Charles Earle [of] Southampton, shall beare our Royall Armes [with] a Baston Sinister Ermine, and for his Crest vp[on a] Chapeau Gules doubled Ermine, a Lyon Passant Gardant Or, with a Ducall Coronnett Azure, a[nd] Gorged with a Coller Compone Ermine and Az[ure]. And for his Supporters on the Dexter Side o[f] said Armes, a Lyon Gardant Or, Crowned & as is the Crest; And on the Sinister Side a Gre[y...] Argent Gorged also as is the Lyon, with a Col[ler] Compone Ermine and Azure. And that our De[are] and Naturall Sonn Henry Earle of Euston [shall] beare our Royall Armes, with a Baston Sini[ster]

[illegible] Armes to ye Ea. of Southampton ye Ea. of Euston & ye L. George FitzRoy

ABOVE: *The armorial bearings of the Earl of Southampton, the Earl of Euston, and of Lord George FitzRoy, natural sons of Charles II.*

RIGHT: *The armorial bearings of the Duchy of Cornwall.*

pallets Sable (the family arms of Mountbatten); (4) *Argent on a rock in base proper a castle triple towered Sable masoned Argent each tower topped by a vane Gules* (Edinburgh). His crest is *Out of a ducal coronet Or a plume of five ostrich feathers alternately Sable and Argent*, and his supporters are *dexter the figure of Hercules proper* and *sinister a lion queue fourché ducally*

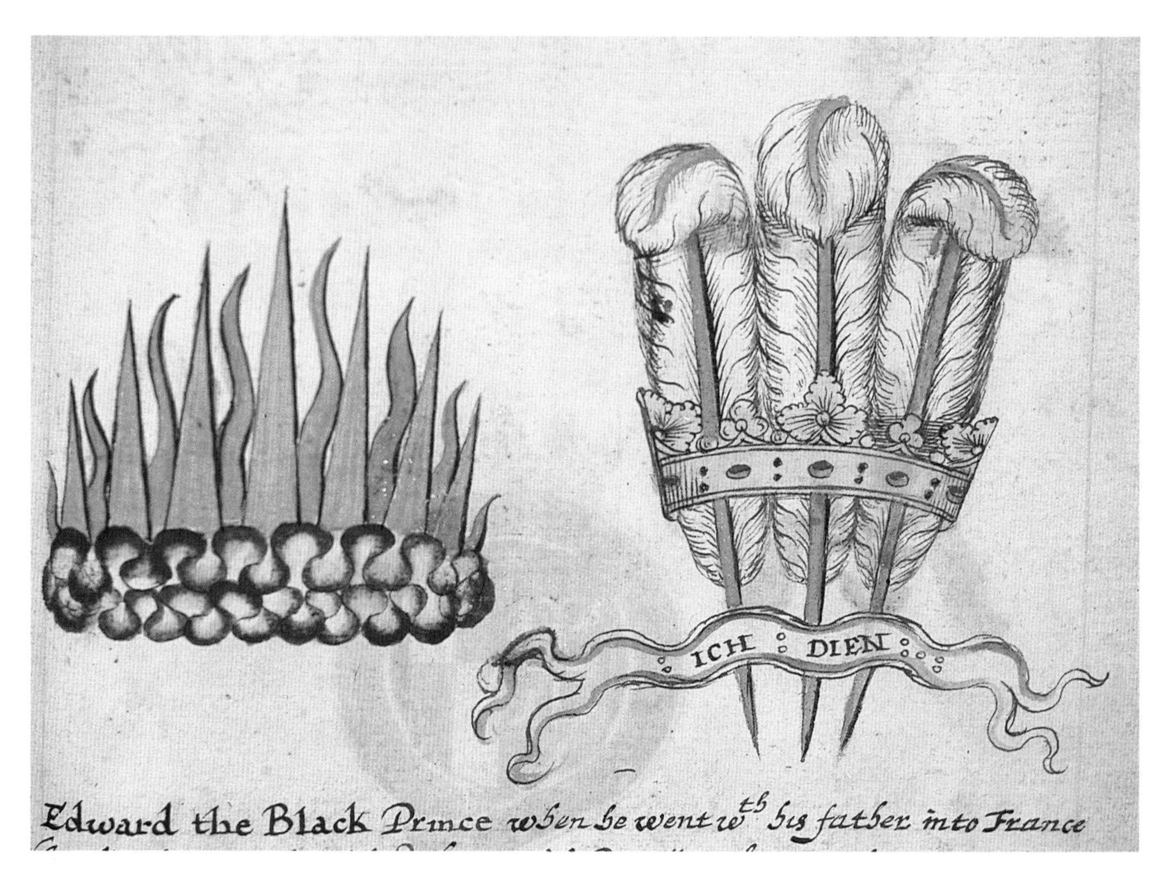

RIGHT: *The Black Prince's badges of the sun arising out of clouds and the ostrich feathers.*

crowned Or gorged with a naval coronet Azure. His motto is: 'God is my help'.

The Prince of Wales bears the Royal Arms with a plain white label to indicate that he is the heir apparent to the throne, with an inescutcheon of the arms of the Principality of Wales ensigned (surmounted) by the heir apparent's coronet. His supporters are the same as the Queen's, but with a plain white label around the necks of the lion and unicorn and the lion wearing the prince's coronet. The crest shows a lion wearing the prince's coronet with a white label standing upon the coronet. In a full achievement of his arms, and below the shield, are the heir apparent's ostrich-feather badge, the arms of the Duchy of Cornwall and the badge of the red dragon of Wales. His motto is *Ich Dien* ('I serve').

The Queen's sister, Princess Margaret, Countess of Snowdon bears the Royal Arms on a lozenge differenced by a label of *three points Argent the centre point charged with a thistle slipped and leaved proper and each of the other points with a Tudor Rose.* Assigned by King George VI in 1944, the lozenge is ensigned by a princely coronet (with no crest) and the supporters are differenced as in the arms, the lion wearing a princely coronet rather than the royal crown.

The Duke of York and Prince Edward have been assigned labels of difference, respectively *a label of three points Argent the centre point charged with an anchor Azure, and a*

ABOVE: *Fragment from the Eleanor Cross at Cheapside, London c.1291-95, showing the arms of England and those of Castile and Leon.*

LEFT: *The armorial bearings of HRH The Princess Royal.*

RIGHT: *The arms of the Black Prince at Canterbury Cathedral.*

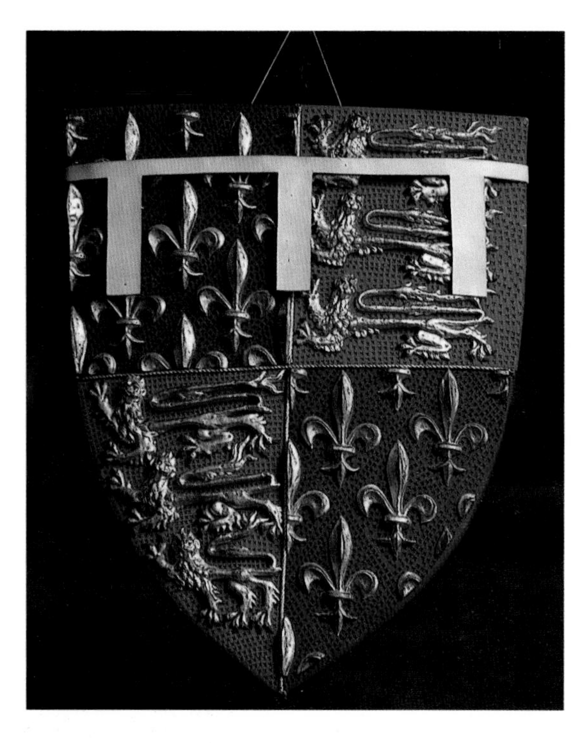

label of three points Argent the centre point charged with a rose Gules barbed proper thereon another rose Argent barbed and seeded proper. The Duke of York's daughters, like the sons of the Prince of Wales, have not yet been assigned arms. The Princess Royal bears arms on a lozenge with *a label of three points Argent the centre point charged with a heart Gules and each of the other points with St George's crosses.* The Princess Royal's children bear the arms of Phillips; they have no royal title and therefore follow the normal rules of heraldry rather than royal rules, although the shields are ensigned with a coronet the finials of which are composed of fleurs-de-lis and alternating strawberry leaves.

A display of the arms of male members of the royal family cannot show the arms of their spouses on the same shield as their own. Instead the spouse's arms are placed on a separate shield alongside, with the husband's supporters, helm, crest and motto. A wife may, however, impale her royal husband's arms with hers, as for example in the Princess of Wales' achievement. This shows the arms of the Prince of Wales on the dexter of the shield, impaling the arms of Spencer on the sinister, supported by the Princess' supporters, which are the Prince of Wales' lion supporter on the dexter, and on the sinister, a *Griffin Ermine winged Erminois beaked and legged Or gorged with a Prince's Coronet thereto a*

RIGHT: *The arms and badges of Richard II.*

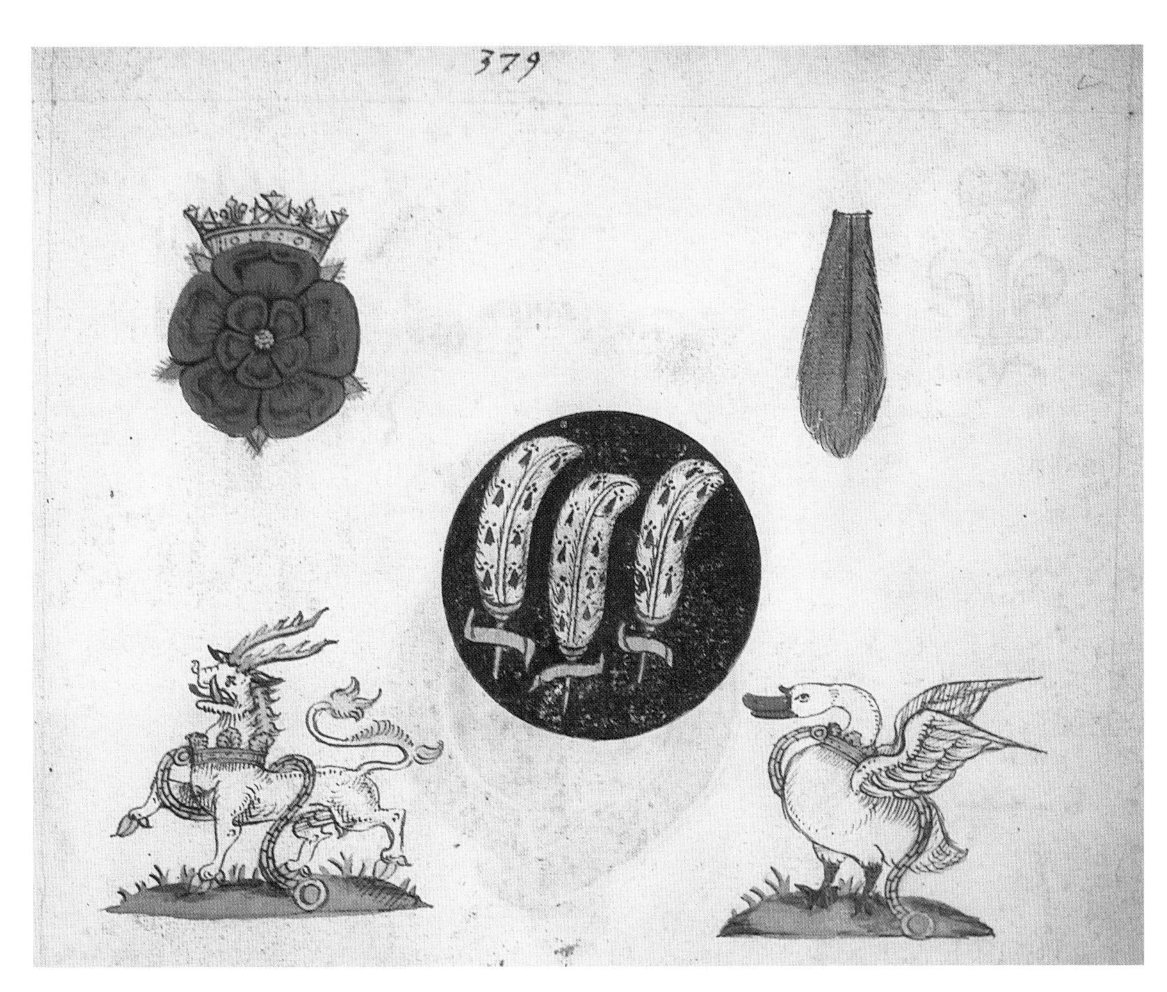

LEFT: *Badges of Henry IV.*

chain reflexed behind the back and ending in a ring all of Gold (a derivation from one of her late father's supporters).

Royal badges have been used since the earliest stages of heraldry. They are always freestanding, in the sense that they are not dependent on shield or crest, and they are invariably simple devices. The earliest heraldic badge is the sprig of broom said to have been worn by Geoffrey of Anjou in his cap. The plant *planta genista* gave Geoffrey his nickname – Plantagenet – and was immortalised as the name of the dynasty which ruled England for over 300 years. The Plantagenet kings used this badge, sometimes combining it with personal devices. Henry II, for example, used the *planta genista*, a genet between two sprigs of broom and an escarb-

BELOW: *King Edward IV, his Queen, Elizabeth Woodville, and the 'Princes in the Tower', c.1482, at Canterbury Cathedral.*

h E
h R
h R

uncle; Edward I the *planta genista* and a gold rose; Edward III a sunburst issuing from a cloud and the base (or stock) of a tree showing roots (for Woodstock).

Ostrich-feather badges were very popular with Edward III and his descendants, and their origin is probably as a pun derived from his wife Philippa of Hainault whose father held the lordship of Ostrevans. Edward, the Prince of Wales (the Black Prince) bore as his shield for peace *Sable three ostrich feathers quilled and piercing scrolls Argent bearing the words* ICH DIEN; he used the Royal Arms on his war shield. Although he placed ostrich feathers on a shield, they were certainly regarded as badges; he described them in his will as 'nos bages des plumes d'ostruce'. (Incidentally, the myth that he captured the ostrich feathers from the blind King of Bohemia at the battle of Crécy has long been exploded.) His son, Richard II, used the feathers, as did John of Gaunt, Henry IV, Thomas, Duke of Gloucester, the Beauforts and other Plantagenets. Gradually they became, in Tudor times, the special badge of the heir apparent to the throne, whether or not he was created Prince of Wales. The Prince of Wales bears this badge today as heir apparent, not as Prince of Wales.

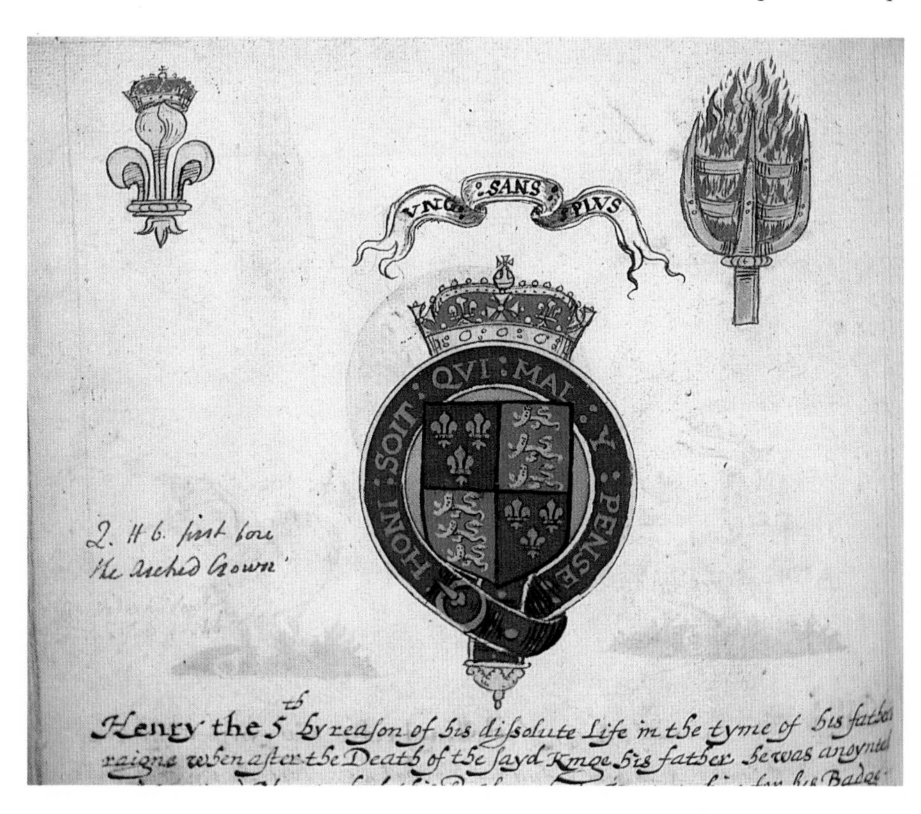

ABOVE: *Arms and badges of Henry V.*

FACING PAGE: *Badges of Henry VII.*

The badges of the red rose of Lancaster and the white rose of York have come to symbol-

LEFT: *The armorial bearings of Henry VII.*

ABOVE: *The armorial bearings of Her Majesty Queen Elizabeth II, borne by each monarch since Queen Victoria.*

ise the fifteenth-century dispute for the throne between the rival branches of the Plantagenets, now known as the Wars of the Roses (a name coined by Sir Walter Scott). They originate in the gold rose borne by Edward I and in the red rose as differenced by his brother Edmund Crouchback, Earl of Lancaster. The Yorkists adopted the white rose as their symbol in their claim to the throne by virtue of their descent from Roger Mortimer, Earl of March, the senior descendant of Edward III. These badges still exist as royal badges; the red rose royally crowned is the badge of office of Lancaster Herald, while the white rose en soleil royally crowned is the badge of office of York Herald.

Richard III's badge was a white boar, the origin of which is obscure. It has been suggested that it was a pun on the Latin name for York, *Ebor*, but he never held the honour of York, nor was he the Duke of York. As Duke of Gloucester, however, he was governor of northern England during the reign of his brother, Edward IV (1461-83), and his seat of government was situated in Yorkshire, where he was very popular. It has also been

RIGHT: *The armorial bearings of Henry VIII.*

suggested that it is a pun on his royal title *Rex Anglie*, for *sanglier* is the French for boar, but he was known to have used a boar as a badge before he became king. In his play *Richard III*, William Shakespeare, the dramatist (and Tudor propagandist) used the pun, referring to Richard by his favourite device 'The wretched, bloody and usurping boar'.

It is said that during Richard's reign many inns displayed the white boar as a mark of allegiance to him, a common-enough practice at the time (and indeed now). After he was killed at the battle of Bosworth in 1485, the white boar inn signs were painted blue to mark a switched allegiance to the Earl of Oxford, whose badge it was, a commander in Henry VII's army at the battle.

Richard's opppressive reign prompted one Collingbourne of Wiltshire to produce a famous couplet:

The Cat, the Rat, and Lovel our Dog
Rule all England under a Hog.

The cat and rat referred to Richard's ministers, Sir William Catesby and Sir Richard Ratcliffe; Lord Lovel's badge was indeed a dog, and the hog referred, of course, to King Richard. The author of this rhyme paid for it with his life.

Mention must be made of the royal badges in use today. Her Majesty the Queen could, of course, by right of inheritance, use any or all of the royal badges ever used by her predecessors. In fact, the badges in use today are limited to that of England, *the red and white*

LEFT: *The armorial bearings of the Duchy of Lancaster.*

LEFT: *The armorial bearings of Australia.*

A·MARI·VSQVE·AD·MARE

FACING PAGE: *The armorial bearings of Canada.*

LEFT: *The armorial bearings of New Zealand.*

rose united, slipped and leaved proper ensigned with the Royal Crown; Scotland, *a thistle slipped and leaved proper ensigned with the Royal Crown*; Northern Ireland, *a shamrock leaf slipped vert ensigned with the Royal Crown*; and *a harp Or stringed Argent ensigned with the Royal Crown*; the United Kingdom, *the rose, thistle and shamrock engrafted on the same stem proper ensigned with the Royal Crown*, and *an escutcheon charged as the Union Flag ensigned with the Royal Crown*; Wales, *within a circular riband Argent fimbriated Or bearing the motto* Y DDRAIG GOCH DDYRY CYCHWYN ['The red dragon gives the lead'] *in letters Vert and ensigned with the Royal Crown an escutcheon per fess Argent and Vert and thereon a Dragon passant Gules*. The badge of the house of Windsor is: *On a mount Vert the Round Tower of Windsor Castle Argent masoned Sable flying thereon the Royal Banner the whole within two branches of Oak fructed and ensigned with a Royal Crown*.

The Prince of Wales' badge as heir apparent is *a plume of three ostrich feathers Argent enfiled by a coronet of crosses paty and fleurs-de-lis Or jewelled proper with the motto upon a scroll Azure fimbriated Or the words* ICH DIEN *in letters also Gold*, and his badge for Wales is *upon a mount Vert a Dragon passant wings elevated Gules gorged with a label of three points Argent*.

Her Majesty the Queen is styled in Great Britain as 'Elizabeth the Second by the Grace of God of the United Kingdom of Great Britain and Northern Ireland and of Her other Realms and Territories Queen Head of

BELOW: *Her Majesty The Queen's personal banner for use in Australia.*

RIGHT: *Her Majesty The Queen's personal banner for use in New Zealand.*

RIGHT: *Her Majesty The Queen's personal banner for use in Canada.*

LEFT: *The armorial bearings of Hong Kong.*

the Commonwealth Defender of the Faith'. In her other realms the style varies, for Her Majesty is separately the Queen of Antigua and Barbuda, Australia, the Commonwealth of the Bahamas, Barbados, Belize, Canada, Grenada, Jamaica, New Zealand, Papua New Guinea, Saint Christopher and Nevis, Saint Lucia, Saint Vincent and the Grenadines, the Solomon Islands and Tuvalu. In Australia, for example, Her Majesty is styled as 'Elizabeth the Second by the Grace of God Queen of Australia and Her other Realms and Territories, Head of the Commonwealth'. In each of her independent realms, the Queen bears different armorial bearings to identify separate sovereignty and authority in each nation. In dependent territories of the United Kingdom which have armorial bearings, such as Hong Kong and the Falkland Islands, the arms are also borne by the Queen in right of these territories. Where a dependent territory has not had arms assigned to it, the Royal Arms of the United Kingdom are borne as arms of dominion and sovereignty. The Queen also flies a personal banner when in her realms other than the United Kingdom, which shows her arms of that country surmounted by the initial letter E, ensigned by the royal crown upon a blue roundel surrounded with a chaplet of roses gold.

LEFT: *The arms of the Falkland Islands.*

Armas de los de Cordoua

Este es vn muy noble linage y procede de dos caualleros Andaluses el vno llamado Fernan Nuñez y el otro Aluar perez, destos salio el grande Capitan llamado Gonçalo Fernandez de Cordoua

8
INTERNATIONAL HERALDRY

Peter Gwynn-Jones

LEFT: *The armorial bearings of Gonzalo Fernandez Cordoba allude to the capture of the Moorish King of Cordoba in 1492. The arms of the kingdom of Aragon (red and gold pallets) are shown in chief, and the shield is surrounded by captured Moorish trophies; painted c.1610.*

It was during the twelfth century that the nobility of Europe began to identify themselves by painting distinctive designs on their shields in bright contrasting colours. This marks the birth of heraldry. Common ground and personal contact were established between the knights of Europe through their affiliation to the Latin church and found a practical outlet in the Crusades.

In 1974 the author wrote an article entitled 'Heraldry and The Wider World' summarising the heraldic characteristics of different European countries, and it serves to quote from this article as follows. 'Much of the science and system of heraldry developed as part of a European rather than national culture. Nonetheless, there remained characteristics peculiar to different individual countries or groups of countries. The proliferation of crests found in Germany, Austria, and much of Switzerland contrasts with the British custom of a single crest and the absence of crests in France and the Iberian countries. In Eastern Europe, whole groups of families or territorial areas adopted the same armorial bearings, a form of clan affiliation unknown elsewhere. Similarly, the East favoured white charges set in a blue or red field, while the extreme West, that is, France and the British Isles, made extensive use of furs and favoured the powdering of their shields with small charges. Again, France and the British Isles were foremost in applying marks of difference to the shield to distinguish between several members or branches of the same family; further East this practice is usually absent.

Regional differences tended to become more emphasised as medieval civilisation gave way to the growth of nationalism and the evolution of strong centralised monarchies which took upon themselves the control of armorial bearings and appointed their own heraldic authorities. Special features of individual countries can now be more readily recognised.

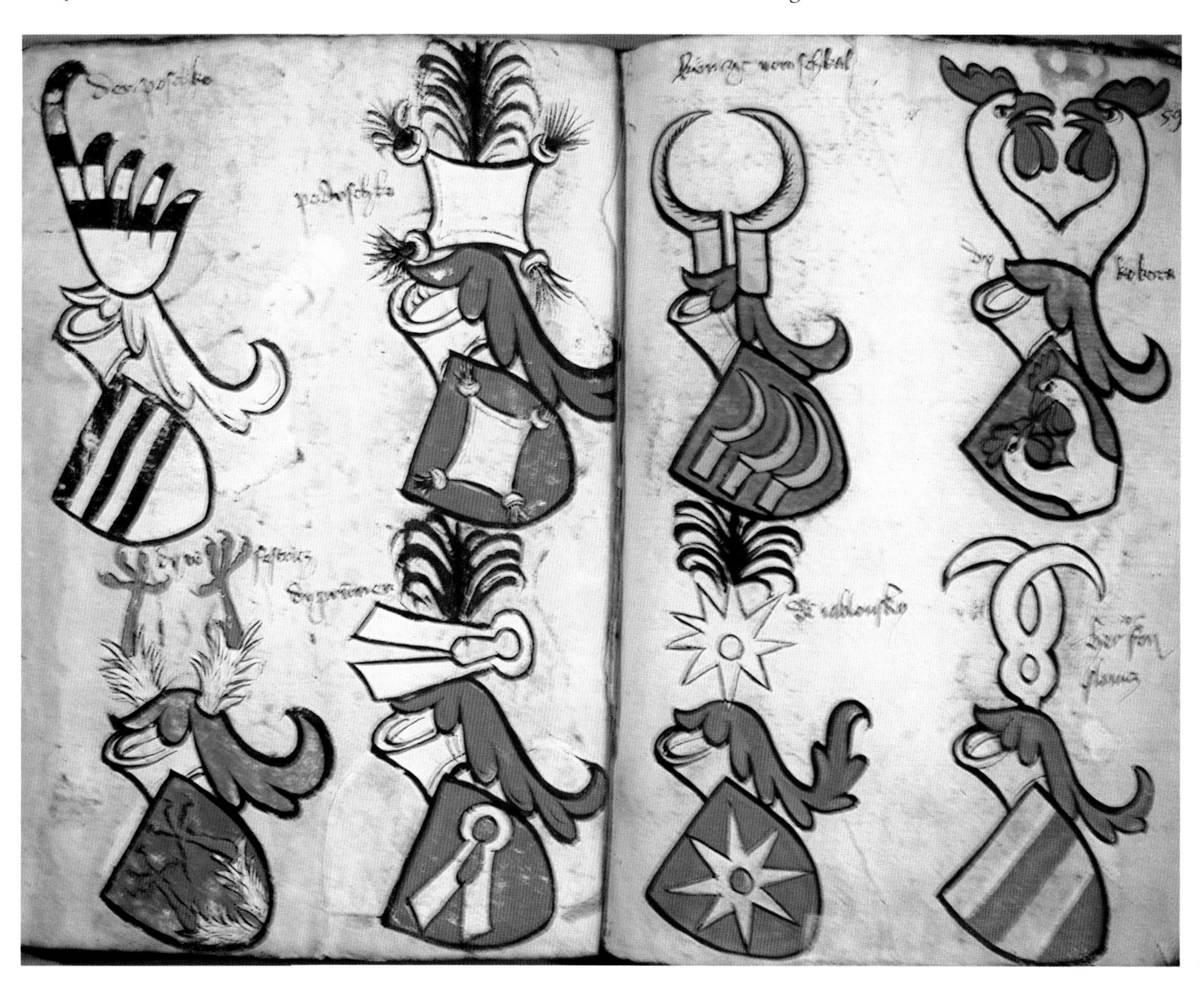

BELOW: *German crests frequently reflect the charges used in the arms as can be seen in Povey's German Roll, painted in the early fifteenth century.*

LEFT: *The arms of the Saxon family Hennenberg provide an obvious pun. The crest is typical of Teutonic heraldry, exaggerating and fancifying the human form, and is adorned with a panache of peacocks' feathers; painted in 1580.*

German or Teutonic heraldry extended its sphere of influence over Central Europe and spread northwards into Scandinavia. Its most striking characteristic lies in the design and treatment of crests. The majority of crests reflect the arms by repeating either the latter's charge or tinctures, or both, in a manner virtually unknown in the British Isles. There is also a predilection for wings and buffalo horns. The merging of crest and mantling in one flowing sweep is another readily recognisable and typical feature.

With the declining use of armorial bearings in a military context at the end of the Middle Ages, Teutonic Europe witnessed the marshalling of many arms on a single shield, each bearing its corresponding crest on a helmet. In the British Isles more than one crest is unusual, and in Latin Europe the use of crests has continuously declined or been abandoned altogether.' The armorial bearings of Notthaft of Podenstein 'exemplify features of design almost unknown in the heraldry of Britain and the latter's sphere of heraldic influence. Chevrons terminating at the top of the arms are a frequent form of continental treatment and contrast with the British custom of keeping the chevron apex in the centre; to embow a chevron and so sweep each of its arms downwards in a concave curve is another ubiquitous characteristic of continental design. Hills and terraces emerging from the base may account for as many as one in 15 of all arms found on the European mainland; in the British Isles they are exceedingly rare. This difference is carried further, with other charges emerging from the sides or bases of shields. In the British heraldic world only the Ordinaries are treated in this way; other charges, whether floral, faunal or inanimate are left freestanding. The absence of any crests in the rendering of the arms of Notthaft, and the use of a coronet of the type borne by a French marquis, suggests that a strong French influence filtered into Bavaria, the homeland of this

BELOW: *A Bavarian claret jug showing the armorial bearings of Notthaft of Podenstein. Hills or terraces and chevrons reaching the middle chief are typical features of continental European heraldry.*

RIGHT: *Dutch heraldry is characteristically simple, with single charges on the arms being frequent. From the* Edele Geslagten in de 7 Provintien, *painted 1738.*

family, and affected the way in which Bavarian nobility portrayed their arms.

Holland and Switzerland stand unrivalled in their widespread use of heraldry. Holland in particular is notable for the great esteem with which Dutch families regard their armorial bearings. Much of this was influenced by the Dutch republic of the sixteenth and seventeenth centuries. Many old medieval families, if not extinguished by the Wars of Independence, often fled to the Spanish Netherlands (modern Belgium), and their place was taken by republican traders and merchants who began an extensive adoption of arms. In comparison with other countries, Dutch heraldry is notable for its pleasant simplicity, many shields bearing only a single charge. In general one shield, one helmet and one crest are found; the practice of marshalling more than one shield in the form of quarterings is uncommon and the use of mottoes is rare.

Belgian shields can be recognised by the practice of suspending them by a strap from the helmet; and in the case of the Belgian nobility a gold medallion and collar is found about the helmet's neck.' Burgher arms which date from the late Middle Ages and the development of the Low Countries as Europe's commercial and industrial centre are characterised by the absence of helmets in Belgian burgher heraldry.

'In France the choice of charges and their arrangement bear close similarity to British heraldry. A major difference is the absence of crests. From the time of the Renaissance families tended to place only their coronets of rank upon their helmets; but by the eighteenth century the helmet had also been abandoned and coronets were placed directly above the shield.

The French revolution of 1789 saw the abolition of French heraldry which was replaced some 15 years later by a new Imperial heraldry.' As might be expected this was characterised by weapons and items of war reflecting the Napoleonic campaigns. Crests, helmets, supporters and mottoes were excluded, but a system of plumed caps to denote rank was introduced. Specific charges and arrangements of design were also laid down for the several grades of nobility and officials, and were even extended to civic heraldry. The plumed caps or toques were supplemented with Napoleonic precision by augmentations to the shield to denote rank. Civic heraldry was similarly graded, with towns being classified with their corresponding chief or canton charged with the symbols favoured by Napoleon, such as the initial N, the Imperial crown and bees.

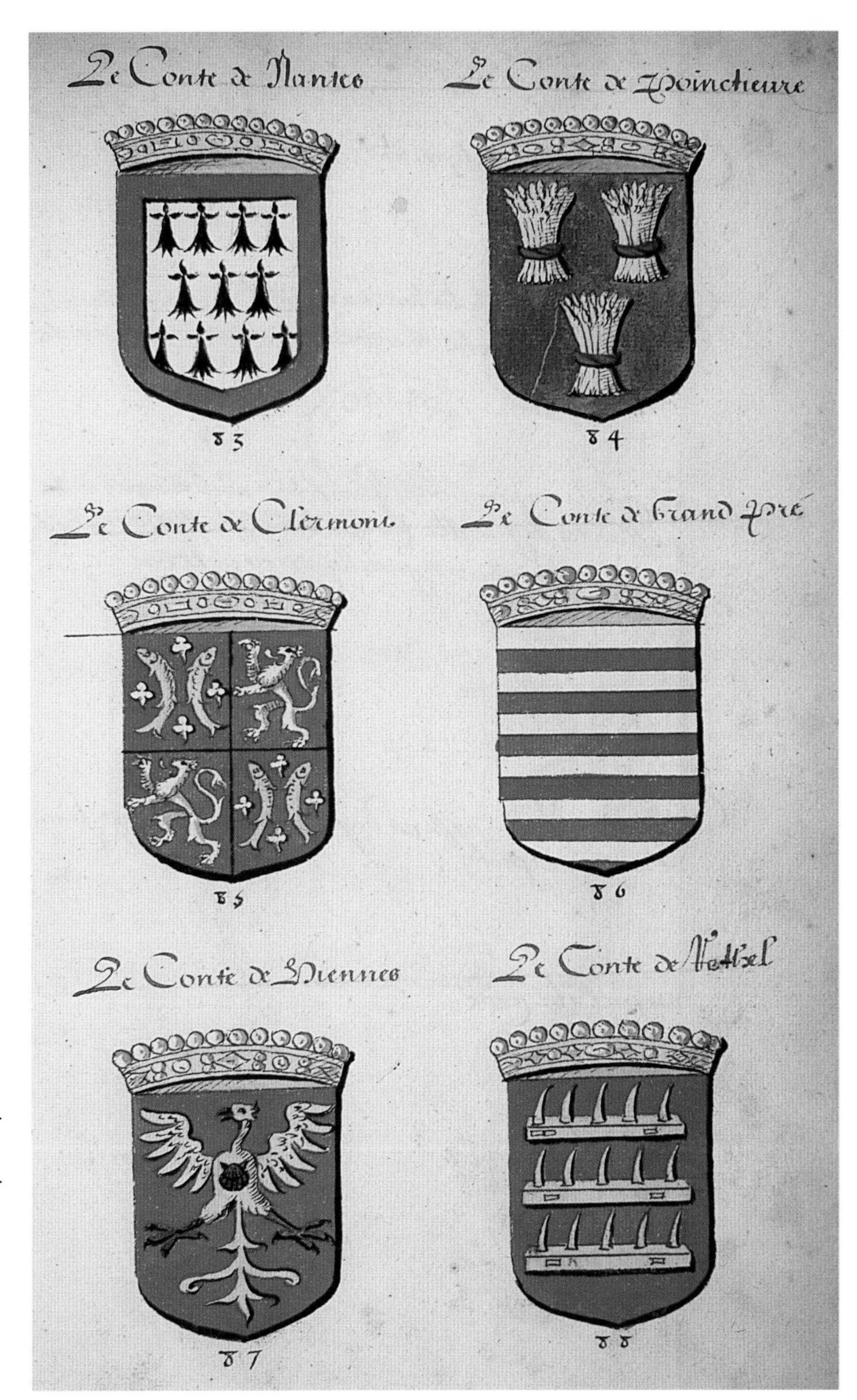

ABOVE: *French heraldry bears some similarity to that of the British Isles, but replaces crests with coronets of rank. From* Hector le Breton, *painted c.1600.*

'Spanish and Portuguese heraldry is characterised by the use of broad shields, often with borders. This practice dates back to earlier times when it was customary for a man to surround his arms with a border charged with single heraldic devices taken from the arms of his wife, or with her complete arms arranged as a series of small shields, usually numbering seven or eight.

Complicated schemes of quarterings have also evolved in Spain and Portugal, for it is

RIGHT AND FAR RIGHT: *Italian crests are uncommon, but when found they are frequently exotic, as typified by those of Sforza of Milan (right) and Dal Verme of Verona (far right).*

BELOW: *The armorial bearings granted to Josef Andres del Portillo Sierra Marroquin y Bringas in 1799. Bordures are charged with additional devices, and a panache of ostrich feathers adorns the helmet instead of a crest, typifying Spanish heraldry.*

held that a woman may transmit the arms of her family whether or not she is an heraldic heiress in the sense accepted in the heraldry of other countries. Crests are rarely found; but an adornment of ostrich feathers is frequently used instead. Other characteristics are the presence of mottoes on the shield itself and the occasional placing of gold on silver or vice versa in a manner quite contrary to heraldic principles elsewhere.

The heraldry of Italy reflects the troubled history of that country, which acted as a battlefield for successive German, French, Spanish and Austrian invaders. All these left

their mark. The rise of the northern city states and the general fragmentation of the country led to a certain duplication of armorial bearings, while the intense Italian cultural activity of the late Middle Ages and the Renaissance lessened the hold of medieval heraldry on the country; charges lack the stylisation found elsewhere and have obtained a more natural and classical form. The chief or top half of the shield often represents a political allegiance, the most frequent being charged with the fleur-de-lis of France and differenced by a label of Anjou, or the eagle of the Holy Roman Empire.

In spite of foreign intervention, Italian heraldry has developed certain characteristics distinctive to itself, in particular the use of almond-shaped or horsehead-shaped shields. The latter were possibly placed on the foreheads of horses at tournaments and resemble the head of a horse when viewed from the front. Crests are rare, but when found, they can obtain an extravagance as exemplified by the crests of Sforza and Dal Verme. Crest wreaths are noticeably thin and are often borne with coronets of rank, a combination rarely found elsewhere in Europe. The hillocks issuing from the base of the shield which are so characteristic of mainland European heraldry, have evolved into elongated pieces which are set one above the other to create a stylised formation found in many Italian arms.'

Central Italian heraldry has been much influenced by the Church. Many families deriving their titles from successive popes have alluded to this by incorporating papal insignia in their arms, notably the papal tiara and the crossed keys.

'Hungarian heraldry is closely akin to that of Austria and Germany, but differs in two particular respects. Firstly there is a marked preference for charges or devices associated with the Turkish wars, which were a perennial feature in Hungarian history from the fifteenth to the eighteenth centuries. More than 15 per cent of all Hungarian armorial bearings feature a gory decapitated Turk's head, usually well moustached and often turbanned. Sabres, swords and lances brandished by arms in armour, lions, gryphons or horsemen are all typical of the warlike quality of Magyar armory. The second characteristic is the occasional extravagance typified by the arms of Hajduboszormeny, charged with a firing gun beneath which are burning logs and above a friendly sun, the whole encircled by a green dragon bearing a patriarchal cross.

BELOW: *The arms of Pope Pius XII (left), Pope Paul VI (centre) and Pope John XXIII (right), showing characteristic Italian shield shapes and stylised hillocks or coupeaux.*

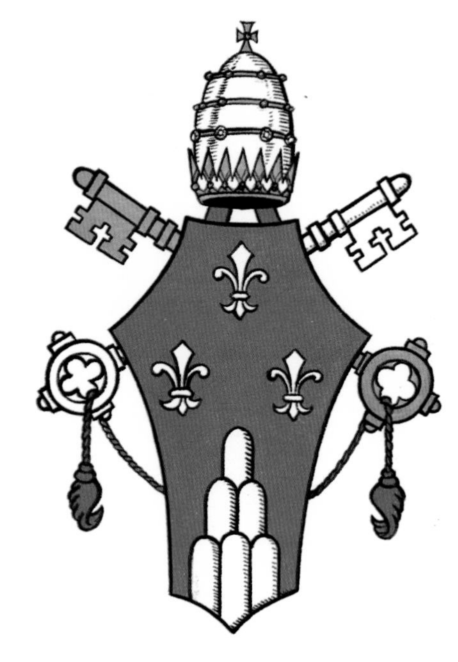

Designs such as these have a certain strangeness about them which seem to border on the eccentric to those accustomed to the more subdued taste found further west.

Poland separates itself from the rest of Europe by reason of the pre-heraldic runic signs which were later absorbed by heraldry and came to constitute its principal feature. These signs were in the form of straight lines or curves. While many remain strictly geometrical, others eventually evolved into a simple charge such as a cross, lance, horseshoe, or crescent. Many arms bearing these charges are not individual to one particular family, but pertain to a whole group of families; for example, nearly 600 families are known to bear a horseshoe enclosing a cross, a situation unlike anything found outside the sphere of Polish heraldic influence.

RIGHT: *The arms of Russian provinces, with Moscow in the centre, on the armorial achievement of Alexander II, Tsar of Russia; painted in 1867.*

Heraldry came late to Russia and was subsequently developed by external rather than internal forces. There was no medieval heraldry, and the simple divisions and charges characteristic of that period are absent. Charges such as animals have avoided stylisation and have retained a natural and arguably unheraldic form; sometimes this natural representation is extended to include a landscape environment. Most of these animals face to the sinister, the opposite direction to their counterparts in the heraldry of other countries. The earliest Russian heraldry is found in Lithuania, which was later to become part of Imperial Russia, and where the nobility began adopting armorial bearings of the Polish type in the fifteenth century. French and German influences date from the westernisation begun by Tsar Peter the Great at the end of the seventeenth century.' Peter established an heraldic authority with a Master of Heraldry in 1722, and 355 grants of armorial bearings were made during the eighteenth century.

LEFT: *The horseshoe enclosing a cross formy is a combination characteristic of the armorial bearings of many Polish families. Here the Bath stall plate of Dr Conrad Swan, CVO, Garter Principal King of Arms.*

Within the British Isles differences can also be discerned. In Scotland the granting of armorial bearings is vested by the Crown in Lord Lyon or Lyon King of Arms. The heraldry of Scotland has always been separate from that of England and has developed its own characteristics. Mottoes, for example, are placed above the crest; in England they are placed beneath. The Scottish system of matriculation does not allow for the same

FAR LEFT AND LEFT: *George Coats and Andrew Coats, younger sons of Thomas Coats of Ferguslie and Maxwelton in the County of Renfrew, matriculated armorial bearings in Scotland in 1908 with suitably differenced bordures. In Scotland mottoes are placed above the crest.*

RIGHT: *Scottish heraldry favours the use of wild men or savages as supporters. A demi savage wielding a club also features in the armorial bearings of successive Barons Livingstone; painted 1625.*

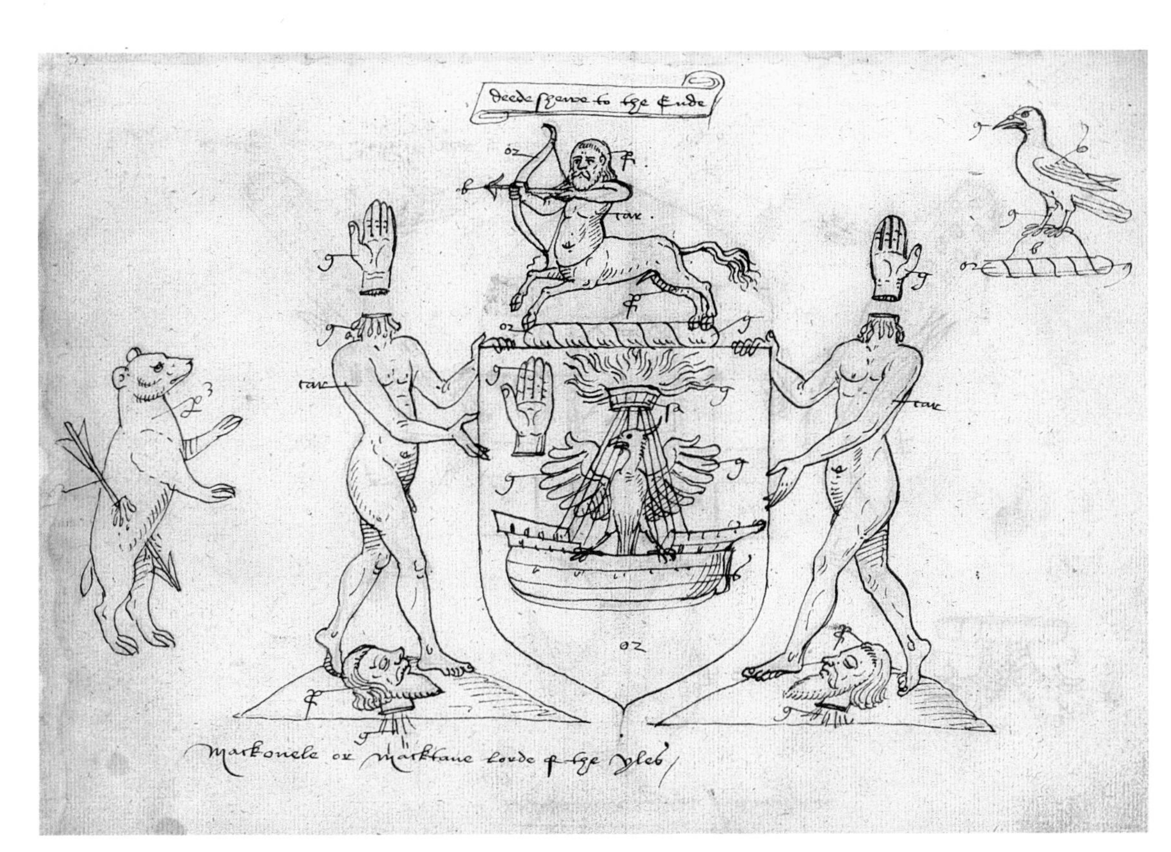

LEFT: *The purpose of supporters is to support the shield of arms, but those of 'Mackonele or Macklane of the Yles' might have experienced some difficulty in doing so; drawn c.1601.*

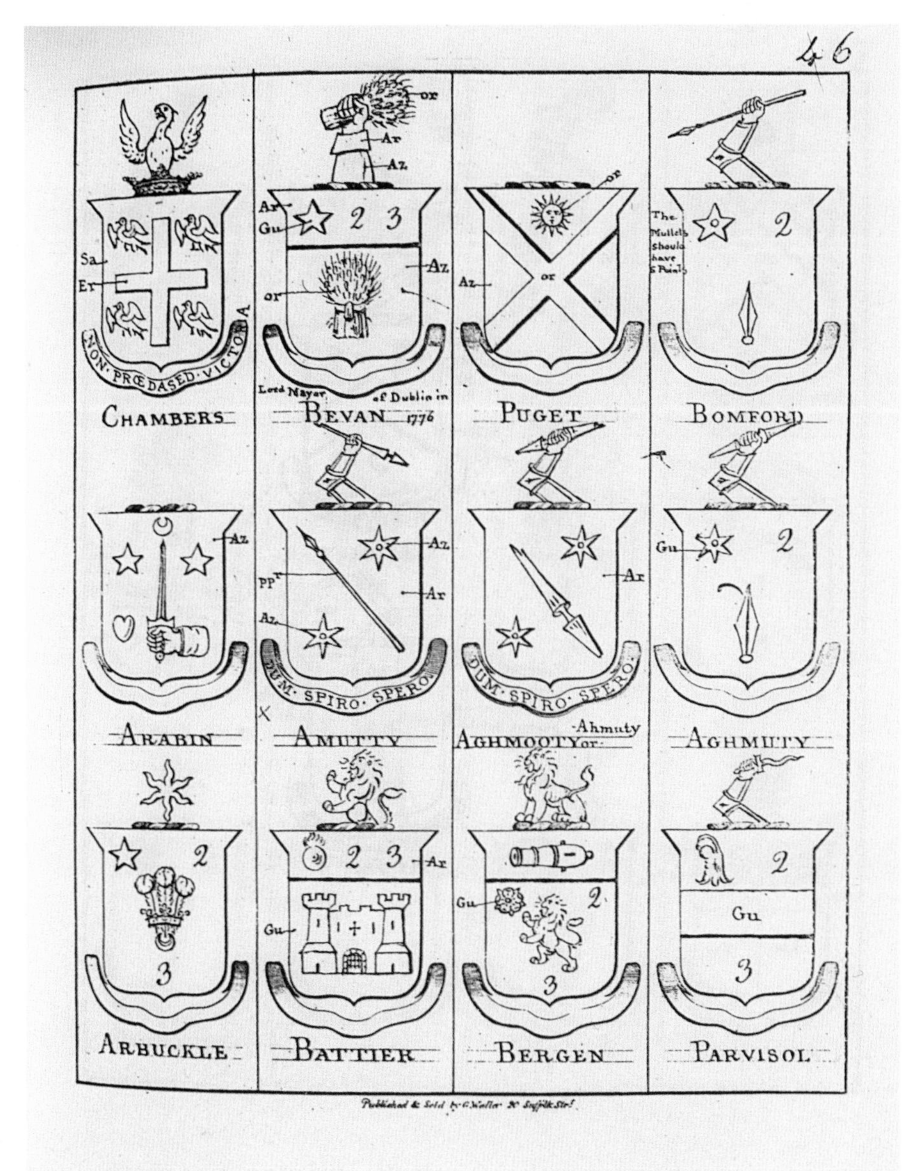

BELOW: *A page from* Kennedy's Book of Irish Arms, *1816, showing the preference of Irish Kings of Arms to grant human arms holding weapons.*

armorial bearings to pertain to all the male-line descendants of the grantee. Younger sons must matriculate and receive a suitably differenced grant of the armorial bearings; this frequently takes the form of a border. Scottish badges are confined to clan chiefs, whereas in England they have no such restriction and are permitted with any new grant of arms.

In Ireland the power to grant arms was once vested in successive Ulster Kings of Arms. On Irish independence this power was transferred to the new office of Chief Herald of Ireland; and the office of Ulster King of Arms was merged with that of Norroy King of Arms in England. Irish heraldry is similar to English medieval or late Tudor heraldry in its general simplicity. Ulster Kings of Arms were disposed to grant the arms of an English family to a person of the same surname in Ireland without proof of connection; and the arms were then often differenced with a trefoil slipped, representing the shamrock. Irish crests show a remarkable preference for the human arm, usually in armour, with the hand grasping a weapon. An analysis of *Kennedy's Book of Irish Arms* shows that approximately a quarter of Irish crests fall within this category.

Heraldry beyond Europe has been much influenced by the English. The cause is not solely past British expansion overseas; of greater significance is the retention of a heraldic authority under the Crown. Where-

ABOVE: *Armorial bearings granted to Tanganyika in 1962, placing the arms on an African shield.*

as such authorities have been generally swept away in continental Europe with the political upheavals of the last two centuries, the English Kings of Arms have continued to grant new armorial bearings to overseas subjects of the Crown. As members of the Royal Household, they are as much the heralds of Australia, for example, as of England. In this respect it is significant that the present Garter King of Arms is a Canadian citizen and holds a Canadian passport.

Living heraldry emanating from England in recent years has adapted to changing circumstances. Countries such as South Africa and Kenya have established their own heraldic authorities on becoming republics and have thus severed their connection with the Crown and the jurisdiction of the English Kings of Arms. In 1988 the Queen established a separate heraldic authority for Canada. The transfer of the right to grant armorial bearings to the Chief Herald of Canada allows for the continued granting of new armorial bearings to Canadian citizens and corporate bodies; and the close relationship between the English and Canadian granting authorities has ensured the smooth continuity of Canadian heraldry. New Zealand also has its own New Zealand Herald Extraordinary, reflecting that country's interest in heraldry, but is still subject to the jurisdiction of the English Kings of Arms.

Heraldry on the American continent arrived with the Spanish. Shortly after the first voyage of Christopher Columbus arms were established for the new continent and were borne on a banner at the marriage of Philip of Hapsburg to Joanna of Spain in 1496, alluding to the original name given to the territories on their discovery, 'The Kingdom of the Fifteen Islands'. Columbus described the vegetation of the West Indies as being green, red and brown, which was duly rendered in heraldic form. Thereafter central and South America retained the characteristics of Spanish and Portuguese heraldry, to which indigenous flora and fauna have been added, together with elements of the native Indian civilisations. After the independence movements of the nineteenth century, a number of charges suggestive of the new freedom were introduced, such as rising suns, caps of liberty and clasped hands of brotherhood.

English heraldry prevailed in North America, the first grant being in 1586 to the City and Corporation of Ralegh in Virginia;

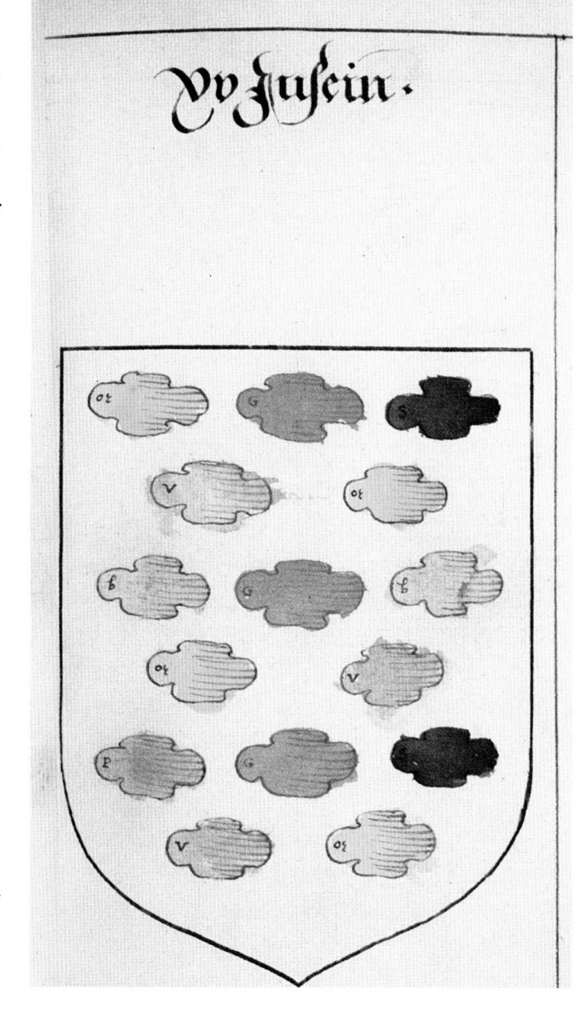

RIGHT: *The first instance of American heraldry: the 15 multi-coloured islands of the arms of the West Indies, borne at the marriage of Philip of Hapsburg to Joanna of Spain, 1496.*

it related to the first English settlement on Roanoke Island, now sited in North Carolina. Although the original grant seemingly made by William Dethick, Garter King of Arms, has not survived, three drafts of the document exist at the College of Arms and include not only arms for the colony, but also for the governor, John White, and each of the 12 assistant governors. Thereafter heraldry was to remain largely dormant in North America, and it was not until 1694 that the first North American resident, Francis Nicholson, 'the Captain General and Governor in Chief of Their Majesties Province of Maryland One of the Chief Governors of a College or University now to be erected or founded in Virginia' received a grant of arms. Shortly afterwards, this university, the College of William and Mary, received its own grant.

In an attempt to further heraldry in America, Laurence Cromp, York Herald, was appointed Carolina Herald in 1705. This appointment is of academic interest only, as Cromp does not appear to have made any grants and provided no stimulus to American heraldry. Ten grants were made to colonists towards the end of the eighteenth century,

LEFT: *Armorial bearings of the College of Arms Foundation, with an 'American' coronet in the crest, featuring mullets (stars) and bars, devised in 1983.*

BELOW: *Indian supporters granted to Sir Jeffery Amherst, commander in chief of His Majesty's Forces in North America, 1761.*

RIGHT: *Armorial bearings of Newfoundland, granted 1638, with Indian supporters* apparaled according to their guise when they go to war.

but this increase in American activity was cut short by the Revolution. Although one or two grants had American connections during the nineteenth century, it was not until the present century that an agreement was reached whereby the English Kings of Arms could issue grants of honorary armorial bearings to American citizens who were able to establish male-line descent from a British subject. In consequence, heraldry in the United States has been revived and is on the increase. A further stimulus was given by an Earl Marshal's Warrant in 1960, which authorised the Kings of Arms to devise armorial bearings for American corporate bodies with the consent of the governor of the relevant state. These have included cities and counties, colleges, ecclesiastical bodies such as the Church of the Advent, Birmingham, Alabama and St Thomas' Church, New York, and leading commercial companies. Growth and interest in heraldry in the United States means that heralds are frequent visitors there; in addition, the College of Arms Foundation was established in the United States in 1983 to disseminate information about heraldry. The armorial bearings granted to the Foundation include a crest which incorporates a new style of American coronet composed of mullets and bars (stars and stripes).

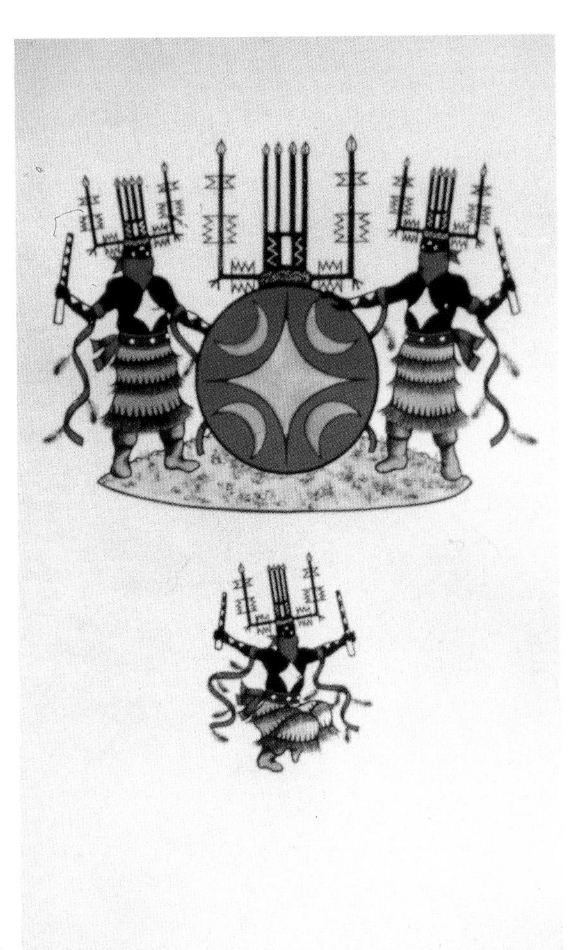

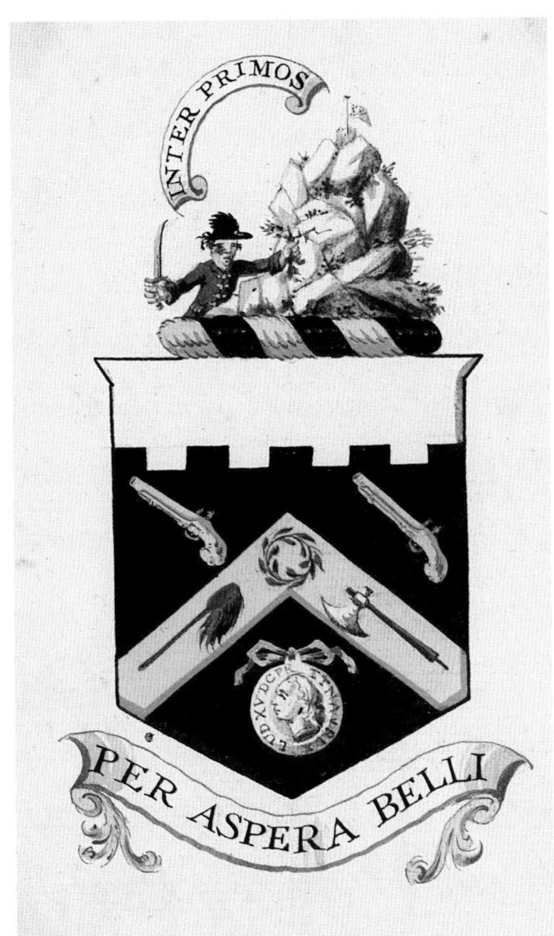

LEFT: *Armorial bearings of Joseph Hopkins of Maryland, who killed and scalped the Chief of the St John's Indians in 1758. Although designed, these were never granted, through failure to pay the fees.*

FAR LEFT: *Armorial bearings of the Mescalero Apache Tribe, devised in 1986 using a circular Apache shield.*

BELOW: *Armorial bearings of Loudon County in the Commonwealth of Virginia, devised in 1968, with supporters of an eighteenth-century Virginian gentleman and a General Officer of the Cavalry of the Army of the Confederacy.*

Much American heraldry uses indigenous flora and fauna, but there are also allusions to American history, with figures such as eighteenth-century Virginian gentlemen and officers from the Civil War. The native American Indian and his artefacts are also popular, and featured in a grant to Newfoundland as early as 1638. Sir John Borough, Garter King of Arms, granted supporters: *two Savages of the Clyme proper armed and appareled according to their guise when they go to war.* The continuous strife between European and Indian is manifest in the grant of supporters in 1761 to Sir Jeffery Amherst, the eighteenth-century commander in chief of the British Army in North America, and in the armorial bearings designed in 1764 for Joseph Hopkins of Maryland, commandant of the Queen's Regiment of American Rangers. The Amherst supporters are blazoned as, *On the Dexter side a Canadian Warr Indian of a Swarthy or bright Copper colour his exterior Arm embowed holding a Warr Axe proper Rings in his nose and Ears and Bracelets on his Arms and wrists Argent over his Shoulders two Buff Belts in Saltire one with his powder horn, the other his Scalping Knife before him a short Apron Azure tied around the Waist with a string Gules having also Blue Gaters seamed Or, the Legs fetterd and fastend by a Chain to the Bracelet on the exterior wrist. On the*

Sinister side a like Canadian holding in his exterior hand a Wand thereon a Scalp proper.

The grant to Joseph Hopkins is blazoned as *Sable on a chevron between two Pistols Or and a Silver Medal with a French King's Bust inscribed Louis XV a Laurel Chaplet in the Centre a Scalp and a Staff on the dexter and a Tomahawk on the sinister proper a chief embattled Argent; crest a rock over the top a Battery in perspective, thereon a French Flagg hoisted, an Officer of the Queen's American Rangers climbing the said rock Sword in hand all proper.* The recital states that 'the said Joseph Hopkins was the first Officer who landed at Louisburgh 8 June 1758 and killed and scalped the Chief of the St John's Indians and took from him an honorary medal given him by the French'. This grant was never entered in the official register at the College of Arms as it was 'never delivered nor entered, not having been paid for'.

BELOW: *Armorial bearings of Richs Incorporated of the City of Atlanta, an example of a devisal for an American commercial body, devised in 1966.*

LEFT: *Armorial bearings of St Thomas' Church, New York, devised in 1975.*

A happier and less belligerent situation now prevails and is exemplified by the armorial bearings of the Mescalero Apache Tribe devised in 1986. This draws upon the precedent of placing arms on tribal shields established by grants of armorial bearings to several African countries. The shield contains tribal emblems and is ensigned with a Mescalero Apache mountain-spirit dancer's crown while mountain-spirit dancers feature in the supporters and badge.

American heraldry has thus survived the vicissitudes of past Anglo-American relations. Today it is contributing to the mainstream of new heraldic creation; it is to be hoped that this contribution will continue to increase and so enrich the culture and heritage of that country.

GLOSSARY

Achievement The complete armorial bearings displayed to show shield, helm, mantling, crest wreath or crest coronet, motto and, where applicable, supporters and compartment.
Addorsed Placed back-to-back. The wings of a bird when extended and almost touching each other behind the bird are termed addorsed. Also two animals back-to-back are so termed.
Adopted children May use their adoptive father's arms, but only by Royal Licence, with the difference of two interlaced links of chain.
Aesculapius, Rod of A snake entwining a rod. Frequently used as a charge by those in the medical profession. Sometimes called 'Aaron's Rod'.
Affronty An animal, monster or helm is so termed when facing the viewer.
Allerion An eagle displayed without legs or beak.
Annulet A ring.
Apaumy A hand or gauntlet is so termed when the palm is facing the viewer.
Arched (or enarched) An Ordinary that has been bent is arched or double-arched (or enarched).
Argent The heraldic metal shown as white or, rarely, silver.
Armed When an animal or bird's claws, talons, horns, beak or tusks are of a different colour to the rest of its body they are blazoned 'armed Gules/Argent' etc.
Armiger One who bears arms, abbreviated to arm. or armig.
Armorial bearings The same as an achievement.
Arms of office Arms borne by virtue of holding office. The Kings of Arms have such arms and can impale their personal arms during tenure of that office.
Astral crown A coronet composed of pairs of wings, each enclosing a mullet of six points and set upon a rim. Associated with the Royal Air Force.
At gaze A term used specifically for deer when standing and regarding the viewer.
Attired A term used to describe antlers of deer when of a different colour to the body.
Attributed arms Arms devised for persons who did not bear them, usually for those living in pre-heraldic times.
Augmentation A small device added to a shield, crest or supporters as a mark of honour, eg for victory in battle.
Azure The heraldic tincture blue.
Badge An heraldic device not associated with arms, crest or supporters, which an armiger may allow to be used by a stranger in blood, employee etc. Originally adopted in the Middle Ages for use by retainers, but since a revival in 1906 may now be granted by the Kings of Arms. An armiger may have more than one badge.
Banner A square or upright-oblong flag showing arms only. It is incorrect to place the whole achievement on a banner. *See also* standard.
Bar An Ordinary, the diminutive of a fess.
Bar gemel Twinned bars usually borne in pairs.
Barbed The sepals of the heraldic rose which appear between each of the five petals. Barbed proper means in their natural colours, ie green.
Barry An even number of bars on a shield. If more or less than six then the number must be specified, eg 'Barry of eight Argent and Azure'.
Barry bendy Divided barry and bendy.
Bar sinister A term used only by those ignorant of heraldry when trying to denote illegitimacy (*see* baton sinister).
Base An area at the bottom of the field.
Baton sinister A bendlet sinister couped or cut off at both ends running from sinister chief to the dexter base, used as a mark of bastardy, usually royal.
Bend An Ordinary, a diagonal strip running from dexter chief to sinister base. When charges are placed upon the shield in a diagonal position they are 'in bend', or 'in bend sinister'.
Bendlet A diminutive of the bend, ie narrower.
Bend sinister An Ordinary, a diagonal strip running from sinister chief to dexter base (*see also* bend).
Bendwise Charges lying in the direction of a bend without the bend being present.
Bendy Divided into an equal number of bends.
Bezant A gold roundel.
Bezanty When the field or charge is strewn with bezants it becomes bezanty.
Bicorporate When an animal or monster has one head attached to two bodies it is termed 'bicorporate'.
Billet An oblong rectangle, the same shape as a ticket (French = *billet*).
Billety Strewn with billets.
Blazon The technical language used to describe arms, crest, mantling, supporters and badge.
Blue Celeste A pale blue tincture, often associated with the Royal Air Force.
Bordure A border running round the edge of a shield which can be plain or charged with devices.
Brock A badger.
Caboshed An animal's head affronty chopped off at the top of the neck is termed caboshed.
Cadency, marks of A small device upon a shield and crest to denote different sons. There are nine such marks. They are also used to denote branches of families.
Caduceus A rod winged at the top and entwined with two snakes. Often confused with the Rod of Aesculapius.
Caltrap A device with three iron spikes so that when thrown onto the ground one spike is always uppermost. It was particularly effective against horses and was termed a 'cheval-trap'.
Canting arms Arms or crest providing a visual pun on the bearer's name (from the Latin *cantus*, song).
Canton A small square situated on the dexter chief corner; if in the sinister chief corner it becomes a canton sinister. Augmentations are often placed upon cantons.
Caparisoned A horse is thus described when fully furnished and decorated with bridle, saddle, armour etc.
Carnation A rare term, denoting a flesh-coloured tincture.
Cartouche The decoration sometimes found round the edge of shield or lozenge.
Celestial crown A crown with a rim, thereon sharp points each terminating with a mullet.
Chapeau A medieval hat of crimson velvet lined and turned-up ermine. It is the forerunner of the velvet cap inside the royal crown. Also called a cap of maintenance and cap of estate.
Chaplet A circular garland of leaves and four flowers, usually heraldic roses.
Charge A device or emblem placed on the shield or Ordinary.
Checky A chequerboard pattern of one tincture and one metal.
Chevron One of the Ordinaries, shaped like an inverted V or gable end of a house.
Chevronel The diminutive of the chevron.
Chevronny Divided into a multiple chevron pattern.
Chief An Ordinary, the top third of the shield. Charges placed in this position are said to be 'in chief'.
Chivalry, Court of The court of law where heraldic disputes can be settled. Presided over by the Earl Marshal of England.

Cinquefoil A stylised flower, having five petals or leaves.
Close A bird is described as close when its wings are folded.
Coat of arms This was originally the surcoat worn over armour depicting the arms of the wearer. Now it refers generally to the achievement or the shield of arms.
Collared Having a collar around the neck.
College of Arms This is the shorthand name of the Corporation of Kings Heralds and Pursuivants of Arms in ordinary to Her Majesty The Queen. It is also abbreviated to the Heralds College. The corporation was founded by King Richard III in 1484 and houses the offices of the officers of arms, together with their official records and collections. It is situated in Queen Victoria Street, London EC4V 4BT.
Combatant Two beasts or monsters facing one another in a rampant position are termed combatant.
Compartment Usually a grassy mound or solid base upon which the supporters stand so that they can perform their function of supporting the shield.
Compony A single row of rectangles tincture alternating with metal. A double row is termed 'countercompony'.
Conjoined The term used when charges touch one another or are joined together.
Corbie A raven, from the French *corbeau*.
Cornucopia The heraldic term for a horn of plenty.
Coronets (1) The crest coronet is not a coronet denoting rank, but forms part of the crest. This category includes the ducal coronet, the ancient coronet, the astral crown, the celestial crown, the mural crown etc, and others of recent invention such as a coronet the finials of which are alternating cinquefoils and crosses patonce.
(2) There are five coronets of rank, one for each of the five ranks of the higher nobility: Duke, Marquis, Earl, Viscount and Baron. These are placed immediately above the shield, below the helm and mantling. The royal crown, the Prince of Wales' coronet and the coronets of princes and princesses do, of course, denote rank but are not treated in the same way as those of nobility in heraldic display.
Cotises The bend, bend sinister, fess, chevron, pale and cross when they have a pair of very thin 'bars' on each side are termed cotised. From the the French *côté*, side.
Couchant This describes a beast or monster lying down, but with its head up.
Counterchanged When a shield is divided by one of the lines of partition, the colours of the field and charges on one side are reversed on the other.
Couped When a beast or monster's head or limb is cut off cleanly with a straight line it is termed couped. This also applies to Ordinaries.
Courant Running at speed.
Coward A beast (or monster, rarely) with its tail between its back legs.
Crescent A new moon with horns uppermost. When the horns are pointing to the dexter, the term becomes 'increscent', when to the sinister, 'decrescent'. The cadency mark for a second son.
Crest An hereditary three-dimensional device situated on top of the helmet.
Crined When the hair of a beast or man is of a different colour to the body, it is termed 'crined', eg 'crined Or'.
Cross One of the Ordinaries. There are many different types of cross in heraldry.
Crusily When cross-crosslets are strewn (semy) over the field or charge, the term 'crusily' is sufficient.
Cubit arm An arm cut off below the elbow.
Dance This is a fess in the form of a wide zigzag pattern.
Dancetty A line of partition of a wide zigzag.
Debruised When a baton or baton sinister is laid over the shield it is termed as 'debruised by a baton'.
Dexter The right side of the shield as held by the bearer, but the left-hand side from the point of view of the spectator. Charges that are capable of facing one direction or another always face the dexter unless described otherwise.
Difference, marks of Synonymous with marks of cadency.
Dimidiation A form of marshalling long since abandoned. When two coats were impaled, the dexter half of the dexter coat was joined with the sinister half of the sinister coat. This could produce unfortunate results.
Displayed Birds, principally eagles, when shown with wings spread open and wing tips uppermost are termed 'displayed'.
Dormant Asleep.
Double-queued A beast or monster having two tails.
Double tressure Twin thin lines following the edge of the shield. Principally known from the Royal Arms of Scotland, where the double tressure is flory counter flory, ie fleurs-de-lis alternatively, pointing outwards and inwards.
Doubled When mantling is blazoned, the lining is described as doubled of a metal.
Earl Marshal of England The great officer of state responsible for state ceremonial and the College of Arms. Also the judge of the Court of Chivalry. The title is hereditary with the dukedom of Norfolk.
Enfile To thread. A charge with a coronet around it is 'enfiling' the coronet, or the cornet is 'enfiled' by the charge. This term easily causes confusion.
Enhanced An Ordinary raised above its normal position.
Ensigned A shield or charge with a crown or coronet above it is termed as 'ensigned' by the crown or coronet.
Eradicated A tree pulled up to show its roots is termed eradicated.
Erased The head or limb of an animal or monster torn from its body and showing a jagged edge is termed erased.
Escarbuncle A charge comprising ornamental spokes emanating from a hub and usually terminating in a fleur-de-lis.
Escutcheon A small shield as a charge in arms, or an escutcheon of pretence if it is a form of marshalling whereby the marital coat is shown indicating that the wife is an heraldic heiress. Also termed inescutcheon.
Fess An Ordinary. A central horizontal strip about one-third of the height of the shield.
Fesswise Lying in the same direction as the fess.
Field The background or surface of the shield.
Fimbriated An Ordinary or charge edged with a different colour.
Flaunches Enarched areas on both sides of the shield.
Fleam A stylised instrument for bloodletting.
Flory When the ends of charges terminate in a fleur-de-lis they are termed flory.
Forcene An adjective used to describe a horse rearing up but not rampant.
Fountain A roundel composed of six bars wavy Argent and Azure, to represent water.
Fourché A tail of an animal that is bifurcated.
Fret A mascle interlaced with a bendlet and a bendlet sinister.
Fretty Bendlets and bendlets sinister interlaced throughout the shield. This looks like netting.
Fructed A tree or plant bearing fruit, or bearing fruit of a different colour, is fructed of that colour.
Fusil A vertically-stretched lozenge.
Fusilly A vertically-stretched version of lozengy.
Gamb The lower part of a beast's leg.
Garb A wheatsheaf.
Garnished A term used for metallic charges, such as helmets, when edged with gold or silver.
Golpe A purple roundel.
Goutte A droplet representing liquid. The term 'goutty' shows droplets splashed upon the field, Ordinary or shield.
Grant of arms A legal document under the hands and seals of the Kings of Arms when exercising the Royal Prerogative, subject to the Earl Marshal's Warrant, granting an individual or corporation the use of armorial bearings or badge. Also called Letters Patent of Armorial Bearings.
Guardant A term used to describe animals and monsters as looking at the viewer.
Gules The heraldic tincture red.
Gyron Half a quarter of the shield, cut per fess and per bend.
Gyronny The shield divided quarterly and per saltire, the eight pieces in alternating tincture and metal.
Hatchment A funerary painting of the armorial achievement of a deceased person, painted on a square canvas (or wood) but turned 90° with points N, S, E, and W.
Haurient A term to describe a fish with head uppermost.
Heiress Or coheiress, a daughter or daughters without brothers (or without surviving brother *sans* issue) who can transmit arms to children as a quartering, providing the husband is armigerous.
Helmet The helmet is always shown in an achievement of arms as a reminder of the martial medie-

val origins of heraldry. The crest is fixed to the top of the helmet. It also denotes rank: a steel tilting helm denotes a gentlemen or esquire (and is used in corporate heraldry), a steel helmet with visor raised denotes a knight or baronet, a silver helmet with gold bars as a visor denotes a peer, and entirely gold helmets are reserved for the sovereign and princes of the blood royal. The tilting helm faces the dexter unless an individual has two crests, when they can face each other; a knight's, baronet's and peer's helm face affronty or to the dexter, and the royal helm is affronty only.
Honorary arms By an Earl Marshal's Warrant, the Kings of Arms are empowered to grant honorary arms to citizens of the United States of America if they can prove a descent in the male line from an ancestor who had been a subject of a British or English sovereign and who must first place such a descent on official record at the College of Arms. Grants of honorary arms may equally be made to foreign citizens already honoured by the Queen.
Hurt A blue roundel.
Impale A term used to describe a shield split vertically down the middle. A husband's arms placed on the dexter side, and a wife's arms placed on the sinister side of the same shield are impaled, showing a marital alliance. Likewise, the head of a corporation may do the same during his tenure of office only, showing the arms of the corporation on the dexter and his or her arms on the sinister, indicating a 'temporary marriage' to that office.
Issuant Issuing from, or coming out of. An animal, monster or other charge is termed as issuant when it arises or comes out of a crest coronet.
Jessed A falcon or hawk is termed 'jessed' if it has leather straps about its legs, and with bells attached it is 'belled and jessed'.
Label The cadency mark of the eldest son. Used in the past as an Ordinary or charge.
Langued Used as a description of the tongue of a beast when of a different colour to the body.
Lodged A deer when lying down is termed 'lodged'.
Lozenge A diamond-shaped charge (but *see also* fusil). Unmarried and divorced ladies depict their arms on a lozenge with or without a cartouche.
Lozengy A term used to describe a shield or charge as divided into a lozengy pattern, ie bendy and bendy sinister, with alternating tincture and metal.
Lymphad A term used to describe an ancient type of seagoing vessel with oars protruding, either in full sail or with sails furled.
Mantling A cape fixed to the top of the helmet, held in place by the wreath. Origins not definitely known. It is possible that it is a version of the Arab head-dress discovered by the crusaders and adopted by them. It is said that its purpose was to keep the sun off the neck, or to deaden blows aimed at the back of the neck. Maybe it was just decorative. It is now depicted in many artistic ways and adds great beauty to an achievement of arms. It is usually described as having a tincture on the outside, lined with a metal. An ermine lining is reserved for peers, and gold mantling-lined ermine is reserved for the sovereign and royal princes.
Marshalling This is the name given to the system whereby arms acquired by marital alliances may be added to the paternal coat by impalement or quartering. It also applies to arms of office impaled with personal arms.
Mascle A voided lozenge.
Masoned A term used to denote that the mortar in a brick or stone wall is of a different colour.
Maunch A stylised depiction of a lady's sleeve, cut off at the shoulder.
Memorial The term given to the petition made by one desiring a grant of arms, addressed to the Earl Marshal of England.
Metals The colours white (*Argent*) and gold (*Or*) are termed metals (*see also* tinctures).
Millrind The metal bracket used for holding a millstone in place.
Motto Usually expressing an uplifting sentiment which is adopted by a grantee, not granted to him. It can be in any language, but Latin, English or French are preferred. In an achievement it is placed upon a scroll below the shield.
Mullet A star of five points, unpierced. The cadency mark of the third son.
Murrey One of the stains, as opposed to the tinctures. A reddish-purple or mulberry colour.
Naiant Swimming; used to describe a fish swimming horizontally (*see also* haurient and urinant).
Naval crown A coronet composed of billowing sails alternating with ships' hulls. Reserved in modern grants for senior naval officers.
Nimbus A halo.
Nowed Snakes and tails of animals when shown in the form of a knot are termed as 'nowed'. Also a type of cross with enlarged circular centre.
Octofoil The same as a cinquefoil, but with eight petals or leaves. The cadency mark of the ninth son.
Or The heraldic term for the metal gold.
Ordinaries a) The basic linear shapes upon a shield, ie the bend, bend sinister, chevron, chief, cross, fess, pale, pile and saltire.
b) An heraldic dictionary, arranged by the charges upon the shield, crest or badge, either in written form (blazon) or pictorial.
Orle Similar to a bordure, but set a little towards the centre of the shield.
Orle, in When charges are arranged around the edges of a shield, but not on a bordure they are termed 'in orle'.
Pairle When a shield is divided in the form of the letter 'Y', or inverted, it is termed 'tierced in pairle' or 'tierced in pairle reversed'.
Pale An Ordinary; it is a vertical band about one-third the width of the shield.
Palewise A charge lying in the direction of a pale.
Palisado crown A coronet in the form of a palisade.
Pall An Ordinary in the shape of the letter 'Y'. It is similar to the ecclesiastical vestment of the same name, or pallium.
Paly A shield divided into an equal number of vertical stripes is termed 'paly'.
Paly bendy A combination of paly and bendy.
Panache A fan of feathers, usually in the crest.
Parted Divided or 'party'.
Partition, lines of See illustration in the chapter on the science of heraldry.
Passant An animal or monster walking, with its dexter forepaw raised.
Paty A cross with the arms splayed towards the edge of the shield is termed 'paty' (or 'patee') or, in modern blazon, 'formy'.
Pean A black fur strewn with gold ermine spots.
Pellet A black roundel.
Pellety Semy of pellets.
Pendant A charge hanging from another is termed pendant.
Pennon A tapering lance-flag.
Pheon A broad arrowhead, the barbs engrailed on the inner edge, shown point downward unless described otherwise.
Pierced A charge pierced with a round central hole is so termed.
Pile An Ordinary, a triangular shape usually starting at the top of the shield with its point in base, but which can also be reversed or can come from either side of the shield.
Plate A white roundel.
Platy Semy of plates.
Potent An early term for a crutch. Ordinaries, particularly the cross, can have crutched ends.
Proper A charge depicted in its natural colours is so termed.
Purpure The heraldic term for the tincture purple.
Quadrate A cross with a square at its centre is termed a 'cross quadrate'.
Quarter A quarter of the shield, in dexter chief unless otherwise blazoned.
Quarterly A term used when describing a shield or charge divided into four quarters coloured with tinctures and metals.
Quatrefoil A four-leaved charge.
Queue fourchy A forked tail, as opposed to 'double-queued' which means two tails.
Quise, à la A bird's leg cut off at the thigh is so described.
Rampant An upright beast with its left hind leg downwards and its other legs splayed to the dexter.
Reflexed This term is usually applied to a chain or line where it is fixed to a collar around the neck of an animal, monster or human and is arranged or reflexed over the back of the creature.
Reguardant An animal looking backwards over his shoulder is reguardant.
Respectant Two animals facing one another. If rampant at the same time the term 'combatant' is used.
Reversed Turned upside-down from its normal position.
Rising A bird about to take off with wings stretched out is described as rising.
Roundel A disc with special names according to the colour – gold (*bezant*), white (*plate*), red (*torteau*), blue (*hurt*), green

(*pomeis*), black (*pellet*), purple (*golpe*), barry wavy Argent and Azure (*fountain*).
Sable The heraldic tincture black.
Salient Animals leaping or springing are described as salient, except horses, which are forcene.
Saltire An Ordinary in the shape of an X.
Segreant Synonymous with rampant, but applied only to a gryphon when in this position.
Sejant Sitting down (not lying down).
Semy Charges evenly strewn over the shield or Ordinary are described as 'semy of . . .'
Sinister The left side of the shield when borne by the owner, the right side when viewed by the spectator.
Slipped Flowers, leaves, and small branches with stalks when pulled off the main stem, are so described.
Stains In addition to metals and tinctures, other colours are occasionally used: sanguine (a bloody colour), tenne (orange) and murrey (mulberry).
Standard This is a long tapering flag with a round end (split for knights, baronets and peers), showing the owner's arms at the hoist, and his badges or crest between his motto upon diagonal bands in the fly. This is not a banner.
Statant An animal standing with all four feet on the ground is so described.
Stock The stump of a tree.
Surcoat A long coat without sleeves, worn over armour, upon which was shown the wearer's arms, hence 'coat of arms'.
Tabard A short surcoat with broad sleeves. The royal tabard is now worn only by heralds on ceremonial duty.
Tierced A shield divided into three parts is so described, as in 'tierced in pairle'.
Tinctures The heraldic colours red (*Gules*), blue (*Azure*), black (*Sable*), green (*Vert*) and purple (*Purpure*) are described collectively as tinctures.
Trick When a pen-and-ink drawing of arms, crest, supporters or badge is shown with colours indicated by lettering, it is said to be 'tricked' or 'a trick'.
Trippant Deer when passant are described as trippant.
Tufted Beasts which have tufts of hair of a different colour are described as tufted of that colour.
Unguled When beasts have hooves of a different colour to their bodies, they are described as unguled of that colour.
Urchin The heraldic term for a hedgehog. It is also called a herisson.
Urinant A term used to describe a fish with its head downwards.
Vambraced A term used to describe a human arm when wearing armour.
Vert The heraldic tincture green.
Voided The heraldic term used to describe a charge which has had its centre cut out, to show only an outline with the background colour showing through, eg 'voided of the field'.
Volant A bird in the act of flying.
Vulned Wounded and showing droplets of blood.
Water bouget A stylised pair of leather bags, joined by a yoke, for carrying water.
Wodehouse A savage or wild man of the woods.
Wreath A circlet of twisted material, holding the mantling on top of the helmet, and disguising how the crest is fixed to the helmet. Conventionally it is depicted as having six twists alternating metal and tincture. When the blazon describes the wreath as 'of the colours', the first metal and first tincture described in the blazon are the colours to be used. A wreath can also be used as a charge, and an Ordinary may also be wreathed.

INDEX

Figures in *italics* refer to illustrations

ACKNOWLEDGMENTS

The publisher would like to thank Martin Bristow for designing this book, Judith Millidge and Clare Haworth-Maden for editing it, Stephen Small for the picture research, Pat Coward for compiling the index, and Godfrey New Photographic for many of the photographs reproduced here.

The authors would like to thank the following for their assistance in the preparation of this book: the Chapter of the College of Arms for permission to reproduce illustrations from the College Records and Collections; the Duke of Norfolk, Earl Marshal; Robert Yorke, Archivist at the College of Arms; Jane Nickels, Assistant Librarian at the College of Arms; Robert Parsons, Linda West and Gillian Barlow, for providing artwork; Herr Heinz Waldner; Dr Elizabeth Hallam; Lady Garrod; Mary-Rose Rogers; Beryl Pendley, Clerk of the Ordinaries at the College of Arms, for her general assistance and acting as referee between the authors.

The following individuals and agencies provided the illustrations:

Gillian Barlow: p.76 top four, 93T (based on College of Arms Carta Marina), 100 top left and top right (based on College of Arms MSS Vincent 187/258 and H13/81), 111 bottom three, 130B, 143 bottom three. **Henry Bedingfeld:** p.11B, 27B, 35, 39T, 48T. **Bibliothèque Nationale, Paris:** p.11T. **Graham Bingham:** p.1, 2 all three, 6 both, 7, 120, 130B. **British Library:** p.12BR, 17, 19, 20, 21T, 25T, 42, 115T. **Canterbury Cathedral:** p.126T, 127B. **College of Arms:** p.8 (Heralds' Roll), 15 (Flower's Ordinary 2G9/105 & 6), 16B (Holles Ordinary), 18 top and bottom (Holles Ordinary), 24 (Westminster Tournament Roll), 25B (Old Grants 2/90), 26, 27 top left and top right, 28 (C36/58), 29T, 37, 38 (Lillywhites Ltd), 39B (Pickering Kenyon), 40, 45B, 46B (M7/62), 48B, 49, 50 (L10/28), 53 (2 L12/7b), 54 (E16/34), 55 top (Jenyn's Ordinary/24b) and bottom (M10/129), 56 (C14/44), 58 top (Smith's Ordinary/34b) and bottom (2G11/1b), 59 top left (Vincent 152/50b) top right (Stall Plates of the Knights of the Garter, St John Hope, 1901, No. LXXII) and bottom (Vincent 152/57), 60 top right and top left (L6/17) and bottom (I 2/62), 61 (Fenwick Roll, Rows 118-121), 62 top (Vincent 153/10b) and bottom (Vincent 153/23), 63 top (Misc. Grants 7/401) and bottom (L10/99), 64 (L10/59), 65 top (Vincent 168/206 & 21) and bottom (L10/58b), 66 (Grants II/449), 67 top (Hare's Ordinary/109b) and bottom (Grants III/250), 68 top (Grants XV/293) and bottom (Grants X/455), 69 top (SML 33/193) and bottom (Grants VIII/148), 70 (Grants XI/21), 71 top (Grants XXXVII/65) and bottom (Grants LXII/292), 72 top (Grants LXII/228) and bottom (Standards I/20), 73 (Culham), 74 (All England Lawn Tennis and Croquet Club), 75 (Royal Philharmonic Orchestra), 76 bottom (Grants CXXXVII/306), 77 (Grants CXLVII/322), 78 (Vincent 152/95), 80 (Vincent 152/92b), 81 (Stall Plates of the Knights of the Garter, St John Hope, 1901, No. VII), 82 (Old Grants 2/79), 83 top (Order of the Bath Vol. 3/104) and bottom (Stall Plates of the Knights of the Garter, St John Hope, 1901, No. LXVIII), 84 top (B 19/25) and bottom (G 2/46), 85 (D 15/2), 86 (Grants LXII/174), 87 top (Grants CXXXIX/51) and bottom (M7/17), 88 (Japan Tobacco (UK) Ltd), 89B (Roberts), 90 top (Grants III/119b) and bottom (L 10/106), 91 (1H 7/59b), 92 top (Grants CXLII/196) and bottom (Vincent 182/111), 93B (CLIII/181), 94 (Grants CLIX/15), 95 top (CXLVIII/62) and bottom (Grants CXXX/136), 96 (L 10/108), 98 top (Heralds' Roll/23) and bottom (2G9/38), 99 (Vincent 152/80), 100B (L10/105b), 101 top (Grants II/453), bottom left (BEDN/48b) and far left (Grants CLI/195), 103 (Grants CXIV/21), 104 top left (153/42), top right (M9/42) and bottom (Grants CLIII/36), 105 top (Grants CXLIII/37) and bottom (EDN 31/351 & 2), 106 (L 10/110), 107 top (C 20/326) and bottom (IM 5/126), 108 top (L 8/1) and bottom (Old Grants 2/77), 109 top (K 9/442) and bottom (Arundel 3/96), 110 top (CXL 11/211) and bottom (CXLVI/102), 111T (Foreign Arms 2/117), 114/115B (Westminster Tournament Roll), 118 top and bottom, 119, 121 (Bath Book/11), 122, 123, (R23/119), 124 top and bottom, 125B, 126B, 127T, 128, 129 top and bottom, 130T, 131 top and bottom, 132, 133 top and bottom, 134 top and bottom, 135 top and bottom, 136 (Hector le Breton/10), 138 (B23/58b & 59), 139T (Vincent 171/27), 140 (Edele Geslagten in de 7 Proviinten/96), 141 (Hector le Breton/15), 142 top (Famiglie Celebri Italiane, Pompeo Litta Vols. 2 & 5) and bottom (Spanish Certificates of Arms), 143T (Famiglie Celebri Italiane, Pompeo Litta Vols. 2 & 5), 144 (Young Collection Vol. 922), 145 bottom left and right (Scotland III/28 & 34), 146 (EDN Scotland's Nobility/51), 147 top (Vincent 172/162b) and bottom (Kennedy's Book of Irish Arms/45), 148 top (I 82/257) and bottom (Arms of Foreign States/21), 149 top (Foreign Arms 2/172) and bottom (Grants X/324), 150 (Misc. Grants 4/7), 151 top left (SML 34/15), top right (Foreign Arms 2/176), bottom (Foreign Arms 2/69), 152 (Foreign Arms 2/63), 153 (Foreign Arms 2/113). **Keith Ellis Collection:** p.34. **Peter Gwynn-Jones:** p.89T, 102, 139B. **Michael Holford:** p.52. **Hulton-Deutsch Collection Ltd:** p.29B. **Lichfield Studios:** p.36. **Lichfield Studios/ Museum of London:** p.125T. **Magdalen College, Oxford University:** p.21B. **Musée de Tessé, Le Mans:** p.14. **Robert Parsons:** p.12T, 44B all 11. **Courtesy of the Public Record Office:** p.12BL, 13. **Royal Collection, Reproduced by Gracious Permission of Her Majesty the Queen:** p.30/31. **Salisbury Cathedral:** p.16T. **Nigel Shuttleworth:** p.10. **Dr Conrad Swan, CVO:** p.145T. **Linda West:** p.43 all 17, 44 top 10, 45T, 46 top three, 47 all three. **By courtesy of the Dean and Chapter of Westminster:** p.57, 112, 116, 117. **Reproduced by permission of the Dean and Canons of Windsor:** p.22, 33.

FOR FURTHER READING

Heralds and Heraldry in the Middle Ages, A R Wagner, Oxford University Press, 1956.

Historic Heraldry of Britain, A R Wagner, Oxford University Press, 1939.

A Catalogue of English Medieval Rolls of Arms (Aspilogia I), A R Wagner, Society of Antiquaries, 1950.

Rolls of Arms, Henry III (Aspilogia II), T D Tremlett, H S London and A R Wagner, Society of Antiquaries, 1967.

Chivalry, Maurice Keen, Yale University Press, 1984.

Lines of Succession, Jiri Louda and Michael Maclagan, Orbis Publishing Ltd, London, 1981.

Die ältesten Wappenbilder, Heinz Waldner, Herold, Berlin, 1992.

The Plantagenet Chronicles, Dr Elizabeth Hallam (ed), Weidenfeld & Nicholson, 1986.

The Complete Peerage, GEC, St Catharine's Press, 1910-40.

Eight Rolls of Arms, Gerard J Brault, Pennsylvania State University Press, 1973.

The College of Arms Monograph, Walter H Godfrey CBE, FSA, FRIBA, assisted by Sir Anthony Wagner, KCVO, DLitt, FSA, Garter King of Arms, with a complete list of the Officers of Arms, prepared by the late H Stanford London FSA, Norfolk Herald Extraordinary, 1963.

Paston Letters and Papers of the Fifteenth Century, Norman Davis (ed), Oxford University Press, 1971 and 1976.

Heralds of England, Sir Anthony Wagner, KCVO, DLitt, Garter King of Arms, HMSO, 1967.

The Records and Collections of the College of Arms, A R Wagner, Burkes Peerage, 1952.

Boutell's Heraldry, revised by J P Brooke-Little, CVO, Norroy and Ulster King of Arms, Frederick Warne & Co Ltd, 1983.

An Heraldic Alphabet, J P Brooke-Little, CVO, Norroy & Ulster King of Arms, Macdonald & Co, 1973 and 1975.

Canada: Symbols of Sovereignty, Conrad Swan, York Herald of Arms, University of Toronto Press, 1977.

The Romance of Heraldry, by Wilfrid Scott-Giles, Fitzalan Pursuivant Extraordinary, J M Dent & Sons Ltd, London, 1967.

Animals and Maps, Wilma George, Secker and Warburg, 1969.

The Magic Zoo, Peter Costello, Sphere Books, 1979.

The Naming of the Beasts, Wilma George and Brunsdon Yapp, Duckworth, 1991.

Medieval Beasts, Ann Payne, The British Library, 1990.

The Heraldic Imagination, Rodney Dennys, Clarkson N Potter Inc, New York, 1975.